# OUR CHRISTIAN FOUNDING FATHERS

"...this is a Christian Nation."

## William Beckman

WESTBOW°
PRESS
A DIVISION OF THOMAS NELSON
& ZONDERVAN

WestBow Press books may be ordered through booksellers or by contacting:

WestBow Press
A Division of Thomas Nelson & Zondervan
1663 Liberty Drive
Bloomington, IN 47403
www.westbowpress.com
1 (866) 928-1240

ISBN: 978-1-4908-7896-6 (sc)
ISBN: 978-1-4908-7898-0 (hc)
ISBN: 978-1-4908-7897-3 (e)

Library of Congress Control Number: 2015908330

Print information available on the last page.

WestBow Press rev. date: 06/19/2015

Dedication

"M"

e-piph-any
/I'pif ə mi/

1. (initial capital letter) a Christian festival, observed on January 6, commemorating the manifestation of Christ to the gentiles in the person of the Magi; Twelfth-day.
2. an appearance or manifestation, especially of a deity.
3. **a sudden, intuitive perception or insight into the reality or essential meaning of something, usually initiated by some simple, homely or commonplace occurrence or experience.** *(Emphasis added)*
4. a literary work or section of a work presenting, usually symbolically, such a moment of revelation and insight.

**Origin:**
1275–1325; Middle English epiphanie < Late Latin *epiphanīa* Late Greek *epiphanīa*. Greek: apparition, equvalent to *epi-* epi- + *phan-* (stem of *phaínein* to appear) + *-eia* -y

Source: Dictionary.com

There were two epiphanies in the early development of our nation that had a major effect on its creation. The first, the military epiphany, occurred at Valley Forge in the winter of 1777-1778. The survival of the troops under General George Washington's leadership gave new hope to not only the survivors, but the colonies as a whole.

The second epiphany, the governmental epiphany, occurred in the Continental-Congress Convention on June 28, 1787, when, "With the oratory degenerating into threats and accusations, Benjamin Franklin appealed for daily prayers." (Religion and the Founding of the American Republic http://loc.gov/exhibits/religion/rel04.html)

# CONTENTS

# ACKNOWLEDGEMENTS

First and foremost, I must acknowledge the Freedom _from_ Religion Foundation for inspiring this compilation. The continual haranguing and court challenges of this group spurred my interest in studying the history of the founding of the United States. Through that study I am satisfied the foundation preaches erroneous history. This _is_ a Christian nation, founded on Christian principles by Christian Founding Fathers, regardless of the twisting of history by some to meet the atheistic objectives of non-believers.

From the standpoint of accomplishment, the foundation has done an excellent job of convincing many people there is no God. Their result is error, but they have developed a very sophisticated religion of non-religion.

There are several other individuals I must mention. These are Christian friends who have encouraged the material presented in a Sunday School class

To be incorporated into what has become this endeavor. They are Jim and Virginia Christiansen, Carl and Linda Kutzke, Tom Pirwitz, Rich Hooper, Mike Durant and Jim Williams. A small group meeting each Sunday morning and studying together the Christian impact on the development of the United States, plus one other staunch supporter, Dr. Bernard Huizenga. I must also thanks Peggy Hooper for editing and correcting.

In addition, I would like to thank Thomas Kindig for allowing me to use his work on the Declaration of Independence signers and

Steve Straub, The Federalist Paper Project, for their Constitution signers.

In digging into factual history of the uniting of the colonies, available from those involved with its creation, it became readily apparent that the history being hinted about today did not match up with what the Founding Fathers said and believed. I say 'hinted about' because so little of our factual history is being taught to the youth of our country. Because of present-day historians such as William Federer, David Barton, Jonathan Cahn and Dinesh D'Souza, to name just a few, we can reach back and find the facts as they *truly* were. We all are indebted to them.

# INTRODUCTION

There is only one reason for this 'compilation'. It's you and your family.

Do you know the *full* role our Founding Fathers played in forming the colonies into what became the United States of America? Do you realize what they gave up to create it? One thing is certain. If you are reading this compilation, it appears you have a desire to know them and understand why they did it.

To many, the Founding Fathers were a group of only three or four men, who had a vision. As we study and learn the history of our country, several things become apparent:

Actually, there were over 250 dedicated individuals who held a vision of liberty among the general population of 3,929,214. This vision came from the group of one third of the population wanting freedom, freedom in many forms[1]

    A. Freedom from the oppressive dictates of Britain and its ruler King George.

    B. Freedom to practice the form of Christianity they chose, not the church chosen by the crown.

    C. Freedom to conduct their affairs according to their individual and corporate beliefs.

    D. Freedom of association without suffering the dictates of a sovereign power.

It is believed only about one third of the colonists desired to separate from the crown. One third wished to remain loyal British subjects, and one third had no opinion one way or the other.

Thus, it appears out of one third of the almost 4 million colonists, 250+ individuals, were responsible for getting all of the colonies to coalesce and form a separate nation. A minority held sway over the majority opinion.

At the time of the pre-revolutionary period, the oppression of Britain had been felt. The trials, tribulations and sacrifices of those seeking liberty are only known to those who are willing to examine and learn of the Founding Fathers' accomplishments.

## Secularists, Deists and Atheists

Another misconception is that the Founding Fathers were either secularists, deists or atheists. Nothing could be farther from the truth. In this compilation, the true role of Christianity in the founding precepts will be shown and documented for your inspection. For example, examine Isaiah 33:22 to find the structure of the new republic.

Christianity played a major position in all thirteen colonies. One of the more important statements of this is the finding of the United States Supreme Court.

Justice David Brewer (1837-1910) writing for the Court, in **Church of the Holy Trinity v. United States**, 143 U.S. 457-458, 465-471, 36 L ed. 226) (1892), stated that:

> "Even the Constitution of the United States, which is supposed to have little touch upon the private life of the individual, contains in the First Amendment a declaration common to the constitutions of all the States, as follows: 'Congress shall make no law respecting an establishment of religion, or prohibiting the free exercise thereof,' etc. And also provides in Article 1, section 7, (a provision common to many constitutions,) that the Executive

shall have ten days (**Sundays excepted**) within which to determine whether he will approve or veto a bill." *(Emphasis added to note recognition of Christian format of a week)*

The Court concluded:

"There is no dissonance in these declarations. There is a universal language pervading them all, having one meaning; they affirm and reaffirm that this is a religious nation. These are not individual sayings, declarations of private persons: they are organic utterances; they speak the voice of the entire people... These, and many other matters which might be noticed, add a volume of unofficial declarations to the mass of organic utterances that **this is a Christian nation.**" *(Emphasis added)*

He also stated in the same case:

"Religion, morality, and knowledge (are) necessary to good government; the preservation of liberty, and the happiness of mankind."

The Founding Fathers used that phrase, "Religion, Morality, and Knowledge" time and time again to promote the idea that the Christian faith (religion) begat morality, both of which were possible only by having the ability to read the Scriptures. Through this knowledge, they could keep the leaders/lawmakers in line. Eliminate the knowledge of the Scriptures and you could eliminate the effect of Christianity and thus, the meaning of morality. Eliminate morality and anything goes. If the citizen cannot read, they have no means of knowing the law for themselves, only what the leaders tell them the law is.

One of the weaknesses of the early Christian church was that the Bible was chained to the church wall and was written in Latin.

The only knowledge of what the Scriptures said was what the priests wanted the people to know.

A simple illustration of the structure the Founding Fathers envisioned is a three-legged stool with legs of Religion, Morality and Knowledge. Eliminate any one of those legs and the entire system collapses. Without the Christian principles the Founding Fathers chose, what would the morality of the new nation be based upon? Man's laws?

As an example of this, during the Nuremberg Trials, the International Military Tribunal held in Count IV of four counts, "...crimes against humanity, including murder, extermination, enslavement, and other inhumane acts committed against civilian populations, as well as every form of political, racial, and religious persecution carried out in furtherance of a crime punishable by the IMT."

In other words, even man's court, the IMT, held that man's laws do not overrule basic morality. There is a need for some standard for morality to follow, and the Founding Fathers chose Christianity as that basis

One has only to look at today's society to see the effect of minimizing or eliminating religion. Immorality reigns; there is no need for God. Yet, the Scriptures state very clearly what will happen to those who do not learn of God's role for His children's lives.

Hosea 4:6 states-

> *My people are destroyed for lack of knowledge;*
> *because you have rejected knowledge,*
> *I reject you from being a priest to me.*
> *And since you have forgotten the law of your God,*
> *I also will forget your children.*

Are people rejecting the learning of God's Word and, thus, disobeying it? Have they decided they can do it better themselves? Do they believe the United States Government and/or the United Nations have the answers? Is there an accepted increase in terror in the world?

For example, imagine you are driving your car at 11 PM in a strange big city. Your spouse is with you as well as your two young children, asleep in the back seat. All of a sudden you realize you've made a wrong turn and find yourself in a seedier section of that strange city, in other words, the slums.

You realize you have to get back on a major thoroughfare to continue on your way home. You attempt to turn around by pulling into an alley and start to back out. That's when it happens. Your car stalls. You are trying to get it started again, when you notice ten or twelve young men in their twenties coming out of a building. In the glare of your headlights, they start coming out of the dark towards your car.

There, in the dark, with your family in a stalled car, what are your first thoughts? Would you feel safe? Would you fear for your family's safety?

As the young men gather around your car, they tap on the car's window and ask if you're having trouble. What is your response? Where is your heart, up in your mouth?

But, what would be your response if you learn they are Christian young men who have just left a Bible study at their church and not some gang meeting?

What would our country look like, if the teachings of Christ would once again create a new Awakening experience amongst Americans? Could it be that, as has happened in the past history of our country following another "Awakening", the prisons would have no inmates? The jailers would be let go because there were no prisoners to watch?

As a contrast, have you noticed an upswing of people applying for concealed carry permits? Why is that? Is the system of law and order, based on the Constitution, collapsing? Does man really know what's best for all the people? What have such beliefs gained for our country in the past and today? Is there a need for an American Epiphany today?

Finally, please recognize that very little of this compilation is original works by yours truly. I have only compiled the works on the Founders, written by several extremely qualified historians, to prove the Christian basis of the original 'united' <u>States</u> of America and the need to return to it.

It is my hope and prayers that enough readers will learn of the commitment the Founding Fathers had to Christ. Perhaps, as children of God, they will be able to return the country to the original standards espoused by those Founding Fathers: based on 'Religion, Morality, Knowledge.' If not, will God's proclamation in Hosea 4:6 become a reality, and will God forget us? Can we seek that epiphany? The choice is ours, isn't it?

WLB

# CHAPTER 1

◆————————◆————————◆

## *What do you know?*

*"Every member of the State ought diligently to read and to study the Constitution of his country... By knowing their rights, they will sooner perceive when they are violated and be the better prepared to defend and assert them." Justice John Jay, Original Chief Justice of the Supreme Court* [1]

Suppose you have a member of your family diagnosed with an ailment that surgery could cure. Suppose you have a choice between two surgeons to perform that surgery. The first is an individual who has had minimal surgical experience, while the second is not only a qualified surgeon, but has had considerable expertise in the problem your family member has. Which would you choose to do the surgery? The answer is obvious: the surgeon with the greater experience.

In every election, whether it is local, state or national, too many of the candidates are elected by voters who are like the first surgeon, understanding very little about either the office or the qualification requirements. They are chosen on the basis of party, campaign material or "I like his looks."

Many candidates seek the office for the power and prestige, with only a smattering of knowledge of the Constitution and its statement of authority.

1

This is easily proven, and has been proven, by ascertaining the level of knowledge of the voter, as to the requirements of the office the individuals are being elected to. Recognizing that local requirements or standards vary from community to community and state to state, there is a simple means of proving the capabilities of the candidate. Simply, it is by an examination of their knowledge of our federal government's structure, as established by our Constitution. If one doesn't know this structure, it is impossible for one to determine the requirements or qualifications for the office. If the voter does not have knowledge of either what is required of the officeholder or the qualifications of the candidate, how can he or she cast an intelligent vote?

We have heard "You must first vote on the measure, before you can read it."

If an intelligent vote cannot be cast, what quality of government can be anticipated? There really can be no room for guessing about a candidate's knowledge about the Constitution, the basis of our country's government, can there?

> *"A nation which does not remember what it was yesterday, does not know what it is today, nor what it is trying to do. We are trying to do a futile thing if we don't know where we have come from or what we have been about,"*
>
> *President Woodrow Wilson.*[2]

Perhaps the history of the United States has not been in the forefront of your 'quest' of knowledge. This is very understandable. If those who choose to educate the youth have not been made aware of the standards set prior to the creation of the United States by the Founders, how can they be expected to pass them on? Without adequate education, Wilson's comment becomes all too true. We attempt to reinvent the wheel, when the best available model is in front of us.

It is also desirable to know something about those who stood together to establish this unique form of government. Who are they? Where did they come from? What is their personal sacrifice in separating from Britain? They are more than just 'names' penned on a piece of parchment. They were living, breathing human beings, and what caused them to create a "new nation under God, with liberty and justice for all"?

"Under God." If there be any doubt, look to the structure and the history of the individuals and the occasions they created and attended.

Most Americans do not realize only two books were used in the education of the children in the colonies; the New England Primer and the Bible. The Primer was used as a teaching tool to learn how to read. The reason for learning to read was to be able to read the Bible. There were three reasons for reading the Bible.

First, to learn and understand the Word of God; second, to incorporate its wisdom into the reader's life; and third, to insure their leaders were following the teachings regarding leadership, found in the Word of God.

Once one accepts Christ as his Savior, it becomes necessary to know what is expected of him and his elected officers. The Bible is the source of that information.

For example, the republican form of government is spelled out in two parts of the Bible. Isaiah 33:22 states "For the LORD is our *judge*, the LORD is our *lawgiver*, the LORD is our *king*; he will save us." (KJV) The Founding Fathers incorporated these ideas into the structure of the new government as the judiciary, legislative and presidential functions. *(Emphasis added)*

The second part incorporated into the new form of government can be found in Exodus 18:18-26;

> "(Moses' father-in-law said) 'You will surely wear
> yourself out, both you and these people with you.
> For the task is too heavy for you; you cannot do it
> alone. Now listen to me. I will give you counsel, and
> God be with you! You should represent the people

3

before God, and you should bring their cases before God; teach them the statutes and instructions and make known to them the way they are to go and the things they are to do. You should also look for able men among all the people, men who fear God, are trustworthy, and hate dishonest gain; **set such men over them as officers over thousands, hundreds, fifties and tens. Let them sit as judges for the people at all times; let them bring every important case to you, but decide every minor case themselves.** So it will be easier for you, and they will bear the burden with you. If you do this, and God so commands you, then you will be able to endure, and all these people will go to their home in peace.' *(Emphasis added)*

"So Moses listened to his father-in-law and did all that he had said. Moses chose able men from all Israel and appointed them as heads over the people, as officers over thousands, hundreds, fifties, and tens. And they judged the people at all times; hard cases they brought to Moses, but any minor case they decided themselves." (NIV)

This is the format incorporated in our representative government (representative democracy), even though it has not adhered to the requirement that the persons chosen are "able men among all the people, men who fear God, are trustworthy, and hate dishonest gain".

Thus, the structure of the government of the 'united' States was laid out by God and utilized in the creation of the Constitution. As they were considering 'uniting' into a federal format, the Founding Fathers often used the spelling, 'united States,' asserting they were states first. In later years, the 'U' was capitalized.

So, what is your knowledge of our form of government? How does it work? What are the limits of the federal v. individual state's rights? What are the *obligations of and limits on* our elected officials? Have the citizens lost control of government, and if so, how can they get it back? Who is the employer, and who is the employee?

There is a test of your knowledge, regarding the United States government. The test was created in 2008 by the Intercollegiate Studies Institute (ISI). It was developed to determine how well a citizen is acquainted with the requirements of that citizenry. Why not take the test and see for yourself how well you understand the basics of our country? Once you know your strengths (and weaknesses), you will also understand where more study may be needed.

Consider listing your answers on a separate sheet, and then let a friend take the test. The answers are also in Appendix A. Finally, make copies of the test and send them to your elected officials and candidates, if for no other reason than to see their response. It might be helpful to you in making your voting decisions.

Here are the first three questions for you to test yourself:

1. **Jamestown, Virginia, was first settled by Europeans during which period?**
   a) 1301-1400
   b) 1401-1500
   c) 1501-1600
   d) 1601-1700
   e) 1701-1800

2. **The Puritans:**
   a) opposed all wars on moral grounds.
   b) stressed the sinfulness of all humanity.
   c) believed in complete religious freedom.
   d) colonized Utah under the leadership of Brigham Young.
   e) were Catholic missionaries escaping religious persecution.

## 3. The Constitution of the United States established what form of government?

   a) Direct democracy
   b) Populism
   c) Indirect democracy
   d) Oligarchy
   e) Aristocracy

Why not see how you can answer all sixty? *(Appendix A)*

# CHAPTER 2

---

## *The Declaration of Independence*

As mentioned, most Americans do not realize just two books were used in education of their youth before and after the creation of the United States; the New England primer and the Bible. Much has been said about the "Separation of Church and State" in order to discredit the role the Bible played in the founding of the United States, but it is a provable fact that the colonies, and the subsequent states, relied heavily upon the principles outlined in the Judeo-Christian teachings of the Bible.

Examine the original intent of the Founders, and see for yourself. An excellent resource for the original intent can be found in David Barton's book, *'The Myth of Separation of Church and State'*, which is listed in the 'Recommended Reading and Viewing' list at the end of this writing. Time and time again, the basis of the country is, "Religion, Morality and Knowledge."

Note also the Christian dependency in the Constitutions of the thirteen colonies/states posted in Chapter 8.

# The Declaration of Independence:
# A History[1]

Nations come into being in many ways. Military rebellion, civil strife, acts of heroism, acts of treachery, a thousand greater and lesser clashes between defenders of the old order and supporters of the new--all these occurrences and more have marked the emergences of new nations, large and small. The birth of our own nation included them all. That birth was unique, not only in the immensity of its later impact on the course of world history and the growth of democracy, but also because so many of the threads in our national history run back through time to come together in one place, in one time, and in one document: the Declaration of Independence.

## Moving Toward Independence

The clearest call for independence up to the summer of 1776 came in Philadelphia on June 7. On that date in session in the Pennsylvania State House (later Independence Hall), the Continental Congress heard Richard Henry Lee of Virginia read his resolution beginning: "Resolved: That these United Colonies are, and of right ought to be, free and independent States, that they are absolved from all allegiance to the British Crown, and that all political connection between them and the State of Great Britain is, and ought to be, totally dissolved."

The Lee Resolution was an expression of what was already beginning to happen throughout the colonies. When the Second Continental Congress, which was essentially the government of the United States from 1775 to 1788, first met in May 1775, King George III had not replied to the petition for redress of grievances that he had been sent by the First Continental Congress. The Congress gradually took on the responsibilities of a national government. In June 1775 the Congress established the Continental Army as well as a continental currency. By the end of July of that year, it created a post office for the "United Colonies."

In August 1775 a royal proclamation declared that the King's American subjects were "engaged in open and avowed rebellion." Later that year, Parliament passed the American Prohibitory Act, which made all American vessels and cargoes forfeit to the Crown. And in May 1776 the Congress learned that the King had negotiated treaties with German states to hire mercenaries to fight in America. The weight of these actions combined to convince many Americans that the mother country was treating the colonies as a foreign entity.

One by one, the Continental Congress continued to cut the colonies' ties to Britain. The Privateering Resolution, passed in March 1776, allowed the colonists "to fit out armed vessels to cruize [sic] on the enemies of these United Colonies." On April 6, 1776, American ports were opened to commerce with other nations, an action that severed the economic ties fostered by the Navigation Acts. A "Resolution for the Formation of Local Governments" was passed on May 10, 1776.

At the same time, more of the colonists themselves were becoming convinced of the inevitability of independence. Thomas Paine's Common Sense, published in January 1776, was sold by the thousands. By the middle of May 1776, eight colonies had decided that they would support independence. On May 15, 1776, the Virginia Convention passed a resolution that "the delegates appointed to represent this colony in General Congress be instructed to propose to that respectable body to declare the United Colonies free and independent states."

It was in keeping with these instructions that Richard Henry Lee, on June 7, 1776, presented his resolution. There were still some delegates, however, including those bound by earlier instructions, who wished to pursue the path of reconciliation with Britain. On June 11 consideration of the Lee Resolution was postponed by a vote of seven colonies to five, with New York abstaining. Congress then recessed for 3 weeks. The tone of the debate indicated that at the end of that time the Lee Resolution would be adopted. Before

Congress recessed, therefore, a Committee of Five was appointed to draft a statement presenting to the world the colonies' case for independence.

## The Committee of Five

The committee consisted of two New England men, John Adams of Massachusetts and Roger Sherman of Connecticut; two men from the Middle Colonies, Benjamin Franklin of Pennsylvania and Robert R. Livingston of New York; and one southerner, Thomas Jefferson of Virginia. In 1823 Jefferson wrote that the other members of the committee "unanimously pressed on myself alone to undertake the draught [sic]. I consented; I drew it; but before I reported it to the committee I communicated it separately to Dr. Franklin and Mr. Adams requesting their corrections... I then wrote a fair copy, reported it to the committee, and from them, unaltered to the Congress." (If Jefferson did make a "fair copy," incorporating the changes made by Franklin and Adams, it has not been preserved. It may have been the copy that was amended by the Congress and used for printing, but in any case, it has not survived. Jefferson's rough draft, however, with changes made by Franklin and Adams, as well as Jefferson's own notes of changes by the Congress, is housed at the Library of Congress.)

Jefferson's account reflects three stages in the life of the Declaration: the document originally written by Jefferson; the changes to that document made by Franklin and Adams, resulting in the version that was submitted by the Committee of Five to the Congress; and the version that was eventually adopted.

On July 1, 1776, Congress reconvened. The following day, the Lee Resolution for independence was adopted by 12 of the 13 colonies, New York not voting. Immediately afterward, the Congress began to consider the Declaration. Adams and Franklin had made only a few changes before the committee submitted the document. The discussion in Congress resulted in some alterations and deletions, but the basic document remained Jefferson's. The process of revision continued through all of July 3 and into the late morning of July 4. Then, at last, church bells rang out over Philadelphia; the Declaration had been officially adopted.

The Declaration of Independence is made up of five distinct parts: the introduction; the preamble; the body, which can be divided into two sections; and a conclusion. The introduction states that this document will "declare" the "causes" that have made it necessary for the American colonies to leave the British Empire. Having stated in the introduction that independence is unavoidable, even necessary, the preamble sets out principles that were already recognized to be "self-evident" by most 18th-century Englishmen, closing with the statement that "a long train of abuses and usurpations... evinces a design to reduce [a people] under absolute Despotism, it is their right, it is their duty, to throw off such Government, and to provide new Guards for their future security." The first section of the body of the Declaration gives evidence of the "long train of abuses and usurpations" heaped upon the colonists by King George III. The second section of the body states that the colonists had appealed in vain to their "British brethren" for a redress of their grievances. Having stated the conditions that made independence necessary and having shown that those conditions existed in British North America, the Declaration concludes that "these United Colonies are, and of Right ought to be Free and Independent States; that they are Absolved from all Allegiance to the British Crown, and that all political connection between them and the State of Great Britain, is and ought to be totally dissolved." [1]

Since many citizens do not recognize the structure and functions of the United States of America, look at what has been neglected in the teaching of the American history and the political structure created by the Founding Fathers.

First, the reasons for the colonies wanting to separate from Britain were clearly spelled out in the Declaration of Independence. Each of the 27 specific reasons for separation, shown below, have been assigned a number for ease in studying their effect (with an expanded explanation of each of the items shown in Appendix B, "Declaration of Independence Accusations" by historian Benson J. Lossing.):

# Declaration of Independence

When in the Course of human events, it becomes necessary for one people to dissolve the political bands which have connected them with another, and to assume among the powers of the earth, the separate and equal station to which the Laws of Nature and of Nature's God entitle them, a decent respect to the opinions of mankind requires that they should declare the causes which impel them to the separation.

We hold these truths to be self-evident, that all men are created equal, that they are endowed by their Creator with certain unalienable Rights, that among these are Life, Liberty and the pursuit of Happiness.-That to secure these rights, Governments are instituted among Men, deriving their just powers from the consent of the governed, --That whenever any Form of Government becomes destructive of these ends, it is the Right of the People to alter or to abolish it, and to institute new Government, laying its foundation on such principles and organizing its powers in such form, as to them shall seem most likely to effect their Safety and Happiness. Prudence, indeed, will dictate that Governments long established should not be changed for light and transient causes; and accordingly all experience hath shewn, that mankind are more disposed to suffer, while evils are sufferable, than to right themselves by abolishing the forms to which they are accustomed. But when a long train of abuses and usurpations, pursuing invariably the same Object evinces a design to reduce them under absolute Despotism, it is their right, it is their duty, to throw off such Government, and to provide new Guards for their future security.-Such has been the patient sufferance of these Colonies; and such is now the necessity which constrains them to alter their former Systems of Government. The history of the present King of Great Britain is a history of repeated injuries and usurpations, all having in direct object the establishment of an absolute Tyranny over these States. To prove this, let Facts be submitted to a candid world.

I.    He has refused his Assent to Laws, the most wholesome and necessary for the public good.

II.    He has forbidden his Governors to pass Laws of immediate and pressing importance, unless suspended in their operation till his Assent should be obtained; and when so suspended, he has utterly neglected to attend to them.

III.    He has refused to pass other Laws for the accommodation of large districts of people, unless those people would relinquish the right of Representation in the Legislature, a right inestimable to them and formidable to tyrants only.

IV.    He has called together legislative bodies at places unusual, uncomfortable, and distant from the depository of their public Records, for the sole purpose of fatiguing them into compliance with his measures.

V.    He has dissolved Representative Houses repeatedly, for opposing with manly firmness his invasions on the rights of the people.

VI.    He has refused for a long time, after such dissolutions, to cause others to be elected; whereby the Legislative powers, incapable of Annihilation, have returned to the People at large for their exercise; the State remaining in the mean time exposed to all the dangers of invasion from without, and convulsions within.

VII.    He has endeavoured to prevent the population of these States; for that purpose obstructing the Laws for Naturalization of Foreigners; refusing to pass others to encourage their migrations hither, and raising the conditions of new Appropriations of Lands.

VIII.    He has obstructed the Administration of Justice, by refusing his Assent to Laws for establishing Judiciary powers.

IX.     He has made Judges dependent on his Will alone, for the tenure of their offices, and the amount and payment of their salaries.

X.     He has erected a multitude of New Offices, and sent hither swarms of Officers to harrass our people, and eat out their substance.

XI.     He has kept among us, in times of peace, Standing Armies without the Consent of our legislatures.

XII.     He has affected to render the Military independent of and superior to the Civil power.

XIII.     He has combined with others to subject us to a jurisdiction foreign to our constitution, and unacknowledged by our laws; giving his Assent to their Acts of pretended Legislation:

XIV.     For Quartering large bodies of armed troops among us:

XV.     For protecting them, by a mock Trial, from punishment for any Murders which they should commit on the Inhabitants of these States:

XVI.     For cutting off our Trade with all parts of the world:

XVII.     For imposing Taxes on us without our Consent:

XVIII. For depriving us in many cases, of the benefits of Trial by Jury:

XIX.     For transporting us beyond Seas to be tried for pretended offences

XX.     For abolishing the free System of English Laws in a neighbouring Province, establishing therein an Arbitrary government, and enlarging its Boundaries so as to render it at once an example and fit instrument for introducing the same absolute rule into these Colonies:

XXI.     For taking away our Charters, abolishing our most valuable Laws, and altering fundamentally the Forms of our Governments:

XXII. For suspending our own Legislatures, and declaring themselves invested with power to legislate for us in all cases whatsoever.

XXIII. He has abdicated Government here, by declaring us out of his Protection and waging War against us.

XXIV. He has plundered our seas, ravaged our Coasts, burnt our towns, and destroyed the lives of our people.

XXV. He is at this time transporting large Armies of foreign Mercenaries to compleat the works of death, desolation and tyranny, already begun with circumstances of Cruelty & perfidy scarcely paralleled in the most barbarous ages, and totally unworthy the Head of a civilized nation.

XXVI. He has constrained our fellow Citizens taken Captive on the high Seas to bear Arms against their Country, to become the executioners of their friends and Brethren, or to fall themselves by their Hands.

XXVII. He has excited domestic insurrections amongst us, and has endeavoured to bring on the inhabitants of our frontiers, the merciless Indian Savages, whose known rule of warfare, is an undistinguished destruction of all ages, sexes and conditions.

In every stage of these Oppressions We have Petitioned for Redress in the most humble terms: Our repeated Petitions have been answered only by repeated injury. A Prince whose character is thus marked by every act which may define a Tyrant, is unfit to be the ruler of a free people.

Nor have We been wanting in attentions to our Brittish brethren. We have warned them from time to time of attempts by their legislature to extend an unwarrantable jurisdiction over us. We have reminded them of the circumstances of our emigration and settlement here. We have appealed to their native justice and magnanimity, and we have conjured them by the ties of our common kindred to disavow these usurpations, which, would inevitably interrupt our connections and correspondence. They too have been deaf to the voice of justice and of consanguinity. We must, therefore, acquiesce in the necessity, which denounces our Separation, and hold them, as we hold the rest of mankind, Enemies in War, in Peace Friends.

We, therefore, the Representatives of the united States of America, in General Congress, Assembled, appealing to the Supreme Judge of the world for the rectitude of our intentions, do, in the Name, and by Authority of the good People of these Colonies, solemnly publish and declare, That these United Colonies are, and of Right ought to be Free and Independent States; that they are Absolved from all Allegiance to the British Crown, and that all political connection between them and the State of Great Britain, is and ought to be totally dissolved; and that as Free and Independent States, they have full Power to levy War, conclude Peace, contract Alliances, establish Commerce, and to do all other Acts and Things which Independent States may of right do. And for the support of this Declaration, with a firm reliance on the protection of divine Providence, we mutually pledge to each other our Lives, our Fortunes and our sacred Honor.

---------

Note that the word "united" is not capitalized in 'We, therefore, the Representatives of the united States of America'. This undoubtedly means that the colony/states chose to retain their individual identity, while becoming a part of the whole.

One more unique element of this Declaration; it was signed by living, breathing human beings. Too often this document, with all of its signatures, is looked upon as purely a document of intention, not realizing that the signers of that document are human beings who put everything they were, hoped to be or possessed on the line when they signed that document. The king of England considered it treason against the crown, rather than a reaction to his unwillingness to treat the colonists with the elements of liberty they believed to enjoy from a higher power.

As listed in *The American Heritage* DVD series by David Barton, the reasons for separating from England were:

Abuse of representative powers 11
Abuse of military powers 7

Abuse of judicial powers 4
Stirring up domestic insurrection 2

Taxation without representation was 17<sup>th</sup> out of 29 listed grievances. Even with so little emphasis in the Declaration, this is the one commonly given as the main reason for the separation.

# CHAPTER 3

---◆---

## *Signers of the Declaration of Independence*

To once again quote President Wilson, "A nation which does not remember what it was yesterday, does not know what it is today, nor what it is trying to do. We are trying to do a futile thing if we don't know where we have come from or what we have been about." How can a nation continue down the path established by the Founding Fathers, if they don't know the intent or reasoning used in founding the country? To understand 'where we have come from', a good starting point would be to examine who the signers of the Declaration were. Look at the signers as human beings, with much to lose by signing that 'parchment'. Take a good look at who these people were and what were the results of their involvement.[1]

## President of Congress

**John Hancock,** Congregationalist, Representing Massachusetts at the Continental Congress
Born: January 12, 1737
Birthplace: Braintree (Quincy), Mass.
Education: Graduated Harvard College (Merchant.)

Elected to the Boston Assembly, 1766; Delegate to, and President of, the Provincial Congress of Massachusetts, circa 1773; Elected to Continental Congress, 1774; Elected President of the Continental Congress, 1775; Member of Massachusetts state Constitutional Convention, elected Governor of Massachusetts, through 1793.

The signature of John Hancock on the Declaration of Independence is the most flamboyant and easily recognizable of all. It is perhaps no surprise that the story of his part in the revolution is equally engaging. Few figures were more well known or more popular than John Hancock.

He played an instrumental role, sometimes by accident, and other times by design, in coaxing the American Revolution into being.

Born in Braintree, Massachusetts in 1737, he was orphaned as a child, and adopted by a wealthy merchant uncle who was childless. Hancock attended Harvard College for a business education and graduated at the age of 17. He apprenticed to his uncle as a clerk and proved so honest and capable that, in 1760, he was sent on a business mission to England.

There he witnessed the coronation of George III and engaged some of the leading businessmen of London. In 1763, his uncle died and John Hancock inherited what was said to be the greatest body of wealth in New England.

This placed him in a society of men who consisted mainly of loyalists, suspected by the working population because of their great affluence and social power.

Hancock, however, soon became very involved in revolutionary politics and his sentiments were, early on and clearly, for independence from Great Britain.

He was in company with the Adamses and other prominent leaders in the republican movement in New England. He was elected to the Boston Assembly in 1766, and was a member of the Stamp Act Congress.

In 1768 his sloop *Liberty* was impounded by customs officials at Boston Harbor, on a charge of running contraband goods. A large group of private citizens stormed the customs post, burned the government boat, and beat the officers, causing them to seek refuge on a ship off shore. Soon afterward, Hancock abetted the Boston Tea Party.

The following year he delivered a public address to a large crowd in Boston, commemorating the Boston Massacre. In 1774, he was elected to the Provincial Congress of Massachusetts and simultaneously to the Continental Congress. When Peyton Randolph resigned in 1776, Hancock assumed the position of President. He retired in 1777 due to problems with gout, but continued public service in his native state by participating in the formation of its constitution. He was then elected to the Governorship of the state where he served for five years, declined reelection, and was again elected in 1787. He served in that office until his death on October 8, 1793. The dignity and character of John Hancock, celebrated by friend and enemy alike, did not suffer for his love of public attention. He was a populist in every sense, who held great confidence in the ability of the common man. He also displayed a pronounced contempt for unreasoned authority. A decree had been delivered from England in early 1776 offering a large reward for the capture of several leading figures. Hancock was one of them.

The story, entirely unfounded, is that on signing the Declaration, Hancock commented, "The British ministry can read that name without spectacles; let them double their reward." An alternate story, also unfounded has him saying, "There, I guess King George will be able to read that!" He was the first to sign and he did so in an entirely blank space.

# 1ST Column Georgia

**Button Gwinnett,** Episcopalian - Congregationalist, Representing Georgia at the Continental Congress
Born: circa 1732-1735
Birthplace: Down Hatherly, England

Education: Mercantile.
Commander of Georgia's Continental Battalion, Elected to Continental Congress, 1776; President of the Georgia Council of Safety, 1777.

Button Gwinnett was born in England around 1735. He came to America, residing briefly in Charleston, and in 1765 acquired a large tract of land in Georgia. Gwinnett enjoyed little success in farming or business, but found a footing in the revolutionary politics of his adopted colony. He was engaged in a long-standing political rivalry with Lachlan McIntosh, a soldier and leader who would attain highest rank in the Georgia militia and in state politics. Gwinnett was respected figure, however. In 1776 he was appointed commander of Georgia's continental militia (a post that he was forced to decline, owing to political faction), and also elected to attend the Continental Congress. Quite soon after he signed the Declaration, he returned home, where he hoped to gain appointment, once again, to the leadership of the Georgia militia. The appointment went instead to his rival. Gwinnett served in the Georgia legislature where he was involved in drafting a constitution for the new state, but also in strenuous efforts to destroy the office of McIntosh. The legislature adjourned in February of 1777 and handed control over to the Council of Safety. Gwinnett succeeded Archibald Bulloch as president of the council soon afterward. He then led an abortive attempt to invade Florida, in order to secure Georgia's southern border. That adventure was thwarted by Lachlan McIntosh and his brother George, and Gwinnett was charged with malfeasance. He was cleared of wrongdoing as he ran an unsuccessful campaign for Governor. Soon afterward, his honor challenged in public by McIntosh, he offered a duel. They met outside of Savanna on May 16, 1777, where both were wounded. McIntosh ultimately survived, Button Gwinnett died three days later at the age of 42.

**Lyman Hall**, Congregationalist, Representing Georgia at the Continental Congress
Born: April 12, 1724
Birthplace: Wallingford, Conn.
Education: Graduated Yale College, (Physician.)
Elected to Continental Congress, 1775; Delegate to the Georgia House of Assembly, Elected Governor of Georgia, 1783; Judge, 1785.

Lyman Hall was born in Connecticut in 1724. He studied medicine at Yale College, graduated in 1756 and went to Charleston, South Carolina, shortly after to establish a medical practice. He bought land in Georgia in 1760 and established a plantation there, while continuing to practice medicine. Two years later he returned to South Carolina, still as a physician. In 1774, by this time partisan in revolutionary politics, he again came to Georgia and earned the unflattering attention of the Royal Governor, James Wright. He also secured election to the Continental Congress, where he was involved in provisioning food and medicine for the Revolutionary Armies. He was reelected to congress through 1780 but retired to his adopted state in 1777 when state matters, including the situation of his longtime friend Button Gwinnett, demanded his attention. A short time later, the war reached Savannah. Hall's property was burned and he stood accused of high treason.

He fled to Charleston, which was also overtaken by the British. He then fled to Connecticut, some say, where he was harbored by family.

He returned to Georgia in 1782, to reclaim his lands, was elected to the House of Assembly in 1783 and then elevated to the office of the Governor. After a single year as Governor, he served one more year in the Assembly, then a year as judge. He then returned to private life and was involved in the continued development of agriculture in the state. Hall died on October 19, 1790, at the age of 66.

**George Walton,** (Christian – Episcopalian) Representing Georgia at the Continental Congress
Born: 1741
Birthplace: Prince Edward County, VA
Education: Informal, perhaps self-taught (Lawyer, Judge)
Admitted to the Bar, 1774; Member, Secretary, Provincial Congress of Georgia, 1776; Member, Georgia Committee of Safety, 1776; Elected to the Continental Congress, 1776, 77, 1780, 81; Colonel of the First Georgia Militia, 1778; Governor of Georgia, 1779; Chief Justice of Georgia, 1783-89; Presidential Elector, Governor of Georgia, 1789; Superior Court Judge, 1789-98, US. Senator, 1795.

George Walton was born in Prince Edward County, Virginia, in 1741. His parents died soon after, and he was adopted by an Uncle who apprenticed him as a carpenter. Little else is known about his early years. He appeared again in 1769 when he moved to Savannah and began to study Law. He was admitted to the Bar in 1774. Deeply involved with the patriot movement in Georgia, he would ultimately serve an important role in the development of the state.

At the formation of the Georgia provincial Congress, Walton was elected Secretary, and made President of the Council of Safety. In 1776 he was elected to the Continental Congress, where he signed the Declaration of Independence. He spent many of the following years engaged in the defense of his state, and in a messy political battle with Button Gwinnett, another signer from Georgia. In 1778 Walton was commissioned a Colonel of the First Regiment of the Georgia Militia. He was injured in Battle and taken prisoner. He gained his freedom in 1779 through a prisoner exchange and was soon after elected Governor of Georgia, an office he held for only two months. Political conflict colored all of Walton's career. He was allied with General Lachlan McIntosh in a fierce struggle against Gwinnett for political dominance of the state. Walton was dispatched from office on several occasions, indicted for alleged criminal activities on others, in an interminable battle between two factions of the patriot movement in Georgia.

He was returned to congress in 1780 and stayed through 1781. He remained in Philadelphia until 1783. That year he was censured by the legislature for his involvement in a duel which led to the death Gwinnett by the hand of his rival, commissioned to treat with the Cherokee nation in Tennessee, and appointed Chief Justice of his state. In 1789 he served in the college of Electors and again was elected Governor. The government was reorganized under a new constitution in November of that year, at which time Walton stepped down. He was immediately appointed a superior court judge. In 1795 he was sent to fill an unfulfilled term in the US Senate. He was not reelected. He then retired to farming. He died in Augusta February 2, 1804, at the age of 64.

## 2nd Column North Carolina

**William Hooper,** Episcopalian Representing North Carolina at the Continental Congress
Born: June 28, 1742
Birthplace: Boston, Massachusetts
Education: Harvard College (Lawyer.)
Elected to General Assembly of North Carolina, 1773; Member of Continental Congress, 1774-1776; Judge of the Federal Court; 1786.

William Hooper was born in Boston Massachusetts in 1742. He graduated from Harvard College in 1760, continued his studies in the law, and settled in Wilmington, North Carolina in 1767. In 1773 he represented Wilmington in the General Assembly of North Carolina. He attended the Continental Congress in 1774. He resigned from the Congress in 1776 and returned home. In 1789 he was appointed to the Federal Bench, but a year later he retired due to failing health. He died on October 14, 1790.

**Joseph Hewes,** Quaker – Episcopalian, Representing North Carolina at the Continental Congress
Born: January 23, 1730
Birthplace: Princeton, New Jersey
Education: Princeton College (Merchant)
Member of the Colonial Assembly of North Carolina, 1766-75. Member of the Committee of Correspondence, member of new Provincial Assembly, 1775; Elected to Continental Congress, 1774-79, Defacto first Secretary of the Navy.

Joseph Hewes was born in Princeton, New Jersey and attended Princeton College. He established a shipping business in Wilmington, North Carolina in 1760 and, by the time of the revolution, had amassed a fortune. He elected to the Provincial Assembly in 1766 and served there until it was dissolved by the royal governor in 1775. He was appointed to the Committee of Correspondence, elected to the Provincial Legislature, and sent along to the Continental Congress in 1775. Hewes was known as a tireless worker in committee and the leading expert on maritime concerns. In 1776 he signed the Declaration of Independence and placed his ships at the service of the Continental Armed Forces.

He served the Congress as the Secretary of the Naval Affairs Committee until 1779, when he fell ill. He died at age 50, on November 10, 1779.

**John Penn**, Episcopalian, Representing North Carolina at the Continental Congress
Born: May 17, 1741
Birthplace: Near Port Royal, Virginia
Education: Informal (Lawyer)
Law Practice in Virginia, 1762; Accepted to the North Carolina Bar, 1774; Member of Continental Congress, 1775-77, 1779-80; Member of the Board of War, 1780.

John Penn was born in Caroline County, Virginia, to a family of means. His father died when he was eighteen years old, and though he had received only a rudimentary education at a country school, he had access to the library of his relative Edmund Pendleton. He was licensed to practice law in the state of Virginia at age twenty-two. In 1774 he moved to Granville County, North Carolina, where he established a law practice and soon became a gentleman member of the political community. He was elected to attend the provincial Congress in 1775 and elected to the Continental Congress that same year. He served there until 1777, participating in committee work. He was again elected in 1779, appointed to the Board of War, where he served until 1780. He declined a judgeship in his native state around that time, due to failing health. In retirement he engaged in his law practice. He died at the age of 48, September 14, 1788.

## South Carolina

**Edward Rutledge,** Episcopalian, Representing South Carolina at the Continental Congress, 1774-76, 1779
Born: November 23, 1749
Birthplace: Charleston, SC
Education: Graduate of Oxford, Studied at Middle Temple (London), Member of the English Bar (Lawyer)
State Legislator, Representative to the Continental Congress, 177476, 1779; Captain, Charleston Battalion of Artillery, 1776-1779; State legislator, 1782-1796; College of Electors, 1788, 1792, 1796; Elected Governor for South Carolina, 1798.

Born to an aristocratic Family in South Carolina, Edward Rutledge was perhaps destined to a life of Public service. He was educated in law at Oxford and studied for and was admitted to the English Bar. He and his brother John were both engaged in the law, and both attended the congress. They supported each other unabashedly, both on the floor and in committee. Edward attended Congress at the remarkable age of 27, and was no doubt pretty excited to find himself in the company of the most eminent men of the colonies.

He took leave of Congress in November of 1776 to join the defense of his colony. He was a member of the Charleston Battalion of Artillery, engaged in several important battles, and attained the rank of Captain. The colonial legislature sent him back to Congress in 1779 to fill a vacancy. He took his leave again in 1780 when the British conducted a third invasion of South Carolina. He resumed his post as Captain in the defense of Charleston, was captured and held prisoner until July of 1781.

In 1782 he returned to the legislature of his native state, where he served until 1796. He was a very active member, intent on the prosecution of British Loyalists. At times he served on as many nineteen committees. He also served as an elector, in 1788, 1792, and in 1796 when, despite his avowed allegiance to the Federalist Party, he voted for Thomas Jefferson. He was then elected to the state Senate, twice, and in 1789 was elected Governor. This would be his last office. His health declining, he was barely able to complete his term as Governor. He died in January 23, 1800, at the age of 50.

**Thomas Heyward, Jr.** Episcopalian, Representing South Carolina at the Continental Congress
Born: July 28, 1746
Birthplace: St. Lukes Parish, SC
Education: Private classical education, Law studies in America and England (Lawyer.) Elected to the Continental Congress, 1775-1778; Judge, 1783-1798.

Thomas Heyward, Jr. was born in South Carolina in 1746. He received a classical education at home and continued in legal studies, which he completed in England. In 1775 he was elected to the Continental Congress, where he signed the Declaration of Independence. In 1778 he returned to South Carolina to serve as a Judge. He was taken prisoner by the British while in command of a Militia force during the siege of Charleston. He resumed his Judgeship following the war, and retired in 1798. He died on March 6, 1809, at the age of 62.

**Thomas Lynch Jr.,** Episcopalian, Representing South Carolina
at the Continental Congress
Born: August 5, 1749
Birthplace: Winyah, SC
Education: Graduated, Cambridge University. (Lawyer)
Captain of a South Carolina Regimental Company, 1775; Delegate
to the Continental Congress, 1776.

Thomas Lynch, Jr., was born in South Carolina on August
5, 1749. He received an education in England and graduated
with honors at Cambridge. He studied law in London and then
returned home in 1772. He was politically engaged as soon as he
returned home, and was commissioned a company commander
in the South Carolina regiment in 1775. Soon afterward he was
elected to a seat in the Continental Congress. He fell ill shortly
after signing the Declaration and retired from the Congress. At
the close of 1776 he and his wife sailed for the West Indies. The
ship disappeared (ca. 1779) and there is no record of his life after
that.

**Arthur Middleton,** Episcopalian, Representing South Carolina
at the Continental Congress
Born: June 26, 1742
Birthplace: Charleston, SC
Education: Graduate of Cambridge, Charleston Council of Safety,
1775; Delegate to the Continental Congress, 1776.

Arthur Middleton was born in South Carolina in 1742. He
was educated in England and graduated from Cambridge in
1773. He was elected to the Council of Safety at Charleston in
1775, and in 1776 was a delegate to the Continental Congress. He
was captured by the British when Charleston was overrun 1781,
and held prisoner for more than a year. Most of his fortune was
destroyed during the Revolution. He was engaged in politics until
his death on the first of January, 1787.

# 3rd Column Maryland

**Samuel Chase,** Episcopalian, Representing Maryland at the Continental Congress
Born: April 17, 1741
Birthplace: Princess Anne, MD
Education: Classical education in Law, Baltimore. (Judge)
Practiced Law in Annapolis; Elected to Continental Congress, 1774-1778; Chief Justice of Criminal Court, district of Baltimore; Chief Justice, state of Maryland, 1788-1796; Justice, US Supreme Court, 1796-1811.

Samuel Chase was born in Maryland on the seventeenth of April, 1741. He received a good classical education in Baltimore. He studied law and began practice in Annapolis. In 1774 he was selected to represent Maryland at the Continental Congress. He was re-elected to that post in 1775, and served there until 1778. In 1786 he moved to Baltimore, where two years later he was appointed chief justice of the Criminal Court of that district. He was later appointed chief justice of the state. In 1796 he was appointed a judge of the Supreme Court of the United States, an office that he filled until his death on the nineteenth of June, 1811.

**William Paca,** Episcopalian, Representing Maryland at the Continental Congress
Born: October 31, 1740
Birthplace: near Abingdon, MD
Education: Philadelphia College, Studied Law at Annapolis. (Judge)
Delegate to the Maryland Legislature, 1771; Member of the Committee of Correspondence, Patriot Leader; Elected to Continental Congress, 1774-78, Chief Justice of Maryland, 1778; Elected Governor of Maryland, 1782; Federal District Judge for the State of Maryland, 1789-99.

William Paca was born in Abington, Maryland on October 30, 1740. His education in law was impressive. He was tutored at home in the classics before attending Philadelphia College at age fifteen, where he graduated at eighteen with a Master's degree. He then studied law in Annapolis at the office of an eminent lawyer.

Before seeking admission to the Bar of Maryland, he attended training at the Inner Temple in England. His political engagement began in his interest in the law. He wrote and organized against a poll-tax originated by the royal governor just prior to the outbreak of hostilities. He was a local leader in the patriot movement in the late 1770s.

Elected to the State Legislature of Maryland in 1771, he was appointed to the Continental Congress in 1774. He was reelected and served there until 1779 when he was appointed chief justice of the State of Maryland. In 1782 he was elected governor of that state. He was appointed federal district judge for the State of Maryland from 1789, until his death, October 23, 1799.

**Thomas Stone,** Episcopalian, Representing Maryland at the Continental Congress
Born: 1743
Birthplace: Charles County, MD
Education: Parish School, Law Studies. (Lawyer)
Admitted to the Maryland Bar, 1764; Elected to the Continental Congress, 1775-78, 1783; Elected to Constitutional Convention (declined), 1785.

Thomas Stone was born at Poynton Manor in Charles County Maryland in 1743. He was educated by a Scottish schoolmaster and later studied law at the office of Thomas Johnson. He was admitted to the Bar in 1764 and set up practice in Frederick Maryland. He was a prosperous landowner and moderately successful lawyer.

Stone was elected to Congress in 1775. He did not speak much in congress, so little is known of his service there, except that he was a member of the committee that framed the Articles of Confederation. He voted for Independence in 1776, and his name is affixed to the Declaration. He was elected to Congress again in

1783 and served as chairman, but retired at the end of his term. He was elected to attend the Constitutional Convention in 1787, but declined the office because of his wife's failing health. She died 1787, and Stone never got over the grief. He decided to travel to England, but died in Alexandria, October 5, 1787, while waiting for the ship. He was forty-four years old. Little else is known about Thomas Stone, as no letters or papers accounting his life have ever been found.

**Charles Carroll of Carrollton,** Episcopalian Representing Maryland at the Continental Congress
Born: September 9, 1737
Birthplace: Annapolis, MD
Education: Jesuits' College at St. Omar, France; seminary in Rheims; Graduate, College of Louis the Grande; Bourges; studies in Paris; Studies, apprenticeship in London. (Scholar, Lawyer)
Member of first Maryland Committee of Safety, Provincial Congress, 1775;
Delayed member of Continental Congress, August, 1776, Signed Declaration of Independence; Appointed to board of War, 1776; Elected to Senate of Maryland, 1781; Elected U.S. Senator from Maryland, 1788, returned to Maryland Senate 1789-'99.

Charles Carroll was born into a wealthy Roman Catholic family in Annapolis Maryland. He began his rather remarkable formal education at the age of 8, when he was packed off to France to attend a Jesuit College at St. Omer. He graduated the College of Louis the Grande at age Seventeen and continued practical studies in Europe until, at the age of 28, he returned to his home. Into the radical climate produced by the Stamp Act, walked a Highly refined Gentleman with all of the education and experience that might be expected of an emissary of the finest courts in Europe. Charles Carroll is said to have identified with the radical cause at once, and he proceeded to work in the circles of American patriots. In 1772 he anonymously engaged the secretary of the colony of Maryland in a series of Newspaper articles protesting the right of the British government to tax the colonies without representation.

Carroll was an early advocate for armed resistance with the object of separation from Gr. Britain. However, his native colony was less certain in this matter and did not even send a representative to the first Continental Congress. He served on the first Committee of Safety, at Annapolis, in 1775, and also in the Provincial Congress. He visited the Continental Congress in 1776, and was enlisted in a diplomatic mission to Canada, along with Franklin and Chase. Shortly after his return, the Maryland Convention decided to join in support for the Revolution. Carroll was elected to represent Maryland on the 4th of July, and though he was too late to vote for the Declaration, he did sign it.

He served in the Continental Congress, on the Board of War, through much of the War of Independence, and simultaneously participated in the framing of a constitution for Maryland. In 1778 he returned to Maryland to participate in the formation of the state government. He was elected to the Maryland Senate in 1781, and to the first Federal Congress in 1788. He returned again to the State Senate in 1790 and served there for 10 years. He retired from that post in 1800.

Charles Carroll was the last surviving member of those who signed the Declaration. He died, the last survivor of the signers of the Declaration, in 1832 at the age of 95 on November 14, 1832.

# Virginia

**George Wythe,** Episcopalian, Representing Virginia at the Continental Congress
Born: 1726
Birthplace: Elizabeth City Co. (Hampton), VA
Education: Informal, Law Studies. (Lawyer, Educator)
Admitted to the Bar in Virginia, 1746; Clerk of the committee on Privileges and Elections of the House of Burgesses, 1747; Attorney General of Virginia, 1753; Member of the House of Burgesses;

1755-65; Member of the Board of Visitors, William and Mary, 1761; Professor of Law, William and Mary, 1769-1789; Elected to Continental Congress, 1775-76; Speaker of the Virginia House, 1777-78; Judge of the Chancery Court of Virginia, 1789-1806.

George Wythe was one of the very most distinguished men of his age, yet due to his modesty and quiet dignity, we learn little about him from the history books. He was born in Elizabeth County Virginia, in 1726, of a wealthy agricultural family. His father died when George was three, but his mother, who was extraordinarily well educated for a woman of that day, tutored him in the classics in a manner that would take him far indeed. His mother died when he was still a teenager and his oldest brother, who took no interest in George, inherited the family property. George entered the college of William and Mary but was unable to keep up with the fees. He dropped out and then managed to secure a study of law at the office of a Stephen Dewey. His studies were so successful that he was admitted to the bar in Spotsylvania County in 1746, at the age of 20.

Everyone who came into contact with him was impressed. He was appointed clerk to the Committee which formed the rules of conduct and elections in the House of Burgesses in 1746. In 1753 the Royal Governor of Virginia made him Attorney General, to fill the shoes of Peyton Randolph while he traveled to England. In 1755 Wythe was elected to represent Williamsburg at the House of Burgesses. At that time, his oldest brother died, and he inherited the family farm. Wythe served in the House of Burgesses until it was dissolved, on the eve of the revolution.

His most valuable contribution to the new nation was his involvement in education. This began in 1761 when he was elected to the Board of Visitors at the College of William and Mary. Eight years later the man who could never gain a degree for want of the money to do it with, became America's first Professor of Law. His students included Thomas Jefferson, Henry Clay, James Monroe, John Marshal, and several dozen other distinguished public servants. He taught for twenty years and admitted to no greater love than that of forming young minds.

In 1775 Wythe was elected to attend the Continental Congress. He served for two years, voted in favor of the Resolution, and for the Declaration. In 1776 he was called back to Virginia in order to help form the new government. He was elected Speaker of the Virginia House of Delegates in 1777. The following year he was made one of the three Chancellors of the State of Virginia, a post that he served in for the rest of his life. George Wythe was revered as a man on great honor and integrity. He was a republican in all things, and a quiet abolitionist. He freed his slaves and made provisions for their support until they could earn a living for themselves. This ended in tragedy-and that tragedy would cost Wythe his own life. A young member of his family, on discovering that Wythe had conditionally willed part of the family property to his slaves, decided to enlarge his own share by poisoning them with arsenic. He incidentally murdered George Wythe in the process. Wythe died on June 8, 1806 at the age of 80.

**Richard Henry Lee,** Episcopalian, Virginia House of Burgesses, Representing Virginia at the Continental Congress
Born: January 20, 1732
Birthplace: Westmoreland County, VA
Education: Private school at Wakefield, Yorkshire, England. (Farmer)
Justice of the peace, 1757; Virginia House of Burgesses, 1757; Continental Congress, 1774; First US Senator for Virginia, 1789.

Richard Henry Lee (brother of F.L. Lee) was born to an aristocratic family at Stratford, in Westmoreland County, Virginia. He attended a private school in England, returning to Virginia in 1751. That being the era of the French and Indian War, Lee formed a militia troop of young men in his neighborhood, was elected the leader, and marched his troop to a council in Alexandria where General Braddock was preparing a campaign on the Ohio River. The young men were rebuffed by the General and returned home. In 1757 Lee was appointed Justice of the Peace, and was shortly thereafter elected to the Virginia House of Burgesses. He was amongst those radical members of the Burgesses who met at the Raleigh tavern when the house was dissolved by the Royal Governor. In 1774 he was elected to attend the first Continental Congress. He enjoyed many important committee appointments. Noted for his oratory skills, it was he who offered the Resolutions for Independence to the committee of the whole in 1776. He served in Congress through the course of the War, while also serving in the House of Burgesses. In 1783 he was selected as president of Congress.

Lee opposed the federal constitution, as he favored strong state rights. He was however elected the first State Senator from Virginia under the new federal government. He retired from that office to his home in Chantilly due to illness, and soon after died at the age of 62, June 19, 1794.

**Thomas Jefferson,** Episcopalian, Deist, Virginia House of Burgesses, Representing Virginia at the Continental Congress
Born: April 13, 1743
Birthplace: Shadwell, VA
Education: William and Mary College (Lawyer)
Admitted to Virginia bar, 1767; Elected to Virginia House of Burgesses, 1769; Delegate to the Continental Congress, 177576; Virginia House of Delegates, 1776-79; Elected Governor of Virginia, 1779, 1780; Dispatched to England to treat for peace with Gr. Britain, 1782; Associate Envoy to France, 1784; Minister to the French Court, 1785; Secretary of State, 1789; Established Democratic-Republican party, 1793; Vice President of the United States, 1796; President, 1801; Established University of Virginia, 1810.

More than a mere renaissance man, Jefferson may actually have been a new kind of man. He was fluent in five languages and able to read two others. He wrote, over the course of his life, over sixteen thousand letters. He was acquainted with nearly every influential person in America, and a great many in Europe as well. He was a lawyer, agronomist, musician, scientist, philosopher, author, architect, inventor, and statesman. Though he never set foot outside of the American continent before adulthood, he acquired an education that rivaled the finest to be attained in Europe. He was clearly the foremost American son of the Enlightenment.

Jefferson was born at Shadwell in Albemarle County, Virginia on April 13, 1743. He was tutored by the Reverend James Maury, a learned man, in the finest classical tradition. He began the study of Latin, Greek, and French at the age of 9. He attended William and Mary College in Williamsburg at sixteen years old, then continued his education in the Law under George Wythe, the first professor of law in America (who later would sign Jefferson's Declaration in 1776). Thomas Jefferson attended the House of Burgesses as a student in 1765 when he witnessed Patrick Henry's defiant stand against the Stamp Act. He gained the Virginia bar and began practice in 1769, and was elected to the House of Burgesses in 1769. It was there that his involvement in revolutionary politics began. He was never a very vocal member, but his writing, his quiet work in committee, and his ability to distill large volumes of information to essence, made him an invaluable member in any deliberative body.

In 1775 when a Virginia convention selected delegates to the Continental Congress, Jefferson was selected as an alternate. It was expected that Payton Randolph, (then Speaker of the Virginia House and president of the Continental Congress too,) would be recalled by the Royal Governor. This did happen and Jefferson went in his place. Thomas Jefferson had a theory about self-governance and the rights of people who established habitat in new lands. Before attending the Congress in Philadelphia he codified these thoughts in an article called A Summary View of the Rights of British America. This paper he sent on ahead of him. He fell ill on the road and was delayed for several days. By the time he arrived, his paper had been published as a pamphlet and sent throughout the colonies and on to England where Edmund

Burke, sympathetic to the colonial condition, had it reprinted and circulated widely. In 1776 Jefferson, then a member of the committee to draft a declaration of independence, was chosen by the committee to write the draft. This he did, with some minor corrections from John Adams and an embellishment from Franklin, the document was offered to the Congress on the first day of July. The congress modified it somewhat, abbreviating certain wording and removing points that were outside of general agreement. The Declaration was adopted on the Fourth of July.

Jefferson returned to his home not long afterward. His wife and two of his children were very ill, he was tired of being remote from his home, and he was anxious about the development of a new government for his native state.

In June of 1779 he succeeded Patrick Henry as Governor of Virginia. The nation was still at war, and the southern colonies were under heavy attack. Jefferson's Governorship was clouded with hesitation. He himself concluded that the state would be better served by a military man. He declined re-election after his first term and was succeeded by General Nelson of Yorktown.

In 1781 he retired to Monticello, the estate he inherited, to write, work on improved agriculture, and attend his wife. It was during this time that he wrote Notes on the State of Virginia, a work that he never completed. Martha Jefferson died in September of 1782. This event threw Jefferson into a depression that, according to his eldest daughter he might never have recovered from. Except that Washington called on him in November of 1782 to again serve his country as Minister Plenipotentiary to negotiate peace with Gr. Britain. He accepted the post, however it was aborted when the peace was secured before he could sail from Philadelphia.

In 1784 Jefferson went to France as an associate Diplomat with Franklin and Adams. It was in that year that he wrote an article establishing the standard weights, measures, and currency units for the United States. He succeeded Franklin as Minister to France the following year. When he returned home in 1789, he joined the Continental Congress for a while, and was then appointed Secretary of State under George Washington.

This placed him in a very difficult position. The character of the executive was being established during the first few terms. Jefferson and many others were critical of the form it was taking under the first Federalist administration. Jefferson was sharply at odds with fellow cabinet members John Adams and Alexander Hamilton, both of whom he found to be too authoritarian and too quick to assume overwhelming power for the part of the executive. He resigned from the cabinet in 1793 and formed the Democrat-republican party. Heated competition continued. Jefferson ran for president in 1796, lost to John Adams, and, most uncomfortably, this made him vice president under a man whom he could no longer abide. After a single meeting, on the street, the two never communicated directly during the whole administration.

Jefferson again ran for the presidency in 1801 and this time he won. He served for two terms and he did ultimately play a deciding role in forming the character of the American Presidency. The 12th amendment to the Constitution changed the manner in which the vice president was selected, so as to prevent arch enemies from occupying the first and second positions of the executive. Jefferson also found the State of the Union address to be too magisterial when delivered in person. He performed one and afterwards delivered them, as required by the constitution, only in writing. He also undertook the Louisiana Purchase, extending the boundaries of the country and establishing the doctrine of manifest destiny.

Thomas Jefferson retired from office in 1808. He continued the private portion of his life's work, and sometime later re-engaged his dearest and longest friend James Madison, in the work of establishing the University of Virginia. In 1815 one of his projects, a Library of Congress, finally bore fruit, when he sold his own personal library to the congress as a basis for the collection. Shortly before his death in 1826, Jefferson told Madison that he wished to be remembered for two things only; as the Author of the Declaration of Independence, and as the founder of the University of Virginia. Jefferson died on the 4th of July, 1826, as the nation celebrated the fiftieth anniversary of his splendid Declaration.

**Benjamin Harrison,** Episcopalian, Representing Virginia at the Continental Congress
Born: April 5, 1726
Birthplace: Berkeley, VA
Education: Attended William and Mary College (Farmer, Politician)
Elected to Virginia House of Burgesses, 1764; Member of the Continental Congress, 1774-77; Reelected to House of Burgesses, 1777, Selected as Speaker, 1778; Elected Governor of Virginia, 1782-84, 1791.

Benjamin Harrison was born in Berkeley Virginia in 1726. He attended William and Mary College in Williamsburg, but was unable to complete his studies due to the sudden death of his father and two sisters in a lightning strike. He was elected to the House of Burgesses at the age of 38. In 1764, when the House defied the Royal Governor and passed the Stamp Act Resolutions, the Governor tried to bribe Harrison with an appointment to the executive council. He refused the appointment and instead declared a devotion to republican principles. Elected to the Continental Congress in 1774, he was one of a party of representatives who, the following year, attended General Washington in Cambridge to plan the future of the American Army.

In 1777 he returned to Virginia to a seat in the House of Burgesses and also to serve as a lieutenant in his county militia. He was chosen Speaker of the House in 1778, and elected Governor of the State of Virginia in 1782. He retired from the Governor's office after five years' service. Harrison suffered with gout during his later years. He died on April 24, 1791, at the age of 65. (His son, William Henry Harrison, was elected ninth President of the United States.)

**Thomas Nelson Jr.,** Episcopalian, Virginia House of Burgesses, Representing Virginia at the Continental Congress
Born: December 26, 1738
Birthplace: Yorktown, Virginia
Died: 1789
Member of the House of Burgesses, 1774; Virginia provincial Convention, 1775; Officer and Commander of the Virginia Militia, 1775; Delegate to the Continental Congress, 1775-77, 1779; Elected Governor of Virginia, 1781.

Thomas Nelson Jr. was born into the aristocratic society of Virginia in December of 1738. Like most of the southern Gentleman of his day, he gained a private education in England, culminating in a degree from Cambridge. He returned in 1761 and soon became involved in service to his colony and his country. Elected to the House of Burgesses in 1774, he was one of eighty nine who convened at the Raleigh tavern when that house was dissolved by the royal Governor. He was a member of the Virginia provincial convention in 1775, and there he undertook the creation of the Virginia Militia. He then assumed duty as its first Commander. Shortly thereafter he was elected to the Continental Congress. Nelson began suffering health problems in 1777 and thought best to retire to his native state. He resumed his military service, much to the benefit of both Virginia and his health. He was reelected to Congress in 1779 but his health again declined and he returned to Virginia several months later.

Once again he resumed service, as commanding General of the Lower Virginia Militia, at a time when British forces began aggressive campaigns against the southern colonies. In 1781, Thomas Jefferson declined reelection as Governor due to his inability to serve the needs of a state under siege. General Nelson succeeded Jefferson and served as both Civil Governor and Commander in chief of the Virginia Militia. Under his command Virginia, both civil and military, became a force to contend with. Both the Continental Army and French forces utilized the skills of the Virginia units in the Siege of Yorktown in the autumn of 1781.

Finally overcome by illness in October of that year, General Nelson retired from public service. He died at one of his estates, in Hanover County, January 4, 1789 at the age of 50.

**Francis Lightfoot Lee,** Episcopalian, Virginia House of Burgesses, Representing Virginia at the Continental Congress
Born: October 14, 1734
Birthplace: Westmoreland County, VA
Education: Private, (Farmer)
Member of the Virginia House of Burgesses 1758-75; Elected to Continental Congress, 1775-79, Member of Virginia Senate.

Francis Lightfoot Lee (brother of R.H. Lee) was born in Westmoreland, Virginia, on the fourteenth of October, 1734. He was educated at home by Doctor Craig, in the manner of an enlightened country gentleman. In 1765 he was elected to the Virginia House of Burgesses, where he served until 1775. He was a noted radical, on the side of Patrick Henry in opposing the Stamp Act. He joined the group who called for a general congress and a Virginia Convention in 1774. He attended that convention and that year was sent to the first Continental Congress. He represented his state there until 1779, working on numerous committees. He retired from the Congress in 1779 and returned to his home. He served for a while in the Virginia Senate and then retired to private life. He died January 11, 1797.

**Carter Braxton,** Episcopalian, Representing Virginia at the Continental Congress
Born: October 14, 1734
Birthplace: Newington Plantation, VA
Education: William and Mary College (Farmer)
Virginia House of Burgesses, 1770-85; Delegate to the Continental Congress, 1774-75; Member, Virginia patriot's Committee of Safety, 1774; Signer of the Declaration of Independence, 1776.

Carter Braxton was born of a wealthy family in Newington Plantation Virginia. He lost nearly all of his wealth in the course of the revolution, partly through his support of the Union, and partly through attack by the British forces. He was educated at William and Mary College. He married at age 19, but his wife died about two years after. He then went to England for a little more than two years. In 1760 he returned, married again, and was appointed to represent King William County in the Virginia House of Burgesses. He was in attendance 1765, when Patrick Henry's Stamp Act resolutions agitated the Assembly. In 1769 he joined the "radical" faction of the Burgesses in support of Virginia's sole right to tax inhabitants. When the house was dissolved in 1774 he joined the patriot's Committee of Safety in Virginia, and represented his county in the Virginia Convention. In 1775, upon the sudden death of <u>Peyton Randolph</u>, Braxton was selected to assume his place in the Continental Congress.

He attended two years, after which he returned to Virginia to continue service to the House of Burgesses. During the War, he had loaned £10,000 sterling to support the revolutionary cause. He had also used his wealth to sponsor shipping and privateering during the conflict, the losses from which eventually resulted in debt. He never recovered, and, in 1786, was forced to leave his inherited country estate for simple quarters in Richmond. He died at age 61, October 10, 1797.

# 4th Column Pennsylvania

**Robert Morris,** Episcopalian, Representing Pennsylvania at the Continental Congress
Born: January 20, 1734
Birthplace: Lancashire, England
Education: Private and Apprenticeship (Merchant)
Delegate to the Continental Congress, 1775, Appointed Special Commissioner of Finance, 1776; Author of the plan for a National Bank, 1781; Financial Agent of the United States, 1781; Delegate to the Pennsylvania Legislature, ca. 1783; Delegate to the

Constitutional Convention, 1787; United States Senator, 1789-95; Appointed Secretary of the Treasury, 1789.

Robert Morris was a man of wealth and integrity in Philadelphia during the revolutionary period. Though not a scholar or a soldier, he was to play an essential role in the success of the War against England, and in placing the new United States on a firm footing in the world. Morris, almost single handed, saw to the financing of the Revolutionary War, and the establishment of the Bank of the United States after.

Born in England in 1734, he came to the Chesapeake Bay in 1744 and attended school in Philadelphia. Young Robert, who seemed ill suited to formal education and too quick for his teacher in any case, was soon apprenticed to the counting room of Charles Willing at the age of 16. Two years later his employer died and Morris entered a partnership with the gentleman's son. In the succeeding thirty nine years that business flourished, and Robert Morris' wealth and reputation were secured. Being an importer, the business was hit hard by the Stamp Act and the colonial revolt against it. Morris and his partner choose the side of the colonials and Robert engaged in the movements against British rule.

Elected to the Continental Congress in 1775, he participated on many of the committees involved in raising capital and provisions for the Continental Army. Early in 1776, he was given a special commission by congress, with authority to negotiate bills of exchange for, and to solicit money by other means for the operation of the war. One of the most successful such devices were the lotteries. In late 1776, with the Continental Army in a state of severe deprivation because of a shortage of capital and the failure of several of the colonies in paying for the war, Morris loaned $10,000 of his own money to the government. This money provisioned the desperate troops, who went on to win the Battle of Trenton (Washington Crossing). Throughout the war he personally underwrote the operations of privateers, ships that ran the British Blockades at great risk and thus brought needed supplies and capital into the colonies.

In 1781 he devised a plan for a National Bank and submitted it to Congress. It was approved and became The Bank of North America, an institution that brought stability to the colonial economy, facilitated continued finance of the War effort, and would ultimately establish the credit of the United States with the nations of Europe. Morris was immediately appointed Financial Agent (Secretary of Treasury) of the United States, in order to direct the operation of the new bank.

Following the war, he served in the Pennsylvania Legislature. He was also a delegate to the Constitutional Convention in 1787, and thereafter an advocate for the new constitution. He was then sent as a Senator for Pennsylvania when that constitution was ratified. In 1789, President George Washington appointed Morris Secretary of the Treasury, but he declined the office and suggested Alexander Hamilton instead. Morris completed his office as Senator and then retired from public service. He never recovered the wealth that he enjoyed before the revolution. What was left of his fortune was soon lost to land speculation in the western part of New York State. He died May 9, 1806, in relative poverty, at the age of 73.

**Benjamin Rush,** Presbyterian, Representing Pennsylvania at the Continental Congress
Born: December 24, 1745
Birthplace: Byberry, PA
Education: B.A. at the College of New Jersey (now Princeton), M.D. at the University of Edinburgh (Physician)
Physician, Professor of Chemistry at the College of Philadelphia, 1769; Writer, Member of the Sons of Liberty in Philadelphia, 1773...; Elected to Pennsylvania provincial conference, Elected to Continental Congress, 1776; Appointed Surgeon-general to the armies of the middle department (of the Continental Army), 1777; Instructor, Physician, University of the State of Pennsylvania, 1778...; Treasurer of the U.S. Mint, 1779-1813; Professor of medical theory and clinical practice, University of Pennsylvania, 1791-1813

Benjamin Rush, eminent Physician, writer, educator, humanitarian, is as interesting a figure as one could find in the formation of the United States. A wildly popular and much loved man, he was nonetheless a fallible character. He was born in December of 1745 in Byberry, Pennsylvania, some twelve miles from Philadelphia. His father died when Benjamin was six, and his mother placed him in the care of his maternal uncle Dr. Finley who became his teacher and advisor for many years. In 1759 he attended the College of Philadelphia, where he ultimately attained a Bachelor of Arts degree. He continued his education with a Dr. Redman of Philadelphia for four years and then crossed the Atlantic to attend to an M.D. at Edinburgh. He spent several years in Europe studying and practicing Medicine, French, Italian, Spanish, and science. He returned in 1769, opened a private practice in Philadelphia, and was appointed Professor of Chemistry at the College of Philadelphia.

Benjamin Rush was soon beloved in the city, where he practiced extensively amongst the poor. His practice was successful, his classes were popular, and he further began to engage in writing that would prove to be of considerable importance to the emerging nation. Rush published the first American textbook on Chemistry. In 1773 he contributed editorial assays to the papers about the Patriot cause and also joined the American Philosophical Society. He was active in the Sons of Liberty in Philadelphia during that time. In June of 1776 he was elected to attend the provincial conference to send delegates to the Continental Congress. He was appointed to represent Philadelphia that year and so signed the Declaration of Independence. In 1777 he was appointed surgeon-general of the middle department of the Continental Army. This office led to some trouble for him; he was critical of the administration of the Army Medical service under Dr. William Shippen. He complained to Washington, who deferred to the Congress. Ultimately Congress upheld Shippen and Rush resigned in disgust. As the war continued and Army forces under General Washington suffered a series of defeats, Rush secretly campaigned for removal of Washington as commander in chief, and went so far as to write an anonymous letter to then Governor Patrick Henry of Virginia.

He was caught in the act and confronted by Washington, at which point he bowed out of any activities related to the war.

In 1789 he wrote in Philadelphia newspapers in favor of adopting the Federal constitution. He was then elected to the Pennsylvania convention which adopted that constitution. He was appointed treasurer of the US Mint where he served from 1797 to 1813.

Rush's teaching career and medical practice continued till the end of his life. He became the Professor of medical theory and clinical practice at the consolidated University of Pennsylvania in 1791, where he was a popular figure at the height of his influence in medicine and in social circles. He was also a social activist, a prominent advocate for the abolition of slavery, an advocate for scientific education for the masses, including women, and for public medical clinics to treat the poor.

Benjamin Rush was a regular writer, and many notes about the less well known signers of the Declaration come from his observations on the floor of congress. Other members of congress, Franklin, and John Adams foremost, had some harsh observations to make about Rush. He was handsome, wellspoken, a gentleman and a very attractive figure-he was also a gossip and was quick to rush to judgment about others. He was supremely confident of his own opinion and decisions, yet shallow and very unscientific in practice. His chief accomplishment as a physician was in the practice of bleeding the patient. It was said that he considered bleeding to be a cure for nearly any ailment. Even when the practice began to decline, he refused to reconsider the dangers of it. He died at the age of 68 at his home in Philadelphia, the most celebrated physician in America, April 19, 1813

**Benjamin Franklin,** Episcopalian, Deist, Representing Pennsylvania at the Continental Congress
Born: January 17, 1706
Birthplace: Boston, MA
Education: Self-taught, apprenticed as a printer. Honorary Doctor of Laws, Universities of Edinburgh and Oxford.
Printer, Publisher, Scientist. Clerk of the Pennsylvania Assembly, 1736; Founded the Library Company of Philadelphia, 1731; Postmaster of Philadelphia, 1737-1753; Member of Pennsylvania Assembly, 1751-1764; Deputy Postmaster general of the British colonies in America, 1753; Founded Academy of Sciences of Philadelphia, 1753; Agent to Europe for Pennsylvania, 1757-1762, for Pennsylvania, Georgia, New Jersey, Massachusetts, 1764-1775; Elected to Continental Congress, 1775; Testified before Parliament concerning the Stamp Act, 1776; Postmaster General of the united colonies, 1775; Commissioner to the French Court, 1776; Minister plenipotentiary to the French Court, 1779; Negotiator in and Member of the Treaties with Gr.Britain, 1781-1783; Member of the Supreme Executive Council of Pennsylvania, President of Pennsylvania Society for the Abolition of Slavery, 1785; Senior member of the Constitutional Convention, 1787.

Benjamin Franklin, born in Boston, Massachusetts, on January 17, 1706, may by his life alone be the most profound statement of what an American strives to be.

With no formal education beyond the age of 10 years, Franklin was celebrated throughout Europe, welcomed in any Royal Court, sought out by every prestigious society. Indeed, when the reputations of George Washington and Thomas Jefferson had yet to be sorted out, Franklin was worshipped wherever his name was known.

He attended grammar school at age eight, but was put to work at ten. He apprenticed as a printer to his brother James, who printed the New England Courant, at age twelve, and published his first article there, anonymously, in 1721. Young Benjamin was an avid reader, inquisitive and skeptical. Through his satirical articles, he poked fun at the people of Boston and soon wore out his welcome, both with his brother and with the city. He ran away to New York and then on to Philadelphia at the age of 16, looking for work as a printer. He managed a commission to Europe for the purpose of buying supplies to establish a new printing house in Philadelphia, but found himself abandoned when he stepped off ship. Through hard work and frugality he bought his fare back to Philadelphia in 1732 and set up shop as a printer. He was appointed clerk of the Pennsylvania Assembly in 1736, and as Postmaster the following year. In 1741 he began publishing Poor Richard's Almanac, a very popular and influential magazine. He was elected to the Pennsylvania Assembly in 1751 and served as an agent for Pennsylvania (and ultimately for three other colonies) to England, France, and several other European powers. He was elected to the Continental Congress in 1775, where he played a crucial role in the rebellion against Gr. Britain, including service to Jefferson in editing the Declaration of Independence. Franklin, who was by this time independently wealthy and retired from publishing, continued to serve an important role in government both local and national. He was the United States first Postmaster General, Minister to the French Court, Treaty agent and signer to the peace with Gr. Britain, Celebrated Member of the Constitutional convention. Benjamin Franklin: Businessman, Writer, Publisher, Scientist, Diplomat, Legislator, and Social activist, was one of the earliest and strongest advocates for the abolition of Slavery, and for the protection of the rights of American aboriginal peoples. He died on the 17th of April in 1790. On that day he was still one of the most celebrated characters in America. So should he always be.

**John Morton,** Episcopalian, Representing Pennsylvania at the Continental Congress
Born: 1724
Birthplace: Ridley, PA
Education: Informal (Judge)
Elected to Provincial Assembly, 1756-1775; Delegate to the Stamp Act Congress, 1765; President of the Provincial Assembly, 1775;

Offices in Pennsylvania: Justice of the Peace, High Sheriff, Presiding Judge of the General Court and the Court of Common Pleas, Associate Judge of the Supreme Court of Pennsylvania; Elected to Continental Congress, 1774-77.

John Morton was born in Ridley, PA in 1724. In his youth he was noted for his quick intelligence and his habit of hard work. His stepfather, a well-educated surveyor from England, gave him a sound education in practical matters and in surveying. In 1756 Morton was elected to the Provincial Assembly, and was elected president of the Assembly in 1775. He attended the Stamp Act Congress in 1765. He filled numerous civil offices in Pennsylvania, including Justice of the Peace, High Sheriff, Presiding Judge of the General Court and the Court of Common Pleas. In 1774 he was appointed Associate Judge of the Supreme Court of Pennsylvania. That year he was elected to the Continental Congress where he was a member of several committees and chairman of the committee which reported the Articles of Confederation. He died soon after that report was presented to Congress, at the age of 53 in April, 1777.

**George Clymer,** Quaker - Episcopalian, Representing Pennsylvania at the Continental Congress
Born: March 16, 1739
Birthplace: Philadelphia, PA
Education: Private (Merchant)
Member of the Philadelphia Committee of Safety, 1773; Elected to the Continental Congress, 1776-1780; Member of Pennsylvania Legislature, Revenue Officer, Federal Indian Agent, 1781-1796; First president of: Philadelphia Bank, Philadelphia Academy of Fine Arts, vice-president of the Philadelphia Agricultural Society.

George Clymer, an orphan at an early age, was reared by a paternal uncle, who gave him a good education. He apprenticed in his uncle's counting room to prepare for a mercantile profession. He was a patriot partisan and leader in the disturbances in

Philadelphia resulting from the Tea Act and the Stamp Act, and a Member of the Philadelphia Council of Safety in 1773. He was elected to the Continental Congress in 1776 and served several years in such important committees as the Board of War and the Treasury Board. He played a large part, along with Robert Morris, in strengthening the authority of General Washington and improving        the pro-visions of the Continental army. In 1781 he was a member of the Legislature of his native state. He returned to the Congress in 1788 under the new constitution where he supported the presidency of George Washington. He was a revenue officer in Pennsylvania during the Whisky Rebellion. His last national public duty was a mission to the Cherokees in 1796. In retirement he was elected first president of Philadelphia Bank, first president of the Philadelphia Academy of Fine Arts, and vice-president of the Philadelphia Agricultural Society. He held all of these posts until his death on January 23 of 1813.

**James Smith,** Presbyterian, Representing Pennsylvania at the Continental Congress
Born: March 16, 1739
Birthplace: Philadelphia, PA
Education: Private (Merchant)
Member of the Philadelphia Committee of Safety, 1773; Elected to the Continental Congress, 1776-1780; Member of Pennsylvania Legislature, Revenue Officer, Federal Indian Agent, 1781-1796; First president of: Philadelphia Bank, Philadelphia Academy of Fine Arts, vice-president of the Philadelphia Agricultural Society.

James Smith was born in Ireland around 1719. He emigrated to Cheshire County Pennsylvania with his family when he was ten or twelve years old. His father was a successful farmer and James benefited from a good, simple, classical education from a local Church Minister. He later studied law at the office of his older brother George, in Lancaster. Smith was admitted to the Pennsylvania Bar at age twenty-six, and set up an office in Cumberland County, near Shippensburg. This was a frontier area at the time, so he spent much of his time engaged in surveying, only practicing law when such work was available. After four or five years he moved back to more populated York, where he might practice law exclusively.

During the 1760s Smith became a leader in the area. He attended a provincial assembly in 1774 where he offered a paper he had written, called "Essay on the Constitutional Power of Great Britain over the Colonies in America." In the essay, he offered a boycott of British goods, and a General Congress of the Colonies, as measures in defense of colonial rights. Later that year he organized a volunteer militia company in York, which elected him Captain. His company later grew to be a battalion, at which point he deferred leadership to younger men.

He was appointed to the provincial convention in Philadelphia in 1775, the state constitutional convention in 1776, and was elected to the Continental Congress the same year. He remained in Congress only two years, and as Congress was meeting in Philadelphia in those days, provided his office for meetings of the Board of War.

James Smith retired from the Congress in 1777, and served in few public offices after: one term in the State assembly, a few months as a judge of the state High Court of Appeals. In 1782 he was appointed Brigadier General of the Pennsylvania militia. He was reelected to Congress in 1785 but declined to attend due to advancing age. Little is known about his work, because a fire destroyed his office and papers shortly before he died Jan 23, 1813.

**George Taylor,** Presbyterian, Representing Pennsylvania at the Continental Congress
Born: circa 1716
Birthplace: Ireland
Education: Ironmaster
Elected to the provincial Assembly, 1764-69; Member of the Committee of Correspondence, Committee of Safety, 1773-76; Elected to Continental Congress, 1775-77.

Little is known about George Taylor. He was a working man and little concerned with politics, though he acted in service to his nation when called. He was born in Northern Ireland and emigrated to America in his early twenties. He was an Ironmaster at the Warwick Furnace and Coventry Forge. Later he and a partner leased an iron furnace in Bucks County. Iron production was his principal concern all of his life.

Taylor was elected to the provincial assembly for Pennsylvania in 1764, and was reelected for five consecutive years. He was a member of the committee to draft the instructions of Pennsylvania delegates to the first Continental Congress, a member of the Committee of Correspondence, and of the Committee of Safety. In 1775 he was appointed to replace a member of the Pennsylvania delegation who refused to support Independence. He arrived too late to vote, but did sign the Declaration. He served Congress through 1777. He was then elected to the new Supreme Council of his state, but served for only six weeks, apparently due to illness. There is no record of any public service afterward. He died February 23, 1781, at the age of 65.

**James Wilson,** Episcopalian – Presbyterian, Representing Pennsylvania at the Continental Congress
Born: September 14, 1742
Birthplace: Carskerdo, Scotland
Education: Attended the Universities of St. Andrews, Glasgow, and Edinburgh; College of Philadelphia. Honorary M.A. from Philadelphia College, studied Law with John Dickinson (Lawyer, Judge), Admitted to the Bar, 1767; Member of the Pennsylvania provincial meeting, Appointed to a Committee of Correspondence, 1774; elected to Provincial Congress, 1775; Commissioned Colonel of the Fourth Cumberland County Battalion, 1775; Elected to the Continental Congress, 1775-77, 1785-87; Director of the Bank of North America, 1781; Member of the Constitutional Convention, 1784; Associate Justice to the US. Supreme Court, 1789-1798.

James Wilson was born in Scotland in 1742. He attended a surprising number of Universities there, and never attained a degree. He emigrated to America in 1766, carrying a number of valuable letters of Introduction with him. Through these connections he began tutoring and then teaching at the Philadelphia College. He petitioned there for a degree and was awarded an honorary Master of Arts several months later.

The most popular career field in those days was the law. Wilson managed to secure studies at the office of John Dickinson a short time later. After two years of study he attained the bar in Philadelphia, and the following year (1767) set up his own practice in Reading. His office was very successful and he managed to earn a small fortune in a few short years. At that point he had bought a small farm near Carlisle, was handling cases in eight local Counties, and lecturing on English Literature at the College of Philadelphia. It was also during this period that he began a lifelong fascination with land speculation.

In 1774 Wilson attended a provincial meeting, as a representative of Carlisle, and was elected a member of the local Committee of Correspondence. He wrote a pamphlet titled "Considerations on the Nature and Extent of the Legislative Authority of the British Parliament." In it, he argued that the Parliament had no authority to pass laws for the colonies. It was published, and later found its way to the Continental Congress, where it was widely read and commented on. In 1775 he was elected to the Continental Congress, where he assumed a position with the most radical members-a demand for separation from Britain. James Wilson's powers of oration, the passion of his delivery and the logic he employed in debate, were commented on favorably by many members of the Congress. He was, however, in a bind. Pennsylvania was divided on the issue of separation, and Wilson refused to vote against the will of his constituents. Many members felt that it was hypocritical to have argued so forcefully and so long for Independence, only to vote against it when the occasion came. Wilson, with the support of three other members who were sympathetic to his position, managed a delay of three weeks, so that he could consult with people back home. When the vote came, he was able to affirm Pennsylvania's wish for Independence.

Following the Declaration, Wilson's attention turned back to his state, where a new constitution was proposed. He was strongly opposed to its form, and argued against it at every opportunity. This placed his office in jeopardy. He was recalled from Congress for about two weeks in 1777 but no one would take his place, so he was restored until the end of his term. Wilson did not return home following his term. He stayed in Annapolis through the winter, settled in Philadelphia. He resumed some of his former law practice there, only now he consulted to corporations. He was a leader in the Democratic - Republican Party. He also resumed his activities in speculation, including profiteering. He borrowed heavily and gambled aggressively. These activities eventually caught up with him in two ways. First, he acquired a great deal of debt and for this he was very nearly arrested on several occasions. Second, he was repeatedly accused of "engrossing," the practice of hoarding goods against the public need in order to drive up prices. During a food shortage in 1779, he and his property were attacked during riots in Philadelphia. He was rescued by a law enforcement troop, but had to hide for some time.

In 1779 Wilson was appointed by France to serve as its US advocate general for maritime and commercial enterprises. He was elected to Congress again in 1782, where he worked closely with Robert Morris on financial matters of state. In 1781, Wilson was appointed a director of the original Bank of North America. In 1784, he was appointed to the Constitutional Convention in Philadelphia. Following ratification of the new Constitution, he searched for an appointment to the Federal government. He appealed directly to Washington, and was appointed an Associate Justice in 1789.

The remainder of his life was miserable. His wife had died in 1786. In 1792 he returned again to speculation in land New York and Pennsylvania. His finances were completely destroyed within a short time and he spent some time in a debtor's prison (while still serving on the Supreme Court!). By 1798 Wilson was destroyed as a man as well. He complained of great mental fatigue and an inability to work any longer. He died while visiting a friend in North Carolina that same year, August 28, 1798.

**George Ross,** Episcopalian, Representing Pennsylvania at the Continental Congress
Born: May 10, 1730
Birthplace: New Castle, DE
Education: Private, Classical. Read law in Philadelphia (Judge), Admitted to Pennsylvania Bar, 1750; Crown Prosecutor for Carlisle, twelve years; Elected to Provincial Assembly, 1768-1776; Elected to Continental Congress, 1774, 1776-77; Colonel in the Continental Army, 1776; Vice president of the Pennsylvania constitutional convention, 1776; Judge of the Admiralty Court of Pennsylvania, 1779

George Ross was born in May of 1730 in Newcastle, Delaware, into very large family. His father was a minister, educated at Edinburgh, and the Ross children received a sound classical education at home. George then proceeded to read law at the office of his older brother, John. George attained the Bar in Philadelphia at the age of 20 and established his own practice in Lancaster. As was typical of many gentlemen of the day, his politics were Tory. He served for some twelve years as Crown Prosecutor (attorney general) to Carlisle, until elected to the provincial legislature of his state in 1768. There he came to understand firsthand the rising conflict between the colonial assemblies and the Parliament. He was an unabashed supporter of the powers of the former. In 1774 he was elected to the provincial conference that would select delegates to attend the General Congress, and was selected as a representative of Pennsylvania that same year. Ross continued to serve his provincial legislature and was a member of the Committee of Safety for his colony in 1775. In 1776 he was again elected to the Continental Congress, while serving as a provincial legislator, and a Colonel in the Continental Army. That year he also undertook negotiations with the Northwestern Indians on behalf of his colony, and took a seat as vicepresident of the first constitutional convention for Pennsylvania. He was reelected to the Continental Congress once more in 1777, but resigned the seat before the close due to poor health. In March of 1779 he was appointed to a judgeship in the Pennsylvania Court of Admiralty. He died in that office July 14, 1779.

# Delaware

**George Read,** Episcopalian, Representing Delaware at the Continental Congress
Born: September 18, 1733
Birthplace: North East, MD
Education: Private school - Chester Pennsylvania, Philadelphia College, Law studies (Judge)
Admitted to Philadelphia Bar, 1753; Attorney General (in Delaware), 1761; Member of Delaware Committee of Correspondence, 1774; Elected to Continental Congress, 17741776; Member of Delaware Constitutional Convention, 1776; Acting Governor of Delaware, 1777; Judge, Court of Appeals, 1780; State Senator 1791, 92; Chief Justice of the State of Delaware, 1793-98.

George Read was born on his family farm near North East, Cecil County, Maryland in 1733. He attended a school in Chester, Pennsylvania then the Philadelphia Academy under Doctor Allison at New London. At fifteen he graduated and proceeded to study law at the office of John Moland in Philadelphia. He was admitted to the Philadelphia Bar in 1753. He moved to New Castle Delaware to establish a new practice the following year. He established quite a reputation there and was appointed Attorney general to three Delaware counties, an office which he resigned in 1774 when he was elected to the first Continental Congress. In 1764, the period leading up to the stamp act protests, Read had joined the Delaware Committee of Correspondence and was active in the patriot movement. At the Continental Congress he found Lee's Resolution for Independence to be too hasty and voted against it. When it was adopted, however, he joined the majority in working toward independence.

In 1776 Read was called upon to join the Constitutional Convention in Delaware, where he served as president of the committee that drafted the document. In 1777 the British captured Delaware governor John McKinly and Read took over as governor in the emergency. He led the state through the crisis of the war, raising money, troops, and supplies for the defense of his state.

In 1779 he suffered a bout of poor health and had to retire from official duties. He recovered, however, and was appointed Judge in Court of Appeals in admiralty cases three years later. Read went on to be twice elected state Senator under the new constitution, and later still was appointed Chief Justice of the State of Delaware. He served in that office until his death September 21, 1798.

**Caesar Rodney,** Episcopalian, Representing Delaware at the Continental Congress
Born: October 7, 1728
Birthplace: Dover, DE
Education: Informal (Judge)
Commissioned High Sheriff of Kent County, 1755; Elected to Colonial Assembly, 1758-70, 1771-76; Delegate to the Stamp Act Congress, 1765; Member of the Delaware Committee of Correspondence, 1765; Elected to Continental Congress, 1774-76, 77; Military Leader, 177477, Elected President of the State of Delaware, 1778-80; Member of the Upper House of the State Assembly, 1776-84;

Caesar Rodney was born on his father's farm near Dover, Delaware, in October of 1728. He was tutored by his parents and may have attended a local Parson's school, but received no formal education. His father died when Caesar was 17. He was placed in the guardianship of Nicholas Ridgely who was a clerk of the peace in Kent County, and this seems to be the root of Rodney's life in politics. In 1755, under the royal government, Rodney was commissioned High Sheriff of Kent County Delaware. This was quite a distinction for a man twenty-two years of age and he apparently honored the distinction, for in succeeding years his official capacities grew to include registrar of wills, recorder of deeds, clerk of the orphan's court, and justice of the peace. At age thirty he attained his first elected office as a representative in the colonial legislature at Newcastle. He served in that position, reelected each year except 1771, until the legislature was dissolved in 1776-and then resumed the seat as a representative to the Upper House of the State of Delaware until 1784.

Rodney was a leading patriot in his colony, a member of the Stamp Act Congress in 1765, a formative member of the Delaware Committee of Correspondence, a military leader in the colonial militia, and a delegate to the Continental Congress from formation until 1777. The following year he was elected President of the State of Delaware for a three year term, a duty that he assumed even as he served as Major-General of the Delaware Militia. In this office he played a crucial part not only in the defense of his own colony but in support of Washington's Continental Army, for Delaware had a record of meeting or exceeding its quotas for troops and provisions throughout the revolutionary conflict. Rodney's health and strength flagged for a time. He suffered from asthma and from a cancerous growth on his face, for which he never attained proper treatment. He saw his colony through the war at the cost of personal neglect.

In 1782 he was again elected to the national Congress, but was forced to decline the office due to failing health. He nonetheless continued to serve as Speaker to the Upper House of the Delaware Assembly. He died in that office June 29, 1784.

**Thomas McKean,** Presbyterian, Delaware, Captain of a South Carolina Regimental Company, 1775; Delegate to the Continental Congress, 1776.

Born: March. 19, 1734

Birthplace: New London, PA

Education: Studied under Francis Allison (Lawyer)

Deputy Attorney General to County Sussex 1756; Admitted to Bar of Pennsylvania Supreme Court, appointed Clerk of the Assembly of Delaware, 1757; Member of Delaware Assembly, 1762-79; Delegate to the Stamp Act Congress, 1765; Collector of Customs and Commissioner of Revenue at New Castle, 1771; Delegate to the Continental Congress, 1774-81; President of Delaware, 1776; Chief Justice of Pennsylvania, 1777-97; Governor of Pennsylvania, 1799-1812

Thomas McKean might just represent an ideal study of how far political engagement can be carried by one man. One can scarcely believe the number of concurrent offices and duties this man performed during the course of his long career. He served three states* and many more cities and county governments, often performing duties in two or more jurisdictions, even while engaged in federal office.

Born in New London, Pennsylvania, he studied law with his cousin David Finney, and then under the eminent Francis Allison. As a student he served as the clerk of the prothonotory Court of Common Pleas for the county of New Castle, Delaware. He was admitted to the bar in Delaware before the age of 21. In 1756 he was commissioned to his first political office, that of deputy Attorney General to county Sussex, in Pennsylvania. The following year he was admitted to the Bar of the Supreme Court of Pennsylvania, and at the same time appointed clerk of the Assembly of Delaware. In 1762 the Assembly appointed him a colleague, along with Caesar Rodney, charged with revising and printing the laws of the province of Delaware. Later that year he was elected a delegate to the Assembly, and was re-elected for seventeen years despite a six year residence outside the commonwealth, in Philadelphia. At the behest of the Assembly he served as a trustee of the provincial loan office from 1764 to 1772. In 1775 he was the delegate for Delaware at the Stamp Act Congress in New York. In 1771 he was appointed collector of customs and commissioner of revenue at New Castle. In 1772 to was chosen Speaker of the Assembly of Delaware. Beginning in 1774 he attended the Continental Congress where he served on the national council throughout the Revolutionary War. He also served on the committee to draw up the Articles of Confederation, was commissioned a colonel in the New Jersey militia, and served as President of the newly independent Delaware. In 1777, still serving in the Congress under the articles of Confederation, he was appointed Chief Justice of Pennsylvania, an office that he held for nearly twenty years. He was elected President of Congress in 1781. In 1787 he attended the ratifying convention for the new Federal Constitution in Pennsylvania. In 1789 he played a role in amending the constitution of Pennsylvania. He was elected Governor of Pennsylvania on the Federalist ticket in 1799. Political enemies tried to impeach him, but were unable to prove any wrong-doing. He filled that office by popular reelection for nine years, retiring in 1812. He died on June 24, 1817 at the age of 83.

*Pennsylvania, Delaware, and New Jersey. Pennsylvania and Delaware were not fully distinct colonies until 1776. From 1701 to 1776, both existed under a common executive, but had separate legislatures.*

## 5th Column New York

**William Floyd,** Presbyterian, Representing New York at the Continental Congress
Born: December 17, 1734
Birthplace: Brookhaven, NY
Soldier; Member of Continental Congress of 1774-76; Member of Congress, 1789-91; State Senator, New York, 1808.

William Floyd was born on Long Island on December 17, 1734. His family had emigrated to America in 1654 and by the time of his birth were well established and wealthy. Though he might have received the best education, his father died when he was in his teens, and William was required to take over the operations of the family farm. He was a member of the Suffolk County Militia in the early conflict with Britain. He attained the rank of major general, though at this late date he spent most of his time in the Continental Congress. In 1774 he was chosen to represent New York in the first Continental Congress. He served there through 1776, while his property was destroyed in the Revolutionary War. He acquired land on the banks of the Mohawk River after the war though it would be a few more years till he would retire there. In 1789 he was elected to congress under the new constitution. He served there, acting several times as a presidential elector, until he returned to his native state in 1791. He was called to the service of his state as a Senator in 1803. After serving his term he retired to his true passion, farming. He died on August 4, 1821.

**Philip Livingston,** Presbyterian, Representing New York at the Continental Congress
Born: January 15, 1716
Birthplace: Albany, NY
Education: Graduate of Yale College (Merchant)
Alderman, New York city; Delegate to the Albany Convention, 1754; Delegate to the Continental Congress, 1776; Later, State Senator in New York, Delegate to Federal Congress until 1778.

Philip Livingston was born in Albany, New York, on the fifteenth of January, 1716. He graduated at Yale College in 1737, and entered into mercantile business in the city of New York. He was a very successful businessman, and served his community as an alderman. In 1754 he attended the Colonial Convention at Albany. He was selected as a delegate to the Continental Congress in 1776, and was in strong favor of the Declaration of Independence. After the adoption of a new Constitution for New York State, he was elected to the state Senate. He died suddenly while in attendance at York, Pennsylvania.

**Francis Lewis,** Episcopalian, Representing New York at the Continental Congress
Born: March, 1713
Birthplace: Llandaff, Wales
Education: Westminster (Merchant) Elected to the Continental Congress, 1775.

Born in Wales in 1713, Francis Lewis was partly educated in Scotland and then attended Westminster in England. He entered a mercantile house in London, and then came to New York to set up a business in 1734. He was taken prisoner and shipped to France while serving as a British mercantile agent in 1756. When he returned to America he became active in politics. He was elected to the Continental Congress in 1775, and served there for several years. He lost all of his property, on Long Island, New York, to the destruction of the Revolutionary war. He died on the thirty first of December, 1802.

**Lewis Morris,** Episcopalian, Representing New York at the Continental Congress
Born: April 8, 1726
Birthplace: Morrisania (Bronx County), NY
Education: Graduate of Yale College (Farmer)
Member of Provincial Legislature; Deputy to New York Convention, 1775; Delegate to the Continental Congress, 1775-77; County judge, Worcester, 1777; Served in New York Legislature, Member of the Board of Regents of the University of the State of New York.

Lewis Morris was born in New York in 1726. He inherited great wealth, most of which was lost during the war. He graduated at Yale College in 1746, and returned to the farm of his father, in Lower West Chester, near Harlem. When his father passed on he became engaged in politics. He served in the Provincial legislature shortly before the troubles with Gr. Britain began and before it was dissolved by the royal governor. Morris joined with the patriots when conflict began, siding, in many cases, against his wealthy neighbors. He convinced local politicians to send representatives to the re-formed Legislature in April of 1775. That congress appointed delegates to the second Continental Congress, and Morris was one. He served on committees for the defense of New York, one for provisioning colonial forces, and another for Indian affairs. These tasks carried him throughout New England in the first few years of the war. He also served as a brigadier general in the New York militia and so was often torn between his duties in congress and those to the defense of his own colony. In 1777, he was succeeded in congress by his brother, Gouverneur Morris. He returned to his local duties, later served as a judge in Worcester, and served intermittently as a member of the upper house of the new legislature until 1790. All of the Morris property and nearly all of his wealth had been destroyed in the revolution. Lewis spend several years working to rebuild his farm. He also served on the first Board of Regents for the University of New York. He died January 22, 1798 at the age of 72.

# New Jersey

**Richard Stockton,** Presbyterian, Representing New Jersey at the Continental Congress
Born: October 1, 1730
Birthplace: near Princeton, NJ
Education: West Nottingham Academy, Graduate of College of New Jersey. (Lawyer)
Justice of the Supreme Court of New Jersey, 1774; Elected to Continental Congress, 1776

Richard Stockton was born near Princeton, on October 1, 1730. He attended the West Nottingham Academy under Dr. Samuel Finley, and then earned his degree at the College of New Jersey (Now Princeton) in 1748. He studied law with David

Ogden of Newark. Stockton became an eminent Lawyer with one of the largest practices in the colonies. He was not much concerned with politics, but applied his talents and person to the revolutionary cause when the day came. He was appointed to the royal council of New Jersey in 1765 and remained a member until the government was reformed. He was a moderate with regard to Colonial autonomy. He argued that the colonies should be represented in the Parliament. With the passage of the Stamp Act, such arguments were overcome by colonial backlash. In 1774 he was appointed Justice of the Supreme Court of New Jersey. In 1776, the New Jersey delegates to the Congress were holding out against Independence. When news of this reached the constituents, New Jersey elected Richard Stockton and Dr. Witherspoon to replace two of the five New Jersey delegates. They were sent with instructions to vote for Independence. Accounts indicate that, despite clear instruction, Justice Stockton wished to hear the arguments on either side of the issue. Once he was satisfied, the New Jersey delegates voted for Independence.

Stockton was appointed to committees supporting the war effort. He was dispatched on a fact finding tour to the northern army. New Jersey was overrun by the British in November of '76, when he was returning from the mission. He managed to move his family to safety, but was captured and imprisoned by the British. He was not released until several years later, badly treated and in very poor condition. He lost all of his extensive library, writings, and all of his property during the British invasion. He died a pauper in Princeton at the age of 51, February 28, 1781.

**John Witherspoon,** Presbyterian, Representing New Jersey at the Continental Congress
Born: February 5, 1723
Birthplace: Gifford, Scotland
Education: Master of Arts, University of Edinburgh; Doctorate of Divinity, University of St. Andrews. (Clergyman, Author, Educator)

President of College of New Jersey, 1768-1792; Delegate to the Continental Congress, 1776-1782; Twice elected to State Legislature of New Jersey.

John Witherspoon brought some impressive credentials and a measure of public acclaim with him when he joined the colonies in 1768, as president of the College of New Jersey (now Princeton).

Born in 1723, he received the finest education available to a bright young gentleman of that era. John attended the preparatory school in Haddington Scotland. He proceeded to Edinburgh where he attained a Master of Arts, then to four years of divinity school. At this point he was twenty. In 1743 he became a Presbyterian Minister at a parish in Beith, where he married, authored three noted works on theology. He was later awarded a Doctorate of Divinity from the University of St. Andrews, in recognition of his theological skills. It was only through a protracted effort on the part of several eminent Americans, including Richard Stockton and Benjamin Rush, that the colonies were able to acquire his service. In colonial American, the best educated men were often found in the clergy. The College of New Jersey needed a first rate scholar to serve as its first president. Witherspoon was at first unable to accept the offer, due to his wife's great fear of crossing the sea. She later had second thoughts, and a visit from the charming Dr. Rush secured the deal. He emigrated to New Jersey in 1768.

Dr. Witherspoon enjoyed great success at the College of New Jersey. He turned it into a very successful institution, and was a very popular man as a result. He also wrote frequent essays on subjects of interest to the colonies. While he at first abstained from political concerns, he came to support the revolutionary cause, accepting appointment to the committees of correspondence and safety in early 1776. Later that year he was elected to the Continental Congress in time to vote for R. H. Lee's Resolution for Independence. He voted in favor, and shortly after voted for the Declaration of Independence. He made a notable comment on that occasion; in reply to another member who argued that the country was not yet ripe for such a declaration, that in his opinion it "was not only ripe for the measure, but in danger of rotting for the want of it." Witherspoon was a very active member of congress, serving on more than a hundred committees through his tenure and debating frequently on the floor.

In November, 1776, he shut down and then evacuated the College of New Jersey at the approach of British forces. The British occupied the area and did much damage to the college, nearly destroyed it. Following the war, Witherspoon devoted his life to rebuilding the College. He also served twice in the state legislature. In the last years of life he suffered injuries, first to one eye then the other, becoming totally blind two years before his death. He died on his farm, "Tusculum," just outside of Princeton in November 15, 1794, a man much honored and beloved by his adopted countrymen.

**Francis Hopkinson,** Episcopalian, Representing New Jersey at the Continental Congress
Born: September 21, 1737
Birthplace: Philadelphia, PA
Education: Graduate of the College of Philadelphia (Lawyer, Judge, Author)
Delegate to the Continental Congress, 1776; Judge of admiralty for Pennsylvania, 1780; Appointed Judge to the US Court for the District of Pennsylvania, 1790.

Francis Hopkinson was a man of extraordinary talent and charm. Born into a family of substance in Philadelphia, he was the first scholar and first Graduate of the College of Philadelphia, which his father, along with good friend Benjamin Franklin, played a role in chartering. He studied Law in the office of Benjamin Chew (later, Chief Justice of Pennsylvania) and then continued his education in England, two years study with the Bishop of Worcester. He was a writer of music, poetry and satire. His notable works include "A Pretty Story," a skeptical examination of the relationship between Great Britain and the colonies, and

"Battle of the Kegs," a satiric taunting of the British. Hopkinson claimed credit for designing the American flag, but the evidence for his claim is not clear. Hopkinson was elected a delegate to the Continental Congress in 1776, where he signed the Declaration. After the War he was an active advocate, in speaking and in writing, for the New Federal constitution. He was commissioned a Judge of Admiralty in Pennsylvania in 1780, and Washington appointed him Federal District Judge for his native state in 1790. He died very suddenly of a massive epileptic seizure on May 9 1791, at the still young age of 53.

**John Hart,** Presbyterian, Representing New Jersey at the Continental Congress
Born: 1713
Birthplace: Hopewell, NJ
Education: (Farmer)
Member of the New Jersey Assembly, 1761-1771; Served on the Committee of Safety, Committee of Correspondence, 1775; Judge of the Court of Common Pleas, Member of Provincial Assembly 1775; Elected to the Continental Congress, 1776.

John Hart was a New Jersey farmer. His exact date of birth is not known. His father had moved from Connecticut to a farm near Hopewell New Jersey. He helped to build, and later inherited, that very successful farm and was a leading member of his community. His first public service was a justice of the peace. In 1761 he was elected the New Jersey Assembly, there annually reelected until the assembly was dissolved in 1771. In 1775 he was appointed to the local Committee of Safety, the Committee of Correspondence, and a judge to the Court of Common Pleas. He was elected to the newly formed Provincial Congress of New Jersey in 1776, and sent as a delegate for New Jersey to the Continental Congress that year. Hart's property was looted in the course of the war. His Wife died on October 8, 1776. When the area was overrun by the British in November of that year, he was forced to hide for a time. He was engaged in public service throughout the war, twice reelected to the Congress and also serving the Committee of Safety and as Speaker of the New Jersey assembly. On June 22ⁿᵈ 1778 he invited the American army to encamp on his farm. Washington had lunch with him, then had his famous Council of War at the nearby Hunt House.

Twelve thousand men camped on his fields-during the growing season. After resting and preparing for battle the troops left on the 24ᵗʰ. On Tuesday, May 11ᵗʰ 1779, he died at the age of 66.

**Abraham Clark,** Presbyterian, Representing New Jersey at the Continental Congress
Birthplace: Elizabethtown, NJ
Education: Self-taught, Surveying, Law (Surveyor, Lawyer, Sheriff)
Land attorney; High Sheriff of Essex County, NJ.; Member of New Jersey Provincial Congress; Elected to the Continental Congress, 1776 ~1784.

Abraham Clark was born into the life of a farmer at what is now Elizabeth, New Jersey. His father saw an aptitude for mathematics and felt that he was too frail for the farm life and so young Abraham was tutored in mathematics and surveying. He continued his own study of the Law while working as a surveyor. He later practiced as an attorney and in this role is said to have been quite popular because of his habit of serving poor farmers in the community in cases dealing with title disputes. In succeeding years he served as the clerk of the Provincial Assembly, High Sheriff of Essex (now divided into Essex and Union) County. Elected to the Provincial Congress in 1775, he then represented New Jersey at the Second Continental Congress in 1776, where he signed the Declaration of Independence. He served in the congress through the Revolutionary War as a member of the committee of Public Safety. He retired and was unable to attend the Federal Constitutional Convention in 1787, however he is said to have been active in community politics until his death on September 15, 1794. Clark Township, New Jersey, is named in his honor.

# 6ᵗʰ Column New Hampshire

**Josiah Bartlett,** Congregationalist, Representing New Hampshire
at the Continental Congress
Born: November 21, 1729
Birthplace: Amesbury, MA
Education: Medicine (Physician, Judge)
Delegate to Continental Congress, 1774-'87; Signed Declaration of
Independence, 1776; Signed Articles of Confederation, 1777; State
court Judge, Member of Federal constitutional convention, 1787;
Elected Governor of New Hampshire.

Josiah Bartlett was born at Amesbury, Massachusetts, in
November, 1729. He studied the science of medicine, and practiced
as a physician at Kingston, in New Hampshire. He became
involved in politics and was elected a member of the Colonial
Legislature. He was noted as a principled legislator, not susceptible
to pressure from the Royal Governor, and as an active advocate
against British oppression. He was a member of a Committee of
Safety, and served as commander of a militia regiment in 1775. In
that year he was also elected to represent New Hampshire in the
Continental Congress. He voted for independence, and was the
first to sign the Declaration, after John Hancock. He continued
to serve in 1777 and participated in the ratification of the Articles
of Confederation. He later filled the offices of Judge of Common
Pleas and of the Supreme Court of his state, and joined the federal
Constitutional Convention in 1787.

He was elected president, and then governor, of New
Hampshire. He died May 19, 1795.

**William Whipple,** Congregationalist, Representing New Hampshire at the Continental Congress
Born: January 14, 1730
Birthplace: Kittery, ME
Education: Common School. (Merchant, Soldier, Judge)
Elected to Provincial Congress, 1775, 76; Member of state Council, Committee of Safety, 1776; Elected to Continental Congress, 1776-79; Commissioned Brigadier General of the New Hampshire Militia, 1777- ca. 1781; Appointed Associate Judge to the Superior Court, 1782.

William Whipple was born at Kittery Maine, in 1730. He was educated at a common school until his early teens, when he went off to sea to find his fortune. He was an able seaman, earning the position of Ship's Master by the age of 21. He worked hard and amassed a great deal of money. In 1759 he landed in Portsmouth and, in partnership with his brother, established himself as a merchant. Calls to public duty began almost immediately. He was elected to several local offices and was involved in the Patriot movement.

In 1775 he was elected to represent his town at the provincial congress. The following year New Hampshire dissolved the Royal government and reorganized with a House of Representatives and an Executive Council. Whipple was made a Council member, a member of the Committee of Safety, and was promptly elected to the Continental Congress. He served there through 1779, though he took much leave for military affairs. In 1777 he was made Brigadier General of the New Hampshire Militia. General Whipple led men in the successful expedition against General Burgoyne at the battles of Stillwater and Saratoga.

After the war Whipple was appointed an associate justice of the Superior Court of New Hampshire. He suffered from a heart ailment for several years and he died, fainting from atop his horse while traveling his court circuit November 28, 1785.

**Matthew Thornton,** Presbyterian, Representing New Hampshire at the Continental Congress
Born: 1714
Birthplace: Ireland
Education: Physician
Appointed surgeon to the New Hampshire Troops, 1745; Member of the Provincial Assembly, 1758-62, ?-1775; Colonel of the Londonderry Militia, Londonderry Town Selectman, 1763-75; Londonderry Committee of Safety, 1775, 76; Speaker of the New Hampshire House of Representatives, Associate Justice of the Superior Court, Delegate to the Continental Congress, 1776.

Matthew Thornton was born in Ireland in 1714. His parents emigrated to America when he was three. They first settled at Wiscasset, in Maine, but soon went to Worcester, Massachusetts, where Mathew received an academic education. He became a physician, and in 1745 was appointed surgeon to the New Hampshire troops in the expedition against Louisburg. He later held royal commissions as justice of the peace and colonel of militia. His medical practice was very successful and he acquired much land, becoming a leading member of the community in Londonderry. There he held many local offices while also representing Londonderry at the Provincial Assembly. Thornton eventually became President of that assembly. As a member of a local committee of Safety in 1775, he was asked to draft a plan of government for New Hampshire after dissolution of the royal government. His plan was adopted immediately and became the first constitution for that state (and was in fact the first new state constitution after the start of hostilities with Britain).

Thornton was then selected as the first President of the New Hampshire House of Representatives, and as a justice to the Superior Court, under the new constitution. He was also sent to the Continental Congress-too late to participate in the debates over Independence, but just in time to sign the Declaration on behalf of New Hampshire. He was selected to attend Congress again in 1777, but declined to attend due to poor health. For the rest of his life, Thornton attended to State duties. He also wrote political essays for the newspapers. He died at the age of 89, while on a visit to his daughter in Newburyport, Massachusetts, in June 24, 1803.

# Massachusetts

**John Adams,** Congregationalist – Unitarian, Representing the colony of Massachusetts at the Continental Congress
Born: October 30, 1735
Birthplace: Braintree, MA
Education: Harvard (Lawyer)
Admitted to Massachusetts Bar, 1761; Elected to Massachusetts Assembly, 1770; Attended First Continental Congress, 1774-'76; Signed Declaration of Independence, 1776; Appointed Diplomat to France, 1776 '79; Member of assembly to form State Constitution of Massachusetts, Minister plenipotentiary in Europe, 1780, '81; Party to the Treaty of Peace with Gr. Britain, 1783; U.S. Minister to the British court, c. 1783- '88; Elected first Vice President, 1789; President, 1796.

Adams began his education in a common school in Braintree. He secured a scholarship to Harvard and graduated at the age of 20.

He apprenticed to a Mr. Putnam of Worcester, who provided access to the library of the Attorney General of Massachusetts, and was admitted to the Bar in 1761. He participated in an outcry against Writs of Assistance. Adams became a prominent public figure in his activities against the Stamp Act, in response to which he wrote and published a popular article, Essay on the Canon and Feudal Law. He was married on Oct. 25, 1764 and moved to Boston, assuming a prominent position in the patriot movement. He was elected to the Massachusetts Assembly in 1770, and was chosen one of five to represent the colony at the First Continental Congress in 1774.

Again in the Continental Congress, in 1775, he nominated Washington to be commander-in-chief on the colonial armies. Adams was a very active member of congress, he was engaged by as many as ninety committees and chaired twenty-five during the second Continental Congress. In May of 1776, he offered a resolution that amounted to a declaration of independence from Gr. Britain. He was shortly thereafter a fierce advocate for the Declaration drafted by Thos. Jefferson. Congress then appointed him ambassador to France, to replace Silas Dean at the French court. He returned from those duties in 1779 and participated in the framing of a state constitution for Massachusetts, where he was further appointed Minister plenipotentiary to negotiate a peace, and form a commercial treaty, with Gr. Britain. In 1781 he participated with Franklin, Jay and Laurens, in development of the Treaty of Peace with Gr. Britain and was a signer of that treaty, which ended the Revolutionary War, in 1783. He was elected Vice President of the United States under Geo. Washington in 1789, and was elected President in 1796. Adams was a Federalist and this made him an arch-rival of Thos. Jefferson and his Republican party. The discord between Adams and Jefferson surfaced many times during Adams' (and, later, Jefferson's) presidency. This was not a mere party contest. The struggle was over the nature of the office and on the limits of Federal power over the state governments and individual citizens. Adams retired from office at the end of his term in 1801. He was elected President of a convention to reform the constitution of Massachusetts in 1824, but declined the honor due to failing health.

He died on July 4, 1826 (incidentally, within hours of the death of Thos. Jefferson.) His final toast to the Fourth of July was "Independence Forever!" Late in the afternoon of the Fourth of July, just hours after Jefferson died at Monticello, Adams, unaware of that fact, is reported to have said, "Thomas Jefferson survives."

**Samuel Adams,** Congregationalist, Representing the colony of Massachusetts at the Continental Congress
Born: September 27, 1722
Birthplace: Boston, MA
Education: Master of Arts, Harvard. (Politician) Tax-collector; Elected to Massachusetts Assembly, 1765; Delegate to the First Continental Congress, 1774; Signed Declaration of Independence, 1776; Member of Massachusetts State constitutional convention, 1781; Appointed Lieutenant Governor of Mass., 1789; Elected Governor of Massachusetts, 1794-'97.

Samuel and John Adams' names are almost synonymous in all accounts of the Revolution that grew, largely, out of Boston. Though they were cousins and not brothers, they were often referred to as the Adams' brothers, or simply as the Adams'. Samuel Adams was born in Boston, son of a merchant and brewer. He was an excellent politician, an unsuccessful brewer, and a poor businessman. His early public office as a tax collector might have made him suspect as an agent of British authority, however he made good use of his understanding of the tax codes and wide acquaintance with the merchants of Boston. Samuel was a very visible popular leader who, along with John, spent a great deal of time in the public eye agitating for resistance. In 1765 he was elected to the Massachusetts Assembly where he served as clerk for many years. It was there that he was the first to propose a continental congress. He was a leading advocate of republicanism and a good friend of Tom Paine. In 1774, he was chosen to be a member of the provincial council during the crisis in Boston. He was then appointed as a representative to the Continental Congress, where he was most noted for his oratory skills, and as a passionate advocate of independence from Britain. In 1776, as a delegate to the Continental Congress, he signed the Declaration of Independence. Adams retired from the Congress in 1781 and returned to Massachusetts to become a leading member of that state's convention to form a constitution. In 1789 he was appointed lieutenant governor of the state. In 1794 he was elected Governor, and was re-elected annually until 1797 when he retired for health reasons. He died in the morning of October 2, 1803, in his home town of Boston.

**Robert Treat Paine,** Congregationalist – Unitarian, Representing Massachusetts at the Continental Congress
Born: March 11, 1731
Birthplace: Boston, MA
Education: Graduate Harvard College (Judge)
Admitted to Massachusetts Bar, 1757; Elected to Provincial Assembly, 1770; Delegate to the Continental Congress, 1774, 1776; Attorney General for Massachusetts, 1777-1796; Judge, Supreme Court of Massachusetts, 1796-1804; State counselor, 1804.

Robert Treat Paine was a native of Massachusetts, born in 1731. He was expected, by family tradition, to become a Minister. He got high marks at the Boston Latin School and was admitted to Harvard College, where he graduated in 1749. He taught school for a while and then began the study of theology. Because of his frail health, Paine set out to build up his strength by working on the sea. He spent some years as a merchant marine visiting the southern colonies, Spain, the Azores, and England. When he returned home he decided to pursue the law. He was admitted to the bar of Massachusetts in 1757. He first set up office in Portland, Maine (then part of Massachusetts) and later relocated to Taunton, Massachusetts. In the trials of British soldiers following the Boston Massacre, Paine served as associate prosecuting attorney.

He was elected to the Provincial Assembly in 1770 and that body selected him in 1774 to attend the first Continental Congress. Paine served on committees which formed the rules of debate, and later served as chairman of the committee charged with acquiring gunpowder for the Continental Army. He also signed the final appeal to the king, known as the Olive Branch Petition, in 1775. Paine was reelected to represent Massachusetts at the Continental Congress of 1776. He participated in the debates leading to the resolution for Independence and his signature appears on the Declaration. According to comments made by Benjamin Rush, Paine was known in Congress as the "Objection Maker," because of his habit of frequent objections to the proposals of others. These objections were eventually taken lightly, for as Rush commented,

"He seldom proposed anything, but opposed nearly every measure that was proposed by other people..."

In 1777 Paine was elected attorney general of the state of Massachusetts. He was then serving on the legislative committee to draft the first constitution of the state under the new federation. He moved back to Boston in 1780 where he helped found the American Academy of Arts and Sciences. Governor Hancock offered him an appointment to the bench of the Supreme Court in 1783 but he declined. That offer was made again in 1796 and he accepted. He retired after some 14 years, in failing health, then died at the age of 83, May 11, 1814.

**Elbridge Gerry,** Episcopalian, Representing Massachusetts at the Continental Congress
Born: July 17, 1744
Birthplace: Marblehead, MA
Education: Graduate of Harvard College (Merchant)
Member, General Court of Massachusetts, 1772; Elected to Massachusetts Legislature, 1773; Provincial Congress, 1774; Continental Congress, 1776-81, 1783-85; Envoy to France, 1797; Governor of Massachusetts, 1810, 1811; Vice President of the United States (with Madison), 1812

Elbridge Gerry was born in Marblehead, Massachusetts, on July 17, 1744. He studied at Harvard to be a merchant, graduating in 1762. He was elected to the Massachusetts Legislature in 1773 and was selected to attend the Provincial Congress in 1774. He was then appointed to the Continental Congress, where he was engaged in committee work on commercial and naval concerns. He attended the Constitutional Convention in 1798 but was opposed to the new Federal Constitution, refusing to sign it. He was elected to the first two Congresses from Massachusetts and, in 1797, was one of several envoys sent to France. He was elected governor of Massachusetts in 1810 and 1811. He was much criticized for redistricting the state to the advantage of his own party (Democratic-Republican). That incident was the source of the term gerrymandering. In 1812 he was elected Vice President of the United States. He died in office, on November 23, 1814, at the age of 70.

# Rhode Island

**Stephen Hopkins,** Episcopalian, Representing Rhode Island at the Continental Congress
Born: March 7, 1707
Birthplace: Providence, RI
Education: (Lawyer, Educator)
Speaker of the Rhode Island Assembly, (circa 1750-2); Delegate to the Albany Convention, 1754; Member of the Continental Congress, 1774-78; Member of Rhode Island Legislature.

Stephen Hopkins was born in Scituate (then a part of Providence), Rhode Island, on the seventh of March, 1707. He was apparently self-educated. He was a member and speaker of the Rhode Island Assembly, and in 1754 was a delegate to the Albany convention in New York where he considered Franklin's early plan of Union. Hopkins spoke out against British tyranny long before the revolutionary period. He attended the first Continental Congress in 1774, and was a party to the Declaration of Independence in 1776. He left that congress in 1778 and returned to his native state to serve in its Legislature. He died on the 13th of July, 1785 at the age of 78.

**William Ellery,** Congregationalist, Representing Rhode Island at the Continental Congress
Born: December 22, 1727
Birthplace: Newport, RI
Education: Harvard College (Lawyer, Judge)
Elected to Continental Congress, 1776-1785; Judge, Supreme Court of Rhode Island, circa 1778-?; First Collector, port of Newport, ?-1820.

William Ellery was born at Newport, Rhode Island, in December of 1727. Under the tutelage of his prominent father, Benjamin Ellery, he attended Harvard College and graduated at the age of 15. He searched for the right career for many years, worked as merchant, then a collector of customs, and later as the Clerk of the Rhode Island General Assembly. It was when he began to practice law in 1770, at the age of 43, that he seemed to find his calling. He was active in the Rhode Island Sons of Liberty, and was sent to the Continental Congress in 1776 to replace Samuel Ward, who had died. He was immediately appointed to the Marine committee and later participated in several others including the committee for foreign relations. Meanwhile he held the office of judge of the Supreme Court of Rhode Island. In 1785 he became a strong and vocal advocate for the abolition of slavery. He was appointed First (customs) Collector of the port of Newport, under the provisions of the Federal Constitution, where he served until his death on February 15 of 1820.

# Connecticut

**Roger Sherman,** Congregationalist, Representing Connecticut at the Continental Congress
Born: April 19, 1721
Birthplace: Newton, MA
Education: Informal, Cobbler, Surveyor, Lawyer. Honorary M.A. from Yale.
Admitted to Bar in New Milford Connecticut, 1754; Justice of the Peace, elected to General Assembly, representing New Milford Connecticut, 1755-58, 1760-61; Commisary for the Connecticut Troops, 1759; Elected to various Upper and Lower House offices representing New Haven, 1760s, 1770s; Judge of the Superior Court of Connecticut, 1766-1789; Elected to Continental Congress, 1774-81, 1783-84; Distinguished member of the Constitutional Convention, 1787; Elected US Senator for Connecticut, 1791-93.

Roger Sherman was born at Newton, near Boston, on April 19, 1721. When he was two his father took the family to what was then a frontier town, Stoughton. His education was very limited. He had access to his father's library, a good one by the standards of the day, and when Roger was about thirteen years old the town built a "grammar school" which he attended for a time. Stoughton was also fortunate to have a parish Minister by the name of Rev. Samuel Danbar, who was trained at Harvard. Danbar helped young Roger acquire some facility with mathematics, sciences, literature, and philosophy.

His first experience with an official office came in 1743 when he was appointed surveyor of New Haven County. A few years later he was commissioned by neighbor to consult a lawyer at the county seat regarding a petition before the court. The lawyer asked if he could examine Sherman's notes and reading them, urged Sherman to set up for the practice of law. At age twenty one he engaged in both civic and religious affairs in New Milford Connecticut, where he and his brother also opened the town's first store. He served as the town clerk there and was also chosen to lobby on behalf of the town at the provincial assembly. Since New Milford did not have a newspaper and reading material was hard to come by, Sherman wrote and published a very popular Almanac each year from 1750 to 1761.

Sherman was accepted to the Bar of Litchfield in 1754, and to represent New Milford in the General Assembly the following year. He was appointed justice of the peace, and four years later justice of the Superior Court of Connecticut. By the age of 40, he had become a very successful landowner and businessman while integrating himself into the social and political fabric of New England. He was appointed commissary to the Connecticut Troops at the start of the Revolutionary war; this was experience that he put to great use when he was elected to the Continental Congress in 1774. Sherman was a very active and much respected Delegate to the congress. He served and numerous committees, including the committee to draft the Declaration of Independence. He served all through the war for Independence. As active as he was in Congress, he simultaneously fulfilled his other offices. In 1776 these efforts began to take their toll on his health. Thus, he appealed to then governor Trumbull to relieve him of some of his state duties while he remained on in Congress through 1781. He left the office in 1781, then returned in 1783 and 84, where he served on the committee forming the Articles of Confederation. His interests in the strength of the federation carried him to the Constitutional Convention in 1787 where he was one of the most vocal and persistent members. Madison's notes on the convention credit him with one hundred and thirty-eight speeches to the convention. His tiny state of Connecticut was in a precarious position, and Sherman, then sixty-one apparently spared no effort in defending the rights of the smaller states.

Many of the most notable figures of the revolution, Adams, Jefferson, Madison, admitted a deep admiration for Roger Sherman and his work. From their notes Sherman appears as a picture of New England pragmatism: stern, taciturn, spare with his words and very direct in his speech, but never hesitating to stand-and stand again-for his principles. On July 23, 1793, Roger Sherman died of typhoid at the age of 72. At the time he served as US Senator from Connecticut under the new constitution that he had helped to build; in the new nation, that he had spent most of his life defending and defining.

**Samuel Huntington,** Congregationalist, Representing Connecticut at the Continental Congress
Born: July 16, 1731
Birthplace: Windham, CT
Education: Self-educated, Lawyer
Admitted to the Bar of Connecticut, 1754; King's attorney, tax collector, town-meeting moderator, justice of the peace, Norwich Connecticut; Appointed to the Superior court, 1773; Elected to provincial Upper House of Assembly, appointed to the Council of Safety, Delegate to the Continental Congress, 1776...; President of the Continental Congress, 1779-81; Lieutenant Governor and

Chief Judge of Superior Court of Connecticut, 178486; Governor of Connecticut, 1786-1796.

Samuel Huntington was one of the several maverick public servants of his era, devoting nearly all of his life to public office. Self-taught, he gained admittance to the Bar of Connecticut at the age of 23, and was soon thereafter appointed King's attorney to the town of Norwich. He served many offices and duties there until 1773, when he was appointed to the superior Court of Connecticut. Huntington was a moderate, with a distinctly upper-class bent, but he became active with the Sons of Liberty in his state in 1774. He then choose a legislative course. Elected to Connecticut's Upper House of Assembly in 1776, he served on the Council of Safety, and was selected a delegate to the Continental Congress that year. He served two terms as President of the Congress during the important adoption of the Articles of Confederation. He was called home in 1784 when he was elected Lieutenant Governor if his state; an office that then included the duties of Chief Judge of its Superior Court. In 1786 he was elected governor. He was very popular in the office and used his influence to develop roads and industry in the state. He was re-elected every term until his death, January 5, 1796.

**William Williams,** Congregationalist, Representing Connecticut at the Continental Congress
Born: April 23, 1731
Birthplace: Lebanon, CT
Education: Graduate of Harvard (Merchant)
Town Clerk, Selectman Provincial Representative, Council to the Legislature. Elected State Legislator, delegate to colonial conferences, 1775; Elected to Continental Congress, 177677; Delegate to the Connecticut convention to ratify the federal Constitution, 1787; Judge of the Windham County Courthouse.

His biography notes that William Williams was a successful merchant, but it is difficult to imagine when he found the time.

Born in 1731, he attained a common school education. He attended Harvard and graduated in 1751. He then studied theology with his father, Pastor of the First Congregational Church in Lebanon. Four years later, he joined his father's cousin in the French and Indian War at Lake George. When he returned, he established himself in Lebanon as a merchant, and also took a job as town clerk. He held that position for forty-four years. He was a Selectman for twenty-five years, served the provincial and later state Legislature for nearly forty years-during which time he was councilor, member, and Speaker of the House.

He was elected to the Continental Congress in 1776. He arrived too late to vote for Independence (he replaced Oliver Wolcott, who became seriously ill), but he did sign the Declaration, and was then appointed a member of the committee to frame the Articles of Confederation. In 1777 he was appointed to the Board of War. After the war, he attended the Hartford convention, where Connecticut ratified the Federal Constitution. Williams spent his remaining years as a County Court judge. He died August 2, 1811.

**Oliver Wolcott,** Congregationalist, Representing Connecticut at the Continental Congress
Born: December 1, 1726
Birthplace: Windsor, CT
Education: Graduate of Yale. (Soldier, Sheriff, Judge)
Sheriff of Litchfield County, ca. 1751-1775; Judge, 1750s, 60s; Militia leader, 1771-1774; Commissioner of Indian Affairs, 1775, 1784-89; Delegate to the Continental Congress, 1775-76, 1778-84; Brigadier General of the Connecticut Militia, 1776... Lt. Governor of Connecticut, 1786-96; Governor, 1796-97.

Oliver Wolcott was the youngest of fourteen children of then Royal Governor Roger Wolcott. Oliver attended Yale, a distinguished student, graduating in 1747. Even before graduating, he was commissioned by Governor Clinton of New York to raise a volunteer militia to assist in the French and Indian War. He did this, graduated Yale, and proceeded as Captain with his volunteer company to serve the crown on the northern frontier.

At the close of the war. Wolcott studied medicine with his brother for a while. As things took their course, he was appointed sheriff of a new Litchfield County, Connecticut, around 1751. He served as sheriff for more than twenty years. In 1771 he rejoined the Militia as revolutionary tensions grew. He was made a Major, and later a Colonel in the Connecticut Militia. Before the course of the war would end, he would become Brigadier General of the entire Connecticut force, under command of the Continental Armies.

In 1774 the Continental Congress appointed him a Commissioner of Indian Affairs in order to secure a treaty at the council at Albany. He was elected to the Congress in 1775. Wolcott was not very active in Congress. He was more concerned with military affairs and did suffer a bought with serious illness in 1776. He was not present for the occasion of the Declaration, but signed it sometime later. He spent all of the time between 1776 and 1778 engaged in military affairs. In 1778 he was again elected to the congress, where he served until 1784.

He then retired, although the congress called him twice more to serve as an Indian Commissioner. Wolcott was much revered in his native state. Yale honored him with a second degree, he was elected president of the Connecticut Society of Arts and Sciences, and in 1786 he was elected Lieutenant Governor of his state. He assumed the Governorship when Samuel Huntington died in January of 1796, and was popularly elected to the post at the following election. He died in that office, December 1, 1797, at the age of 71.

## Religious Affiliation of the Signers of the Declaration of Independence[59]

| Religious Affiliation | # of Signers | % of Signers |
| --- | --- | --- |
| Episcopalian/Anglican | 32 | 57.1 |
| Congregationalist | 13 | 23.2 |
| Presbyterian | 12 | 21.4 |
| Quaker | 2 | 3.6 |
| Unitarian or Universalist | 2 | 3.6 |
| Catholic | 1 | 1.8 |
| Total | 56 | 100.0 |

(The actual total is 62, because six signers had listings of two Denominations)

The following is a portion of Bill Federer's *"American Minute – Declaration of Independence – What price did the Signers pay?"*[60]

> 33-year-old Thomas Jefferson's original rough draft of the Declaration contained a line condemning slavery: "He has waged cruel war against human nature itself...in the persons of a distant people who never offended him, captivating and carrying them into slavery in another hemisphere, or to incur miserable death in their transportation thither... suppressing every legislative attempt to prohibit or to restrain this execrable commerce determining to keep open a market where MEN should be bought and sold."
>
> A few delegates objected, and as the Declaration needed to pass unanimously and time was running short with the British invading New York, the line condemning slavery was unfortunately omitted.
>
> John Hancock, the 39-year-old President of the Continental Congress, signed the Declaration first,

reportedly saying "the price on my head has just doubled."

Next to sign was Secretary, Charles Thomson, age 47.

70-yearold Benjamin Franklin said: "We must hang together or most assuredly we shall hang separately.

The Declaration referred to God: "Laws of Nature and of **Nature's God**... All Men are created equal, that they are endowed by their **Creator** with certain unalienable Rights...

Appealing to the **Supreme Judge of the World** for the Rectitude of our Intentions..."

And for the support of this Declaration, with a firm reliance on the protection of **Divine Providence**, we mutually pledge to each other our Lives, our Fortunes, and our sacred Honor."

Many of the 56 signers sacrificed their prosperity for their posterity. Of the Signers:

17 served in the military (30%),

11 had their homes destroyed (20%),

5 were hunted and captured (9%) and

9 died during the war (16%).

27-year-old George Walton signed, and at the Battle of Savannah was wounded and captured.

Signers Edward Rutledge, age 27, Thomas Heyward, Jr., age 30, and Arthur Middleton, age 34, were made prisoners at the Siege of Charleston.

38-year-old signer Thomas Nelson had his home used as British headquarters during the siege of Yorktown. Nelson reportedly offered five guineas to the first man to hit his house.

Signer Carter Braxton, age 40, lost his fortune during the war.

42-year-old signer Thomas McKean wrote that he was "hunted like a fox by the enemy, compelled to remove my family five times in three month."

46-year-old Richard Stockton signed and was dragged from his bed at night and jailed.

50-year-old signer Lewis Morris had his home taken and used as a barracks.

50-year-old signer Abraham Clark had two sons tortured and imprisoned on the British starving ship Jersey.

**More Americans died on British starving ships than died in battle during the Revolution.** *(Emphasis added)*

53-year-old signer John Witherspoon's son, James, was killed in the Battle of Germantown.

60-year-old signer Philip Livingston lost several properties to British occupation and died before the war ended.

63-year-old signer Francis Lewis had his wife imprisoned and treated so harshly, she died shortly after her release.

65-year-old signer John Hart had his home looted and had to remain in hiding, dying before the war ended.

41-year-old John Adams wrote of the Declaration: "I am apt to believe that it will be celebrated, by succeeding generations, as the great anniversary Festival. It ought to be commemorated, as the Day of Deliverance by solemn acts of devotion to **God Almighty**. It ought to be solemnized with pomp and parade, with shews, games, sports, guns, bells, bonfires and illuminations from one End of this Continent to the other from this time forward forever more." *(Emphasis added)*

John Adams continued: "You will think me transported with enthusiasm but I am not. I am well aware of the toil and blood and treasure, that it will cost us to maintain this Declaration, and support and defend these States. Yet through all the gloom I can see the rays of ravishing light and glory. I can see that the end is more than worth all the means, and that Posterity will triumph in that Days Transaction, even although we should rue it, which **I trust in God** We shall not." *(Emphasis added)*

When 54-year-old Samuel Adams signed the Declaration, he said: "We have this day restored the **Sovereign** to whom all men ought to be obedient. **He** reigns in heaven and from the rising to the setting of the sun, let **His kingdom** come." *(Emphasis added)*

# CHAPTER 4

---

# *Religion and the Congress of the Confederation, 1774-89*

The Continental-Confederation Congress, a legislative body that governed the United States from 1774 to 1789, contained an extraordinary number of deeply religious men. The amount of energy that Congress invested in encouraging the practice of religion in the new nation exceeded that expended by any subsequent American national government. Although the Articles of Confederation did not officially authorize Congress to concern itself with religion, the citizenry did not object to such activities. This lack of objection suggests that both the legislators and the public considered (it acceptable).

Congress thought it appropriate for the national government to promote a nondenominational, non-polemical Christianity chaplains for itself and the armed forces, sponsored the publication of a Bible, imposed Christian morality on the armed forces, and granted public lands to promote Christianity among the Indians. National days of thanksgiving and of "humiliation, fasting, and prayer" were proclaimed by Congress at least twice a year throughout the war. Congress was guided by "covenant theology," a Reformation doctrine especially dear to New England Puritans, which held that God bound himself in an agreement with a nation and its people. This agreement stipulated that they "should be prosperous or afflicted, according as their general Obedience or Disobedience thereto appears." Wars and revolutions were, accordingly, considered afflictions, as divine punishments for sin, from which a nation could rescue itself by repentance and reformation.

The first national government of the United States, was convinced that the "public prosperity" of a society depended on the vitality of its religion. Nothing less than a "spirit of universal reformation among all ranks and degrees of our citizens," Congress declared to the American people, would "make us a holy, that so we may be a happy people."[1]

# CHAPTER 5

---◆--------◆--------◆---

# A More Perfect Union;
# The Creation of the U.S. Constitution[1]

May 25, 1787, Freshly spread dirt covered the cobblestone street in front of the Pennsylvania State House, protecting the men inside from the sound of passing carriages and carts. Guards stood at the entrances to ensure that the curious were kept at a distance. Robert Morris of Pennsylvania, the "financier" of the Revolution, opened the proceedings with a nomination--Gen. George Washington for the presidency of the Constitutional Convention. The vote was unanimous. With characteristic ceremonial modesty, the general expressed his embarrassment at his lack of qualifications to preside over such an august body and apologized for any errors into which he might fall in the course of its deliberations.

To many of those assembled deliberations., especially to the small, boyish-looking, 36-year-old delegate from Virginia, James Madison, the general's mere presence boded well for the convention, for the illustrious Washington gave to the gathering an air of importance and legitimacy But his decision to attend the convention had been an agonizing one. The Father of the Country had almost remained at home.

Suffering from rheumatism, despondent over the loss of a brother, absorbed in the management of Mount Vernon, and doubting that the convention would accomplish very much or that many men of stature would attend, Washington delayed accepting the invitation to attend for several months. Torn between the hazards of lending his reputation to a gathering perhaps doomed to failure and the chance that the public would view his reluctance to attend with a critical eye, the general finally agreed to make the trip. James Madison was please

## The Articles of Confederation

The determined Madison had for several years insatiably studied history and political theory searching for a solution to the political and economic dilemmas he saw plaguing America. The Virginian's labors convinced him of the futility and weakness of confederacies of independent states. America's own government under the Articles of Confederation, Madison was convinced, had to be replaced. In force since 1781, established as a "league of friendship" and a constitution for the 13 sovereign and independent states after the Revolution, the articles seemed to Madison woefully inadequate. With the states retaining considerable power, the central government, he believed, had insufficient power to regulate commerce. It could not tax and was generally impotent in setting commercial policy. It could not effectively support a war effort. It had little power to settle quarrels between states. Saddled with this weak government, the states were on the brink of economic disaster. The evidence was overwhelming. Congress was attempting to function with a depleted treasury; paper money was flooding the country, creating extraordinary inflation--a pound of tea in some areas could be purchased for a tidy $100; and the depressed condition of business was taking its toll on many small farmers. Some of them were being thrown in jail for debt, and numerous farms were being confiscated and sold for taxes.

In 1786 some of the farmers had fought back. Led by Daniel Shays, a former captain in the Continental army, a group of armed men, sporting evergreen twigs in their hats, prevented the circuit court from sitting at Northampton, MA, and threatened to seize muskets stored in the arsenal at Springfield. Although the insurrection was put down by state troops, the incident confirmed the fears of many wealthy men that anarchy was just around the corner. Embellished day after day in the press, the uprising made upper-class Americans shudder as they imagined hordes of vicious outlaws descending upon innocent citizens. From his idyllic Mount Vernon setting, Washington wrote to Madison: "Wisdom and good examples are necessary at this time to rescue the political machine from the impending storm."

Madison thought he had the answer. He wanted a strong central government to provide order and stability. "Let it be tried then," he wrote, "whether any middle ground can be taken which will at once support a due supremacy of the national authority," while maintaining state power only when "subordinately useful." The resolute Virginian looked to the Constitutional Convention to forge a new government in this mold.

The convention had its specific origins in a proposal offered by Madison and John Tyler in the Virginia assembly that the Continental Congress be given power to regulate commerce throughout the Confederation. Through their efforts in the assembly a plan was devised inviting the several states to attend a convention at Annapolis, MD, in September 1786 to discuss commercial problems. Madison and a young lawyer from New York named Alexander Hamilton issued a report on the meeting in Annapolis, calling upon Congress to summon delegates of all of the states to meet for the purpose of revising the Articles of Confederation. Although the report was widely viewed as a usurpation of congressional authority, the Congress did issue a formal call to the states for a convention. To Madison it represented the supreme chance to reverse the country's trend. And as the delegations gathered in Philadelphia, its importance was not lost to others. The squire of Gunston Hall, George Mason, wrote to his son, "The Eyes of the United States are turned upon this Assembly and their Expectations raised to a very anxious Degree. May God

Grant that we may be able to gratify them, by establishing a wise and just Government."

## The Delegates

Seventy-four delegates were appointed to the convention, of which 55 actually attended sessions. Rhode Island was the only state that refused to send delegates. Dominated by men wedded to paper currency, low taxes, and popular government, Rhode Island's leaders refused to participate in what they saw as a conspiracy to overthrow the established government. Other Americans also had their suspicions. Patrick Henry, of the flowing red Glasgow cloak and the magnetic oratory, refused to attend, declaring he "smelt a rat." He suspected, correctly, that Madison had in mind the creation of a powerful central government and the subversion of the authority of the state legislatures. Henry along with many other political leaders, believed that the state governments offered the chief protection for personal liberties. He was determined not to lend a hand to any proceeding that seemed to pose a threat to that protection.

With Henry absent, with such towering figures as Jefferson and Adams abroad on foreign missions, and with John Jay in New York at the Foreign Office, the convention was without some of the country's major political leaders. It was, nevertheless, an impressive assemblage. In addition to Madison and Washington, there were Benjamin Franklin of Pennsylvania-crippled by gout, the 81-year-old Franklin was a man of many dimensions printer, storekeeper, publisher, scientist, public official, philosopher, diplomat, and ladies' man; James Wilson of Pennsylvania--a distinguished lawyer with a penchant for ill-advised land-jobbing schemes, which would force him late in life to flee from state to state avoiding prosecution for debt, the Scotsman brought a profound mind steeped in constitutional theory and law; Alexander Hamilton of New York--a brilliant, ambitious former aide-de-camp and secretary to Washington during the Revolution who had, after his marriage into the Schuyler family of New York, become a powerful political figure; George Mason of Virginia--the author of the Virginia Bill of Rights whom Jefferson later called "the Cato of his country without the avarice of the Roman"; John Dickinson of Delaware-the quiet, reserved author of the "Farmers' Letters" and chairman of the congressional committee that framed the articles; and Gouverneur Morris of Pennsylvania-- well versed in French literature and language, with a flair and bravado to match his keen intellect, who had helped draft the New York State Constitution and had worked with Robert Morris in the Finance Office.

There were others who played major roles - Oliver Ellsworth of Connecticut; Edmund Randolph of Virginia; William Paterson of New Jersey; John Rutledge of South Carolina; Elbridge Gerry of Massachusetts;

Roger Sherman of Connecticut; Luther Martin of Maryland; and the Pinckneys, Charles and Charles Cotesworth, of South Carolina. Franklin was the oldest member and Jonathan Dayton, the 27-year-old delegate from New Jersey was the youngest. The average age was 42. Most of the delegates had studied law, had served in colonial or state legislatures, or had been in the Congress. Well versed in philosophical theories of government advanced by such philosophers as James Harrington, John Locke, and Montesquieu, profiting from experience gained in state politics, the delegates composed an exceptional body, one that left a remarkably learned record of debate. Fortunately we have a relatively complete record of the proceedings, thanks to the indefatigable James Madison. Day after day, the Virginian sat in front of the presiding officer, compiling notes of the debates, not missing a single day or a single major speech. He later remarked that his self-confinement in the hall, which was often oppressively hot in the Philadelphia summer, almost killed him.

The sessions of the convention were held in secret--no reporters or visitors were permitted. Although many of the naturally loquacious members were prodded in the pubs and on the streets, most remained surprisingly discreet. To those suspicious of the convention, the curtain of secrecy only served to confirm their anxieties. Luther Martin of Maryland later charged that the conspiracy in Philadelphia needed a quiet breeding ground. Thomas Jefferson wrote John Adams from Paris, "I am sorry they began their deliberations by so abominable a precedent as that of tying up the tongues of their members."

## The Virginia Plan

On Tuesday morning, May 29, Edmund Randolph, the tall, 34-year- old governor of Virginia, opened the debate with a long speech decrying the evils that had befallen the country under the Articles of Confederation and stressing the need for creating a strong national government. Randolph then outlined a broad plan that he and his Virginia compatriots had, through long sessions at the Indian Queen tavern, put together in the days preceding the convention. James Madison had such a plan on his mind for years. The proposed government had three branches- -legislative, executive, and judicial--each branch structured to check the other. Highly centralized, the government would have veto power over laws enacted by state legislatures. The plan, Randolph confessed, "meant a strong *consolidated* union in which the idea of states should be nearly annihilated." This was, indeed, the rat so offensive to Patrick Henry.

The introduction of the so-called Virginia Plan at the beginning of the convention was a tactical coup. The Virginians had forced the debate into their own frame of reference and in their own terms.

For 10 days the members of the convention discussed the sweeping and, to many delegates, startling Virginia resolutions. The critical issue, described succinctly by Gouverneur Morris on May 30, was the distinction between a federation and a national government, the "former being a mere compact resting on the good faith of the parties; the latter having a compleat and *compulsive* operation." Morris favored the latter, a "supreme power" capable of exercising necessary authority not merely a shadow government, fragmented and hopelessly ineffective.

## The New Jersey Plan

This nationalist position revolted many delegates who cringed at the vision of a central government swallowing state sovereignty. On June 13 delegates from smaller states rallied around proposals offered by New Jersey delegate William Paterson. Railing against efforts to throw the states into "hotchpot," Paterson proposed a "union of the States merely federal." The "New Jersey resolutions" called only for a revision of the articles to enable the Congress more easily to raise revenues and regulate commerce. It also provided that acts of Congress and ratified treaties be "the supreme law of the States."

For 3 days the convention debated Paterson's plan, finally voting for rejection. With the defeat of the New Jersey resolutions, the convention was moving toward creation of a new government, much to the dismay of many small-state delegates. The nationalists, led by Madison, appeared to have the proceedings in their grip. In addition, they were able to persuade the members that any new constitution should be ratified through conventions of the people and not by the Congress and the state legislatures- another tactical coup. Madison and his allies believed that the constitution they had in mind would likely be scuttled in the legislatures, where many state political leaders stood to lose power. The nationalists wanted to bring the issue before "the people," where ratification was more likely.

## Hamilton's Plan

On June 18 Alexander Hamilton presented his own ideal plan of government. Erudite and polished, the speech, nevertheless, failed to win a following. It went too far. Calling the British government "the best in the world," Hamilton proposed a model strikingly similar an executive to serve during good behavior or life with veto power over all laws; a senate with members serving during good behavior; the legislature to have power to pass "all laws whatsoever." Hamilton later wrote to Washington that the people were now willing to accept "something not very remote from that which they have lately quitted." What the people had "lately quitted," of course, was monarchy. Some members of the convention fully expected the country to turn in this direction. Hugh Williamson of North Carolina, a wealthy physician, declared that it was "pretty certain... that we should at some time or other have a king." Newspaper accounts appeared in the summer of 1787 alleging that a plot was under way to invite the second son of George III, Frederick, Duke of York, the secular bishop of Osnaburgh in Prussia, to become "king of the United States."

Strongly militating against any serious attempt to establish monarchy was the enmity so prevalent in the revolutionary period toward royalty and the privileged classes. Some state constitutions had even prohibited titles of nobility. In the same year as the Philadelphia convention, Royall Tyler, a revolutionary war veteran, in his play, The Contract, gave his own jaundiced view of the upper classes:

> Exult each patriot heart! this night is shewn
> A piece, which we may fairly call our own;
> Where the proud titles of "My Lord!" "Your Grace!"
> To humble Mr. and plain Sir give place.

Most delegates were well aware that there were too many Royall Tylers in the country, with too many memories of British rule and too many ties to a recent bloody war, to accept a king. As the debate moved into the specifics of the new government, Alexander Hamilton and others of his persuasion would have to accept something less.

By the end of June, debate between the large and small states over the issue of representation in the first chamber of the legislature was becoming increasingly acrimonious. Delegates from Virginia and other large states demanded that voting in Congress be according to population; representatives of smaller states insisted upon the equality they had enjoyed under the articles. With the oratory degenerating into threats and accusations, Benjamin Franklin appealed for daily prayers. Dressed in his customary gray homespun, the aged philosopher pleaded that "the Father of lights... illuminate our understandings." Franklin's appeal for prayers was never fulfilled; the convention, as Hugh Williamson noted, had no funds to pay a preacher.

*(Editor's Note: However the group did turn to prayer, which had a calming effect on the delegates. He made his appeal on June 28, 1787. Many believe this is the turning point, the epiphany, of the Convention; the governmental epiphany. And it appears prayer and attendance at church services were utilized to calm the tempers and stick to the creation of "...a new nation." Franklin is called a Deist? Would a Deist truly suggest prayer?)*

"Mr. President:

"The small progress we have made after 4 or five weeks close attendance & continual reasonings with each other -- our different sentiments on almost every question, several of the last producing as many noes as ays, is methinks a melancholy proof of the imperfection of the Human Understanding. We indeed seem to feel our own wont of political wisdom, since we have been running about in search of it. We have gone back to ancient history for models of government, and examined the different forms of those Republics which having been formed with the seeds of their own dissolution now no longer exist. And we have viewed Modern States all round Europe, but find none of their Constitutions suitable to our circumstances.

"In this situation of this Assembly groping as it were in the dark to find political truth, and scarce able to distinguish it when to us, how has it happened, Sir, that we have not hitherto once thought of humbly applying to the **Father of lights** to illuminate our understandings? In the beginning of the contest with G. Britain, when we were sensible of danger we had **daily prayer** in this room for the Divine Protection. -- **Our prayers**, Sir, were heard, and they were graciously answered. All of us who were engaged in the struggle must have observed frequent instances of **a Superintending providence** in our favor. To that kind providence we owe this happy opportunity of consulting in peace on the means of establishing our future national felicity. And have we now forgotten that **powerful friend**? or do we imagine that we no longer need **His assistance.**

"I have lived, Sir, a long time and the longer I live, the more convincing proofs I see of this truth.... that <u>***God***</u> *governs in the affairs of men.* And if a sparrow cannot fall to the ground without his notice, is it probable that an empire can rise without his aid? We have been assured, Sir, in the sacred writings that "except the Lord build they labor in vain that build it." **I firmly believe this;** and I also believe that without his concurring aid we shall succeed in this political building no better than the Builders of Babel: We shall be divided by our little partial local interests; our projects will be confounded, and we ourselves shall be become a reproach and a bye word down to future age. And what is worse, mankind may hereafter this unfortunate instance, despair of establishing Governments by Human Wisdom, and leave it to chance, war, and conquest.

"I therefore beg leave to move -- **that henceforth prayers imploring the assistance of Heaven, and its blessings on our deliberations, be held in this Assembly every morning before we proceed to business, and that one or more of the Clergy of this City be requested to officiate in that service."** *(Emphasis added)*

On June 29 the delegates from the small states lost the first battle. The convention approved a resolution establishing population as the basis for representation in the House of Representatives, thus favoring the larger states. On a subsequent small-state proposal that the states have equal representation in the Senate, the vote resulted in a tie. With large-state delegates unwilling to compromise on this issue, one member thought that the convention "was on the verge of dissolution, scarce held together by the strength of an hair."

By July 10 George Washington was so frustrated over the deadlock that he bemoaned "having had any agency" in the proceedings and called the opponents of a strong central government "narrow minded politicians... under the influence of local views." Luther Martin of Maryland, perhaps one whom Washington saw as "narrow minded," thought otherwise. A tiger in debate, not content merely to parry an opponent's argument but determined to bludgeon it into eternal rest, Martin had become perhaps the small states' most effective, if irascible, orator. The Marylander leaped eagerly into the battle on the representation issue declaring, "The States have a right to an equality of representation. This is secured to us by our present articles of confederation; we are in possession of this privilege."

## The Great Compromise

Also crowding into this complicated and divisive discussion over representation was the North-South division over the method by which slaves were to be counted for purposes of taxation and representation. On July 12 Oliver Ellsworth proposed that representation for the lower house be based on the number of free persons and three-fifths of "all other persons," a euphemism for slaves. In the following week the members finally compromised, agreeing that direct taxation be according to representation and that the representation of the lower house be based on the white inhabitants and three-fifths of the "other people." With this compromise and with the growing realization that such compromise was necessary to avoid a complete breakdown of the convention, the members then approved Senate equality. Roger Sherman had remarked that it was the wish of the delegates "that some general government should be established." With the crisis over representation now settled, it began to look again as if this wish might be fulfilled.

For the next few days the air in the City of Brotherly Love, although insufferably muggy and swarming with blue-bottle flies, had the clean scent of conciliation. In this period of welcome calm, the members decided to appoint a Committee of Detail to draw up a draft constitution. The convention would now at last have something on paper. As Nathaniel Gorham of Massachusetts, John Rutledge, Edmund Randolph, James Wilson, and Oliver Ellsworth went to work, the other delegates voted themselves a much needed 10-day vacation.

During the adjournment, Gouverneur Morris and George Washington rode out along a creek that ran through land that had been part of the Valley Forge encampment 10 years earlier. While Morris cast for trout, Washington pensively looked over the now lush ground where his freezing troops had suffered, at a time when it had seemed as if the American Revolution had reached its end. The country had come a long way.

## The First Draft

On Monday August 6, 1787, the convention accepted the first draft of the Constitution. Here was the article-by-article model from which the final document would result some 5 weeks later. As the members began to consider the various sections, the willingness to compromise of the previous days quickly evaporated. The most serious controversy erupted over the question of regulation of commerce. The southern states, exporters of raw materials, rice, indigo, and tobacco, were fearful that a New England dominated Congress might, through export taxes, severely damage the South's economic life. C. C. Pinckney declared that if Congress had the power to regulate trade, the southern states would be "nothing more than overseers for the Northern States."

On August 21 the debate over the issue of commerce became very closely linked to another explosive issue--slavery. When Martin of Maryland proposed a tax on slave importation, the convention was thrust into a strident discussion of the institution of slavery and its moral and economic relationship to the new government. Rutledge of South Carolina, asserting that slavery had nothing at all to do with morality, declared, "Interest alone is the governing principle with nations." Sherman of Connecticut was for dropping the tender issue altogether before it jeopardized the convention. Mason of Virginia expressed concern over unlimited importation of slaves but later indicated that he also favored federal protection of slave property already held. This nagging issue of possible federal intervention in slave traffic, which Sherman and others feared could irrevocably split northern and southern delegates, was settled by, in Mason's words, "a bargain." Mason later wrote that delegates from South Carolina and Georgia, who most feared federal meddling in the slave trade, made a deal with delegates from the New England states. In exchange for the New Englanders' support for continuing slave importation for 20 years, the southerners accepted a clause that required only a simple majority vote on navigation laws, a crippling blow to southern economic interests.

The bargain was also a crippling blow to those working to abolish slavery. Congregationalist minister and abolitionist Samuel Hopkins of Connecticut charged that the convention had sold out: "How does it appear... that these States, who have been fighting for liberty and consider themselves as the highest and most noble example of zeal for it, cannot agree in any political Constitution, unless it indulge and authorize them to enslave their fellow men... Ah! these unclean spirits, like frogs, they, like the Furies of the poets are spreading discord, and exciting men to contention and war." Hopkins considered the Constitution a document fit for the flames.

On August 31 a weary George Mason, who had 3 months earlier written so expectantly to his son about the "great Business now before us," bitterly exclaimed that he "would sooner chop off his right hand than put it to the Constitution as it now stands." Mason despaired that the convention was rushing to saddle the country with an ill-advised, potentially ruinous central authority He was concerned that a "bill of rights," ensuring individual liberties, had not been made part of the Constitution. Mason called for a new convention to reconsider the whole question of the formation of a new government. Although Mason's motion was overwhelmingly voted down, opponents of the Constitution did not abandon the idea of a new convention. It was futilely suggested again and again for over 2 years.

One of the last major unresolved problems was the method of electing the executive. A number of proposals, including direct election by the people, by state legislatures, by state governors, and by the national legislature, were considered. The result was the Electoral College, a master stroke of compromise, quaint and curious but politically expedient. The large states got proportional strength in the number of delegates, the state legislatures got the right of selecting delegates, and the House the right to choose the president in the event no candidate received a majority of electoral votes. Mason later predicted that the House would probably choose the president 19 times out of 20.

In the early days of September, with the exhausted delegates anxious to return home, compromise came easily. On September 8 the convention was ready to turn the Constitution over to a Committee of Style and Arrangement. Gouverneur Morris was the chief architect. Years later he wrote to Timothy Pickering: "That Instrument was written by the Fingers which wrote this letter." The Constitution was presented to the convention on September 12, and the delegates methodically began to consider each section. Although close votes followed on several articles, it was clear that the grueling work of the convention in the historic summer of 1787 was reaching its end.

Before the final vote on the Constitution on September 15, Edmund Randolph proposed that amendments be made by the state conventions and then turned over to another general convention for consideration. He was joined by George Mason and Elbridge Gerry. The three lonely allies were soundly rebuffed. Late in the afternoon the roll of the states was called on the Constitution, and from every delegation the word was "Aye."

On September 17 the members met for the last time, and the venerable Franklin had written a speech that was delivered by his colleague James Wilson. Appealing for unity behind the Constitution, Franklin declared, "I think it will astonish our enemies, who are waiting with confidence to hear that our councils are confounded like those of the builders of Babel; and that our States are on the point of separation, only to meet hereafter for the purpose of cutting one another's throats." With Mason, Gerry, and Randolph withstanding appeals to attach their signatures, the other delegates in the hall formally signed the Constitution, and the convention adjourned at 4 o'clock in the afternoon.

Weary from weeks of intense pressure but generally satisfied with their work, the delegates shared a farewell dinner at City Tavern. Two blocks away on Market Street, printers John Dunlap and David Claypoole worked into the night on the final imprint of the six-page Constitution, copies of which would leave Philadelphia on the morning stage. The debate over the nation's form of government was now set for the larger arena.

As the members of the convention returned home in the following days, Alexander Hamilton privately assessed the chances of the Constitution for ratification. In its favor were the support of Washington, commercial interests, men of property, creditors, and the belief among many Americans that the Articles of Confederation were inadequate. Against it were the opposition of a few influential men in the convention and state politicians fearful of losing power, the general revulsion against taxation, the suspicion that a centralized government would be insensitive to local interests, and the fear among debtors that a new government would "restrain the means of cheating Creditors."

## The Federalists and the Anti-Federalists

Because of its size, wealth, and influence and because it was the first state to call a ratifying convention, Pennsylvania was the focus of national attention. The positions of the Federalists, those who supported the Constitution, and the anti-Federalists, those who opposed it, were printed and reprinted by scores of newspapers across the country. And passions in the state were most warm. When the Federalist-dominated Pennsylvania assembly lacked a quorum on September 29 to call a state ratifying convention, a Philadelphia mob, in order to provide the necessary numbers, dragged two anti-Federalist members from their lodgings through the streets to the State House where the bedraggled representatives were forced to stay while the assembly voted. It was a curious example of participatory democracy.

On October 5 anti-Federalist Samuel Bryan published the first of his "Centinel" essays in Philadelphia's Independent Gazetteer. Republished in newspapers in various states, the essays assailed the sweeping power of the central government, the usurpation of state sovereignty, and the absence of a bill of rights guaranteeing individual liberties such as freedom of speech and freedom of religion. "The United States are to be melted down," Bryan declared, into a despotic empire dominated by "well-born" aristocrats. Bryan was echoing the fear of many anti-Federalists that the new government would become one controlled by the wealthy established families and the culturally refined. The common working people, Bryan believed, were in danger of being subjugated to the will of an all-powerful authority remote and inaccessible to the people. It was this kind of authority, he believed, that Americans had fought a war against only a few years earlier.

The next day James Wilson, delivering a stirring defense of the Constitution to a large crowd gathered in the yard of the State House, praised the new government as the best "which has ever been offered to the world." The Scotsman's view prevailed. Led by Wilson, Federalists dominated in the Pennsylvania convention, carrying the vote on December 12 by a healthy 46 to 23.

The vote for ratification in Pennsylvania did not end the rancor and bitterness. Franklin declared that scurrilous articles in the press were giving the impression that Pennsylvania was "peopled by a set of the most unprincipled, wicked, rascally and quarrelsome scoundrels upon the face of the globe." And in Carlisle, on December 26, anti-Federalist rioters broke up a Federalist celebration and hung Wilson and the Federalist chief justice of Pennsylvania, Thomas McKean, in effigy; put the torch to a copy of the Constitution; and busted a few Federalist heads. In New York the Constitution was under siege in the press by a series of essays signed "Cato." Mounting a counterattack, Alexander Hamilton and John Jay enlisted help from Madison and, in late 1787, they published the first of a series of essays now known as the Federalist Papers. The 85 essays, most of which were penned by Hamilton himself, probed the weaknesses of the Articles of Confederation and the need for an energetic national government. Thomas Jefferson later called the *Federalist Papers* the "best commentary on the principles of government ever written."

Against this kind of Federalist leadership and determination, the opposition in most states was disorganized and generally inert. The leading spokesmen were largely statecentered men with regional and local interests and loyalties. Madison wrote of the Massachusetts anti-Federalists, "There was not a single character capable of uniting their wills or directing their measures.... They had no plan whatever." The antiFederalists attacked wildly on several fronts: the lack of a bill of rights, discrimination against southern states in navigation legislation, direct taxation, the loss of state sovereignty. Many charged that the Constitution represented the work of aristocratic politicians bent on protecting their own class interests. At the Massachusetts convention one delegate declared, "These lawyers, and men of learning and moneyed men, that... make us poor illiterate people swallow down the pill... they will swallow up all us little folks like the great Leviathan; yes, just as the whale swallowed up Jonah!" Some newspaper articles, presumably written by anti-Federalists, resorted to fanciful predictions of the horrors that might emerge under the new Constitution pagans and deists could control the government; the use of Inquisition like torture could be instituted as punishment for federal crimes; even the pope could be elected president.

One anti-Federalist argument gave opponents some genuine difficulty--the claim that the territory of the 13 states was too extensive for a representative government. In a republic embracing a large area, anti-Federalists argued, government would be impersonal, unrepresentative, dominated by men of wealth, and oppressive of the poor and working classes. Had not the illustrious Montesquieu himself ridiculed the notion that an extensive territory composed of varying climates and people, could be a single republican state? James Madison, always ready with the Federalist volley, turned the argument completely around and insisted that the vastness of the country would itself be a strong argument in favor of a republic. Claiming that a large republic would counterbalance various political interest groups vying for power, Madison wrote, "The smaller the society the fewer probably will be the distinct parties and interests composing it; the fewer the distinct parties and interests, the more frequently will a majority be found of the same party and the more easily will they concert and execute their plans of oppression." Extend the size of the republic, Madison argued, and the country would be less vulnerable to separate factions within it.

## Ratification

By January 9, 1788, five states of the nine necessary for ratification had approved the Constitution--Delaware, Pennsylvania, New Jersey, Georgia, and Connecticut. But the eventual outcome remained uncertain in pivotal states such as Massachusetts, New York, and Virginia. On February 6, with Federalists agreeing to recommend a list of amendments amounting to a bill of rights, Massachusetts ratified by a vote of 187 to 168. The revolutionary leader, John Hancock, elected to preside over the Massachusetts ratifying convention but unable to make up his mind on the Constitution, took to his bed with a convenient case of gout. Later seduced by the Federalists with visions of the vice presidency and possibly the presidency,

Hancock, whom Madison noted as "an idolater of popularity," suddenly experienced a miraculous cure and delivered a critical block of votes. Although Massachusetts was now safely in the Federalist column, the recommendation of a bill of rights was a significant victory for the anti-Federalists. Six of the remaining states later appended similar recommendations.

When the New Hampshire convention was adjourned by Federalists who sensed imminent defeat and when Rhode Island on March 24 turned down the Constitution in a popular referendum by an overwhelming vote of 10 to 1, Federalist leaders were apprehensive. Looking ahead to the Maryland convention, Madison wrote to Washington, "The difference between even a postponement and adoption in Maryland may... possibly give a fatal advantage to that which opposes the constitution." Madison had little reason to worry. The final vote on April 28 - 63 for, 11 against. In Baltimore, a huge parade celebrating the Federalist victory rolled through the downtown streets, highlighted by a 15foot float called "Ship Federalist." The symbolically seaworthy craft was later launched in the waters off Baltimore and sailed down the Potomac to Mount Vernon.

On July 2, 1788, the Confederation Congress, meeting in New York, received word that a reconvened New Hampshire ratifying convention had approved the Constitution. With South Carolina's acceptance of the Constitution in May, New Hampshire thus became the ninth state to ratify. The Congress appointed a committee "for putting the said Constitution into operation." In the next 2 months, thanks largely to the efforts of Madison and Hamilton in their own states, Virginia and New York both ratified while adding their own amendments. The margin for the Federalists in both states, however, was extremely close. Hamilton figured that the majority of the people in New York actually opposed the Constitution, and it is probable that a majority of people in the entire country opposed it. Only the promise of amendments had ensured a Federalist victory.

# CHAPTER 6

◆━━━━━•••◆•••━━━━━◆

## *Continental Congress Delegates*

On September 17, 1789, the delegates to the Continental Congress adopted what became known as the Constitution of the United States of America. In went into effect March 4, 1789. Since there are many sources for analysis of the Constitution, it will not be replicated here. However, once again, it must be realized that this "Constitution" was agreed upon by individuals, who were human beings who lived and died as participants in the creation of a new country.

They knew the price the Signers of the Declaration of Independence paid, yet they were willing to step up and put *their* "lives, their fortunes and their sacred honor" on the line, also. So as to understand who they were and where they came from, their names and background, as well as Christian affiliation, are included here.[1]

## Connecticut

**Oliver Ellsworth\***, Congregationalist, Connecticut[2]
Oliver Ellsworth was born on April 29, 1745, in Windsor, CT, to Capt. David and Jemima Ellsworth. He entered Yale in 1762 but transferred to the College of New Jersey (later Princeton) at the end

of his second year. He continued to study theology and received his A.B. degree after 2 years. Soon afterward, however, Ellsworth turned to the law. After 4 years of study, he was admitted to the bar in 1771. The next year Ellsworth married Abigail Wolcott. *(The Non-Signers are indicated with \*.)*

From a slow start Ellsworth built up a prosperous law practice. His reputation as an able and industrious jurist grew, and in 1777 Ellsworth became Connecticut's state attorney for Hartford County. That same year he was chosen as one of Connecticut's representatives in the Continental Congress. He served on various committees during six annual terms until 1783. Ellsworth was also active in his state's efforts during the Revolution. As a member of the Committee of the Pay Table, Oliver Ellsworth was one of the five men who supervised Connecticut's war expenditures. In 1779 he assumed greater duties as a member of the council of safety, which, with the governor, controlled all military measures for the state.

When the Constitutional Convention met in Philadelphia in 1787 Ellsworth once again represented Connecticut and took an active part in the proceedings. During debate on the Great Compromise, Ellsworth proposed that the basis of representation in the legislative branch remain by state, as under the Articles of Confederation. He also left his mark through an amendment to change the word "national" to "United States" in a resolution. Thereafter, "United States" was the title used in the convention to designate the government.

Ellsworth also served on the Committee of Five that prepared the first draft of the Constitution. Ellsworth favored the three-fifths compromise on the enumeration of slaves but opposed the abolition of the foreign slave trade. Though he left the convention near the end of August and did not sign the final document, he urged its adoption upon his return to Connecticut and wrote the Letters of a Landholder to promote its ratification.

Ellsworth served as one of Connecticut's first two senators in the new federal government between 1789 and 1796. In the

Senate he chaired the committee that framed the bill organizing the federal judiciary and helped to work out the practical details necessary to run a new government. Ellsworth's other achievements in Congress included framing the measure that admitted North Carolina to the Union, devising the nonintercourse act that forced Rhode Island to join, drawing up the bill to regulate the consular service, and serving on the committee that considered Alexander Hamilton's plan for funding the national debt and for incorporating the Bank of the United States.

In the spring of 1796 he was appointed Chief Justice of the Supreme Court and also served as commissioner to France in 1799 and 1800. Upon his return to America in early 1801, Ellsworth retired from public life and lived in Windsor, CT. He died there on November 26, 1807, and was buried in the cemetery of the First Church of Windsor.

**William Samuel Johnson,** Episcopalian, Presbyterian, Connecticut[3]

William Samuel Johnson was the son of Samuel Johnson, the first president of King's College (later Columbia College and University). William was born at Stratford, CT, in 1727. His father, who was a well-known Anglican clergyman-philosopher, prepared him for college and he graduated from Yale in 1744. About 3 years later he won a master of arts degree from the same institution and an honorary master's from Harvard.

Resisting his father's wish that he become a minister, Johnson embraced law instead--largely by educating himself and without benefit of formal training. After admittance to the bar, he launched a practice in Stratford, representing clients from nearby New York State as well as Connecticut, and before long he established business connections with various mercantile houses in New York City. In 1749, adding to his already substantial wealth, he married Anne Beach, daughter of a local businessman. The couple was to have five daughters and six sons, but many of them died at an early age.

Johnson did not shirk the civic responsibilities of one of his station.

In the 1750s he began his public career as a Connecticut militia officer. In 1761 and 1765 he served in the lower house of the colonial assembly. In 1766 and 1771 he was elected to the upper house. At the time of the Revolution, Johnson was disturbed by conflicting loyalties. Although he attended the Stamp Act Congress in 1765, moderately opposed the Townshend Duties of 1767, and believed that most British policies were unwise, he retained strong transatlantic ties and found it difficult to choose sides. Many of his friends resided in Britain; in 1765 and 1766 Oxford University conferred honorary master's and doctor's degrees upon him; he had a strong association with the Anglican Church; he acted as Connecticut's agent in Britain during the years 1767-71; and he was friendly with men such as Jared Ingersoll, Sr., who were affiliated with the British administration.

Johnson finally decided to work for peace between Britain and the colonies and to oppose the extremist Whig faction. On that basis, he refused to participate in the First Continental Congress, to which he was elected in 1774, following service as a judge of the Connecticut colonial supreme court (1772-74). When hostilities broke out, he confined his activities to peacemaking efforts. In April 1775 Connecticut sent him and another emissary to speak to British Gen. Thomas Gage about ending the bloodshed. But the time was not ripe for negotiations and they failed. Johnson fell out of favor with radical patriot elements who gained the ascendancy in Connecticut government and they no longer called upon his service. Although he was arrested in 1779 on charges of communicating with the enemy, he cleared himself and was released.

Once the passions of war had ebbed, Johnson resumed his political career. In the Continental Congress (1785-87), he was one of the most influential and popular delegates. Playing a major role in the Constitutional Convention, he missed no sessions after arriving on June 2; espoused the Connecticut Compromise; and chaired the Committee of Style, which shaped the final document. He also worked for ratification in Connecticut.

Johnson took part in the new government, in the U.S. Senate where he contributed to passage of the Judiciary Act of 1789. In 1791, the year after the government moved from New York to Philadelphia, he resigned mainly because he preferred to devote all his energies to the presidency of Columbia College (1787-1800), in New York City. During these years, he established the school on a firm basis and recruited a fine faculty.

Johnson retired from the college in 1800, a few years after his wife died, and in the same year wed Mary Brewster Beach, a relative of his first bride. They resided at his birthplace, Stratford. He died there in 1819 at the age of 92 and was buried at Old Episcopal Cemetery.

**Roger Sherman,** Congregationalist, Connecticut[4]

In 1723, when Sherman was 2 years of age, his family relocated from his Newton, MA, birthplace to Dorchester (present Stoughton). As a boy, he was spurred by a desire to learn and read widely in his spare time to supplement his minimal education at a common school. But he spent most of his waking hours helping his father with farming chores and learning the cobbler's trade from him. In 1743, 2 years after his father's death, Sherman joined an elder brother who had settled in New Milford, CT.

Purchasing a store, becoming a county surveyor, and winning a variety of town offices, Sherman prospered and assumed leadership in the community. In 1749 he married Elizabeth Hartwell, by whom he had seven children. Without benefit of a formal legal education, he was admitted to the bar in 1754 and embarked upon a distinguished judicial and political career. In the period 1755-61, except for a brief interval, he served as a representative in the colonial legislature and held the offices of justice of the peace and county judge. Somehow he also eked out time to publish an essay on monetary theory and a series of almanacs incorporating his own astronomical observations and verse.

In 1761, Sherman abandoned his law practice, and moved to New Haven, CT. There, he managed two stores, one that catered to Yale students, and another in nearby Wallingford. He also became a friend and benefactor of Yale College, and served for many years as its treasurer. In 1763, or 3 years after the death of his first wife, he wed Rebecca Prescott, who bore eight children.

Meanwhile, Sherman's political career had blossomed. He rose from justice of the peace and county judge to an associate judge of the Connecticut Superior Court and to representative in both houses of the colonial assembly. Although opposed to extremism, he promptly joined the fight against Britain. He supported nonimportation measures and headed the New Haven committee of correspondence.

Sherman was a longtime and influential member of the Continental Congress (1774-81 and 1783-84). He won membership on the committees that drafted the Declaration of Independence and the Articles of Confederation, as well as those concerned with Indian affairs, national finances, and military matters. To solve economic problems, at both national and state levels, he advocated high taxes rather than excessive borrowing or the issuance of paper currency.

While in Congress, Sherman remained active in state and local politics, continuing to hold the office of judge of the Connecticut Superior Court, as well as membership on the council of safety (1777-79). In 1783 he helped codify Connecticut's statutory laws. The next year, he was elected mayor of New Haven (1784-86).

Although on the edge of insolvency, mainly because of wartime losses, Sherman could not resist the lure of national service. In 1787 he represented his state at the Constitutional Convention, and attended practically every session. Not only did he sit on the Committee on Postponed Matters, but he also probably helped draft the New Jersey Plan and was a prime mover behind the Connecticut, or Great, Compromise, which broke the deadlock between the large and small states over representation. He was, in addition, instrumental in Connecticut's ratification of the Constitution.

Sherman concluded his career by serving in the U.S. House of Representatives (1789-91) and Senate (1791-93), where he espoused the Federalist cause. He died at New Haven in 1793 at the age of 72 and is buried in the Grove Street Cemetery.

# Georgia

**Abraham Baldwin,** Congregationalist - Episcopalian, Georgia[5]

Baldwin was born at Guilford, Conn., in 1754, the second son of a blacksmith who fathered 12 children by 2 wives. Besides Abraham, several of the family attained distinction. His sister Ruth married the poet and diplomat Joel Barlow, and his half-brother Henry attained the position of justice of the U.S. Supreme Court. Their ambitious father went heavily into debt to educate his children.

After attending a local village school, Abraham matriculated at Yale, in nearby New Haven. He graduated in 1772. Three years later, he became a minister and tutor at the college. He held that position until 1779, when he served as a chaplain in the Continental Army. Two years later, he declined an offer from his alma mater of a professorship of divinity. Instead of resuming his ministerial or educational duties after the war, he turned to the study of law and in 1783 gained admittance to the bar at Fairfield, CT.

Within a year, Baldwin moved to Georgia, won legislative approval to practice his profession, and obtained a grant of land in Wilkes County. In 1785 he sat in the assembly and the Continental Congress. Two years later, his father died and Baldwin undertook to pay off his debts and educate, out of his own pocket, his half-brothers and half-sisters.

That same year, Baldwin attended the Constitutional Convention, from which he was absent for a few weeks. Although usually inconspicuous, he sat on the Committee on Postponed Matters and helped resolve the large-small state representation crisis. At first, he favored representation in the Senate based upon property holdings, but possibly because of his close relationship with the Connecticut delegation he later came to fear alienation of the small states and changed his mind to representation by state.

After the convention, Baldwin returned to the Continental Congress (1787-89). He was then elected to the U.S. Congress, where he served for 18 years (House of Representatives, 1789-99; Senate, 1799-1807). During these years, he became a bitter opponent of Hamiltonian policies and, unlike most other native New Englanders, an ally of Madison and Jefferson and the Democratic-Republicans. In the Senate, he presided for a while as president pro tem.

By 1790 Baldwin had taken up residence in Augusta. Beginning in the preceding decade, he had begun efforts to advance the educational system in Georgia. Appointed with six others in 1784 to oversee the founding of a state college, he saw his dream come true in 1798 when Franklin College was founded. Modeled after Yale, it became the nucleus of the University of Georgia.

Baldwin, who never married, died after a short illness during his 53d year in 1807. Still serving in the Senate at the time, he was buried in Washington's Rock Creek Cemetery.

**William Few,** Methodist, Georgia[6]

Few was born in 1748. His father's family had emigrated from England to Pennsylvania in the 1680s, but the father had subsequently moved to Maryland, where he married and settled on a farm near Baltimore. William was born there. He encountered much hardship and received minimal schooling. When he was 10 years of age, his father, seeking better opportunity, moved his family to North Carolina.

In 1771 Few, his father, and a brother associated themselves with the "Regulators," a group of frontiersmen who opposed the royal governor. As a result, the brother was hanged, the Few family farm was destroyed, and the father was forced to move once again, this time to Georgia. William remained behind, helping to settle his father's affairs, until 1776 when he joined his family near Wrightsboro, Ga. About this time, he won admittance to the bar, based on earlier informal study, and set up practice in Augusta.

When the War for Independence began, Few enthusiastically aligned himself with the Whig cause. Although largely self-educated, he soon proved his capacity for leadership and won a lieutenant colonelcy in the dragoons. In addition, he entered politics. He was elected to the Georgia provincial congress of 1776 and during the war twice served in the assembly, in 1777 and

1779. During the same period, he also sat on the state executive council besides holding the positions of surveyor-general and Indian commissioner. He also served in the Continental Congress (178088), during which time he was reelected to the Georgia Assembly (1783).

Four years later, Few was appointed as one of six state delegates to the Constitutional Convention, two of whom never attended and two others of whom did not stay for the duration. Few himself missed large segments of the proceedings, being absent during all of July and part of August because of congressional service, and never made a speech. Nonetheless, he contributed nationalist votes at critical times. Furthermore, as a delegate to the last sessions of the Continental Congress, he helped steer the Constitution past its first obstacle, approval by Congress. And he attended the state ratifying convention.

Few became one of his state's first U.S. senators (1789-93). When his term ended, he headed back home and served again in the assembly. In 1796 he received an appointment as a federal judge for the Georgia circuit. For reasons unknown, he resigned his judgeship in 1799 at the age of 52 and moved to New York City.

Few's career continued to blossom. He served 4 years in the legislature (1802-5) and then as inspector of prisons (180210), alderman (1813-14), and U.S. commissioner of loans (1804). From 1804 to 1814 he held a directorship at the Manhattan Bank and later the presidency of City Bank. A devout Methodist, he also donated generously to philanthropic causes.

When Few died in 1828 at the age of 80 in Fishkill-on-the-Hudson (present Beacon), he was survived by his wife (born Catherine Nicholson) and three daughters. Originally buried in the yard of the local Reformed Dutch Church, his body was later reinterred at St. Paul's Church, Augusta, GA.

## William Houston*, Episcopalian, Georgia[7]

William Houston was the son of Sir Patrick Houston, a member of the council under the royal government of Georgia. He was born in 1755 in Savannah, GA. Houston received a liberal education, which included legal training at Inner Temple in London. The War for Independence cut short his training, and Houston returned home to Georgia. For many years members of Houston's family had been high officials in the colony. With the onset of war, many remained loyal to the crown, but William, a zealous advocate of colonists' rights, was among the first to counsel resistance to British aggression.

Houston represented Georgia in the Continental Congress from 1783 through 1786. He was chosen as one of Georgia's agents to settle a boundary dispute with South Carolina in 1785 and was one of the original trustees of the University of Georgia at Athens.

When the Constitutional Convention convened in 1787, Houston presented his credentials as one of Georgia's delegates. He stayed for only a short time, from June 1 until about July 23, but he was present during the debate on the representation question. Houston split Georgia's vote on equal representation in the Senate, voting "nay" against Abraham Baldwin's "aye." Houston died in Savannah on March 17, 1813, and was interred in St. Paul's Chapel, New York City.

**William Leigh Pierce\***, Episcopalian, Georgia[8]

Very little is known about William Pierce's early life. He was probably born in Georgia in 1740, but he grew up in Virginia. During the Revolutionary War Pierce acted as an aide-de-camp to Gen. Nathanael Greene and eventually attained the rank of brevet major. For his conduct at the battle of Eutaw Springs, Congress presented him with a ceremonial sword.

The year Pierce left the army, 1783, he married Charlotte Fenwick of South Carolina. They had two sons, one of whom died as a child. Pierce made his home in Savannah, where he engaged in business. He first organized an import-export company, Pierce, White, and Call, in 1783, but it dissolved less than a year later. He made a new start with his wife's dowry and formed William Pierce & Company. In 1786 he was a member of the Georgia House of Representatives and was also elected to the Continental Congress.

At the Constitutional Convention Pierce did not play a large role, but he exerted some influence and participated in three debates. He argued for the election of one house of the federal legislature by the people and one house by the states; he favored a 3-year term instead of a 7-year term in the second house. Because he agreed that the Articles had been insufficient, he recommended strengthening the federal government at the expense of state privileges as long as state distinctions were not altogether destroyed. Pierce approved of the resulting Constitution, but he found it necessary to leave in the middle of the proceedings. A decline in the European rice market adversely affected his business. Soon after he returned to Savannah he went bankrupt, having "neither the skill of an experienced merchant nor any reserve capital." Only 2 years later, on December 10, 1789, Pierce died in Savannah at age 49 leaving tremendous debts.

Pierce's notes on the proceedings of the convention were published in the Savannah Georgian in 1828. In them he wrote incisive character sketches that are especially valuable for the information they provide about the lesser-known delegates.

# Massachusetts

**Elbridge Gerry\***, Episcopalian, Massachusetts[9]

Gerry was born in 1744 at Marblehead, MA, the third of 12 children. His mother was the daughter of a Boston merchant; his father, a wealthy and politically active merchant-shipper who had once been a sea captain. Upon graduating from Harvard in 1762, Gerry joined his father and two brothers in the family business, exporting dried codfish to Barbados and Spain. He entered the colonial legislature (1772-74), where he came under the influence of Samuel Adams, and took part in the Marblehead and Massachusetts committees of correspondence. When Parliament closed Boston harbor in June 1774, Marblehead became a major port of entry for supplies donated by patriots throughout the colonies to relieve Bostonians, and Gerry helped transport the goods.

Between 1774 and 1776 Gerry attended the first and second provincial congresses. He served with Samuel Adams and John Hancock on the council of safety and, as chairman of the committee of supply (a job for which his merchant background ideally suited him) wherein he raised troops and dealt with military logistics. On the night of April 18, 1775, Gerry attended a meeting of the council of safety at an inn in Menotomy (Arlington), between Cambridge and Lexington, and barely escaped the British troops marching on Lexington and Concord.

In 1776 Gerry entered the Continental Congress, where his congressional specialties were military and financial matters. In Congress and throughout his career his actions often appeared contradictory. He earned the nickname "soldiers' friend" for his advocacy of better pay and equipment, yet he vacillated on the issue of pensions. Despite his disapproval of standing armies, he recommended long-term enlistments.

Until 1779 Gerry sat on and sometimes presided over the congressional board that regulated Continental finances. After a quarrel over the price schedule for suppliers, Gerry, himself a supplier, walked out of Congress. Although nominally a member, he did not reappear for 3 years. During the interim, he engaged in trade and privateering and served in the lower house of the Massachusetts legislature.

As a representative in Congress in the years 1783-85, Gerry numbered among those who had possessed talent as Revolutionary agitators and wartime leaders but who could not effectually cope with the painstaking task of stabilizing the national government. He was experienced and conscientious but created many enemies with his lack of humor, suspicion of the motives of others, and obsessive fear of political and military tyranny. In 1786, the year after leaving Congress, he retired from business, married Ann Thompson, and took a seat in the state legislature.

Gerry was one of the most vocal delegates at the Constitutional Convention of 1787. He presided as chairman of the committee that produced the Great Compromise but disliked the compromise itself. He antagonized nearly everyone by his inconsistency and, according to a colleague, "objected to everything he did not propose." At first an advocate of a strong central government, Gerry ultimately rejected and refused to sign the Constitution because it lacked a bill of rights and because he deemed it a threat to republicanism. He led the drive against ratification in Massachusetts and denounced the document as "full of vices." Among the vices, he listed inadequate representation of the people, dangerously ambiguous legislative powers, the blending of the executive and the legislative, and the danger of an oppressive judiciary. Gerry did see some merit in the Constitution, though, and believed that its flaws could be remedied through amendments. In 1789, after he announced his intention to support the Constitution, he was elected to the First Congress where, to the chagrin of the Antifederalists, he championed Federalist policies.

Gerry left Congress for the last time in 1793 and retired for 4 years. During this period he came to mistrust the aims of the Federalists, particularly their attempts to nurture an alliance with Britain, and sided with the pro-French Democratic-Republicans.

In 1797 President John Adams appointed him as the only non-Federalist member of a three-man commission charged with negotiating a reconciliation with France, which was on the brink of war with the United States. During the ensuing XYZ affair (1797-98), Gerry tarnished his reputation. Talleyrand, the French foreign minister, led him to believe that his presence in France would prevent war, and Gerry lingered on long after the departure of John Marshall and Charles Cotesworth Pinckney, the two other commissioners. Finally, the embarrassed Adams recalled him, and Gerry met severe censure from the Federalists upon his return.

In 1800-1803 Gerry, never very popular among the Massachusetts electorate because of his aristocratic haughtiness, met defeat in four bids for the Massachusetts governorship but finally triumphed in 1810. Near the end of his two terms, scarred by partisan controversy, the Democratic-Republicans passed a redistricting measure to ensure their domination of the state senate. In response, the Federalists heaped ridicule on Gerry and coined the pun "gerrymander" to describe the salamander-like shape of one of the redistricted areas.

Despite his advanced age, frail health, and the threat of poverty brought on by neglect of personal affairs, Gerry served as James Madison's Vice President in 1813. In the fall of 1814, the 70-year old politician collapsed on his way to the Senate and died. He left his wife, who was to live until 1849, the last surviving widow of a signer of the Declaration of Independence, as well as three sons and four daughters. Gerry is buried in Congressional Cemetery at Washington, DC.

**Nathaniel Gorham,** Congregationalist, Massachusetts[10]

Gorham, an eldest child, was born in 1738 at Charlestown, MA, into an old Bay Colony family of modest means. His father operated a packet boat. The youth's education was minimal. When he was about 15 years of age, he was apprenticed to a New London, CT, merchant. He quit in 1759, returned to his hometown and established a business which quickly succeeded. In 1763 he wed Rebecca Call, who was to bear nine children.

Gorham began his political career as a public notary but soon won election to the colonial legislature (1771-75). During the Revolution, he unswervingly backed the Whigs. He was a delegate to the provincial congress (1774-75), member of the Massachusetts Board of War (1778-81), delegate to the constitutional convention (1779-80), and representative in both the upper (1780) and lower (1781-87) houses of the legislature, including speaker of the latter in 1781, 1782, and 1785. In the last year, though he apparently lacked formal legal training, he began a judicial career as judge of the Middlesex County court of common pleas (1785-96). During this same period, he sat on the Governor's Council (1788-89).

During the war, British troops had ravaged much of Gorham's property, though by privateering and speculation he managed to recoup most of his fortune. Despite these pressing business concerns and his state political and judicial activities, he also served the nation. He was a member of the Continental Congress

(1782-83 and 1785-87), and held the office of president from June 1786 until January 1787.

The next year, at age 49, Gorham attended the Constitutional Convention. A moderate nationalist, he attended all the sessions and played an influential role. He spoke often, acted as chairman of the Committee of the Whole, and sat on the Committee of Detail. As a delegate to the Massachusetts ratifying convention, he stood behind the Constitution.

Some unhappy years followed. Gorham did not serve in the new government he had helped to create. In 1788 he and Oliver Phelps of Windsor, CT, and possibly others, contracted to purchase from the Commonwealth of Massachusetts 6 million acres of unimproved land in western New York. The price was $1 million in devalued Massachusetts scrip. Gorham and Phelps quickly succeeded in clearing Indian title to 2,600,000 acres in the eastern section of the grant and sold much of it to settlers. Problems soon arose, however. Massachusetts scrip rose dramatically in value, enormously swelling the purchase price of the vast tract. By 1790 the two men were unable to meet their payments. The result was a financial crisis that led to Gorham's insolvency--and a fall from the heights of Boston society and political esteem.

Gorham died in 1796 at the age of 58 and is buried at the Phipps Street Cemetery in Charlestown, MA.

**Rufus King,** Episcopalian, Congregationalist, Massachusetts[11]

King was born at Scarboro (Scarborough), MA (present Maine), in 1755. He was the eldest son of a prosperous farmer-merchant. At age 12, after receiving an elementary education at local schools, he matriculated at Dummer Academy in South Byfield, MA, and in 1777 graduated from Harvard. He served briefly as a general's aide during the War for Independence. Choosing a legal career, he read for the law at Newburyport, MA, and entered practice there in 1780.

King's knowledge, bearing, and oratorical gifts soon launched him on a political career. From 1783 to 1785 he was a member of the Massachusetts legislature, after which that body sent him to the Continental Congress (1784-86). There, he gained a reputation as a brilliant speaker and an early opponent of slavery. Toward the end of his tour, in 1786, he married Mary Alsop, daughter of a rich New York City merchant. He performed his final duties for Massachusetts by representing her at the Constitutional Convention and by serving in the commonwealth's ratifying convention.

At age 32, King was not only one of the most youthful of the delegates at Philadelphia, but was also one of the most important. He numbered among the most capable orators. Furthermore, he attended every session. Although he came to the convention unconvinced that major changes should be made in the Articles of Confederation, his views underwent a startling transformation during the debates. With Madison, he became a leading figure in the nationalist caucus. He served with distinction on the Committee on Postponed Matters and the Committee of Style. He also took notes on the proceedings, which have been valuable to historians.

About 1788 King abandoned his law practice, moved from the Bay State to Gotham, and entered the New York political forum. He was elected to the legislature (1789-90), and in the former year was picked as one of the state's first U.S. senators. As political divisions grew in the new government, King expressed ardent sympathies for the Federalists. In Congress, he supported Hamilton's fiscal program and stood among the leading proponents of the unpopular Jay's Treaty (1794).

Meantime, in 1791, King had become one of the directors of the First Bank of the United States. Reelected to the U.S. Senate in 1795, he served only a year before he was appointed as Minister to Great Britain (17961803).

King's years in this post were difficult ones in Anglo-American relations. The wars of the French Revolution endangered U.S. commerce in the maritime clashes between the French and the British. The latter in particular violated American rights on the high seas, especially by the impressment of sailors. Although King was unable to bring about a change in this policy, he smoothed relations between the two nations.

In 1803 King sailed back to the United States and to a career in politics. In 1804 and 1808 fellow-signer Charles Cotesworth Pinckney and he were the Federalist candidates for President and Vice President, respectively, but were decisively defeated. Otherwise, King largely contented himself with agricultural pursuits at King Manor, a Long Island estate he had purchased in 1805. During the War of 1812, he was again elected to the U.S. Senate (1813-25) and ranked as a leading critic of the war. Only after the British attacked Washington in 1814 did he come to believe that the United States was fighting a defensive action and to lend his support to the war effort.

In 1816 the Federalists chose King as their candidate for the presidency, but James Monroe beat him handily. Still in the Senate, that same year King led the opposition to the establishment of the Second Bank of the United States. Four years later, believing that the issue of slavery could not be compromised but must be settled once and for all by the immediate establishment of a system of compensated emancipation and colonization, he denounced the Missouri Compromise.

In 1825, suffering from ill health, King retired from the Senate. President John Quincy Adams, however, persuaded him to accept another assignment as Minister to Great Britain. He arrived in England that same year, but soon fell ill and was forced to return home the following year. Within a year, at the age of 72, in 1827, he died. Surviving him were several offspring, some of whom also gained distinction. He was laid to rest near King Manor in the cemetery of Grace Episcopal Church, Jamaica, Long Island, NY.

**Caleb Strong***, Congregationalist, Massachusetts[12]

Strong was born to Caleb and Phebe Strong on January 9, 1745 in Northampton, MA. He received his college education at Harvard, from which he graduated with highest honors in 1764. Like so many of the delegates to the Constitutional Convention,

Strong chose to study law and was admitted to the bar in 1772. He enjoyed a prosperous country practice.

From 1774 through the duration of the Revolution, Strong was a member of Northampton's committee of safety. In 1776 he was elected to the Massachusetts General Court and also held the post of county attorney for Hampshire County for 24 years. He was offered a position on the state supreme court in 1783 but declined it.

At the Constitutional Convention, Strong counted himself among the delegates who favored a strong central government. He successfully moved that the House of Representatives should originate all money bills and sat on the drafting committee. Though he preferred a system that accorded the same rank and mode of election to both houses of Congress, he voted in favor of equal representation in the Senate and proportional in the House. Strong was called home on account of illness in his family and so missed the opportunity to sign the Constitution. However, during the Massachusetts ratifying convention, he took a leading role among the Federalists and campaigned strongly for ratification.

Massachusetts chose Strong as one of its first U.S. senators in 1789. During the 4 years he served in that house, he sat on numerous committees and participated in framing the Judiciary Act. Caleb Strong wholeheartedly supported the Washington administration. In 1793 he urged the government to send a mission to England and backed the resulting Jay's Treaty when it met heated opposition.

Caleb Strong, the Federalist candidate, defeated Elbridge Gerry to become Governor of Massachusetts in 1800. Despite the growing strength of the Democratic party in the state, Strong won reelection annually until 1807. In 1812 he regained the governorship, once again over Gerry, and retained his post until he retired in 1816. During the War of 1812 Strong withstood pressure from the Secretary of War to order part of the Massachusetts militia into federal service. Strong opposed the war and approved the report of the Hartford Convention, a gathering of New England Federalists resentful of Jeffersonian policies.

Strong died on November 7, 1819, 2 years after the death of his wife, Sarah. He was buried in the Bridge Street Cemetery in Northampton. Four of his nine children survived him.

# New Jersey

**David Brearly,** Episcopalian, New Jersey

Brearly (Brearley) was descended from a Yorkshire, England family, one of whose members migrated to New Jersey around 1680. Signer Brearly was born in 1745 at Spring Grove near Trenton, was reared in the area, and attended but did not graduate from the nearby College of New Jersey (later Princeton). He chose law as a career and originally practiced at Allentown, NJ. About 1767 he married Elizabeth Mullen.

Brearly avidly backed the Revolutionary cause. The British arrested him for high treason, but a group of patriots freed him. In 1776 he took part in the convention that drew up the state constitution. During the War for Independence, he rose from a captain to a colonel in the militia.

In 1779 Brearly was elected as chief justice of the New Jersey supreme court, a position he held until 1789. He presided over the precedent-setting case of Holmes v. Walton. His decision, rendered in 1780, represented an early expression of the principle of judicial review. The next year, the College of New Jersey bestowed an honorary M.A. degree on him.

Brearly was 42 years of age when he participated in the Constitutional Convention. Although he did not rank among the leaders, he attended the sessions regularly. A follower of Paterson, who introduced the New Jersey Plan, Brearly opposed proportional representation of the states and favored one vote for each of them in Congress. He also chaired the Committee on Postponed Matters.

Brearly's subsequent career was short, for he had only 3 years to live. He presided at the New Jersey convention that ratified the Constitution in 1788, and served as a presidential elector in 1789.

That same year, President Washington appointed him as a federal district judge, and he served in that capacity until his death.

When free from his judicial duties, Brearly devoted much energy to lodge and church affairs. He was one of the leading members of the Masonic Order in New Jersey, as well as state vice president of the Society of the Cincinnati, an organization of former officers of the Revolutionary War. In addition, he served as a delegate to the Episcopal General Conference (1786) and helped write the church's prayer book. In 1783, following the death of his first wife, he had married Elizabeth Higbee.

Brearly died in Trenton at the age of 45 in 1790. He was buried there at St. Michael's Episcopal Church.

**Jonathan Dayton,** Presbyterian, Episcopalian, New Jersey[14]

Dayton was born at Elizabethtown (present Elizabeth), NJ, in 1760. His father was a storekeeper who was also active in local and state politics. The youth obtained a good education, graduating from the College of New Jersey (later Princeton) in 1776. He immediately entered the Continental Army and saw extensive action. Achieving the rank of captain by the age of 19 and serving under his father, Gen. Elias Dayton, and the Marquis de Lafayette, he was a prisoner of the British for a time and participated in the Battle of Yorktown, VA.

After the war, Dayton returned home, studied law, and established a practice. During the 1780s he divided his time between land speculation, legal practice, and politics. He sat in the assembly in 1786-87. In the latter year, he was chosen as a delegate to the Constitutional Convention after the leaders of his political faction, his father and his patron, Abraham Clark, declined to attend. Dayton did not arrive at Philadelphia until June 21 but thereafter faithfully took part in the proceedings. He spoke with moderate frequency during the debates and, though objecting to some provisions of the Constitution, signed it.

After sitting in the Continental Congress in 1788, Dayton became a foremost Federalist legislator in the new government. Although elected as a representative, he did not serve in the First

Congress in 1789, preferring instead to become a member of the New Jersey council and speaker of the state assembly. In 1791, however, he entered the U.S. House of Representatives (1791-99), becoming Speaker in the Fourth and Fifth Congresses. During this period, he backed Hamilton's fiscal program, suppression of the Whisky Rebellion, Jay's Treaty, and a host of other Federalist measures.

In personal matters Dayton purchased Boxwood Hall in 1795 as his home in Elizabethtown and resided there until his death. He was elevated to the U.S. Senate (1799-1805). He supported the Louisiana Purchase (1803) and, in conformance with his Federalist views, opposed the repeal of the Judiciary Act of 1801.

In 1806 illness prevented Dayton from accompanying Aaron Burr's abortive expedition to the Southwest, where the latter apparently intended to conquer Spanish lands and create an empire. Subsequently indicted for treason, Dayton was not prosecuted but could not salvage his national political career. He remained popular in New Jersey, however, continuing to hold local offices and sitting in the assembly (1814-15).

In 1824 the 63-year-old Dayton played host to Lafayette during his triumphal tour of the United States, and his death at Elizabeth later that year may have been hastened by the exertion and excitement. He was laid to rest at St. John's Episcopal Church in his hometown. Because he owned 250,000 acres of Ohio land between the Big and Little Miami Rivers, the city of Dayton, was named after him--his major monument. He had married Susan Williamson, but the date of their wedding is unknown. They had two daughters.

**William C. Houston\*,** Presbyterian, New Jersey[15]

William Houston was born about 1746 to Margaret and Archibald Houston. He attended the College of New Jersey (later Princeton) and graduated in 1768 and became master of the college grammar school and then its tutor. In 1771 he was appointed professor of mathematics and natural philosophy.

From 1775 to 1776 Houston was deputy secretary of the Continental Congress. He also saw active military service in 1776 and 1777 when, as captain of the foot militia of Somerset County, he engaged in action around Princeton. During the Revolution, Houston also served in the New Jersey Assembly (1777) and the New Jersey Council of Safety (1778). In 1779 he was once again elected to the Continental Congress, where he worked mainly in the areas of supply and finance. In addition to serving in Congress, Houston remained active in the affairs of the College of New Jersey and also found time to study law. He was admitted to the bar in 1781 and won the appointment of clerk of the New Jersey Supreme Court in the same year. Houston resigned from the college in 1783 and concentrated on his Trenton law practice. He represented New Jersey in Congress once again in 1784 and 1785.

Houston represented New Jersey at both the Annapolis and Philadelphia conventions. Though illness forced him to leave after 1 week, he did serve on a committee to consider the distribution of seats in the lower house. Houston did not sign the Constitution, but he signed the report to the New Jersey legislature.

On August 12, 1788, William Houston succumbed to tuberculosis and died in Frankford, PA., leaving his wife Jane, two daughters, and two sons. His body was laid to rest in the Second Presbyterian Churchyard in Philadelphia.

**William Livingston,** Presbyterian, New Jersey[16]

Livingston was born in 1723 at Albany, NY. His maternal grandmother reared him until he was 14, and he then spent a year with a missionary among the Mohawk Indians. He attended Yale and graduated in 1741.

Rejecting his family's hope that he would enter the fur trade at Albany or mercantile pursuits in New York City, young Livingston chose to pursue a career in law at the latter place. Before he completed his legal studies, in 1745 he married Susanna French, daughter of a well-to-do New Jersey landowner. She was to bear 13 children.

Three years later, Livingston was admitted to the bar and quickly gained a reputation as the supporter of popular causes against the more conservative factions in the city. Associated with the Calvinists in religion, he opposed the dominant Anglican leaders in the colony and wielded a sharply satirical pen in verses and broadsides. Livingston attacked the Anglican attempt to charter and control King's College (later Columbia College and University) and the dominant De Lancey party for its Anglican sympathies, and by 1758 rose to the leadership of his faction. For a decade, it controlled the colonial assembly and fought against parliamentary interference in the colony's affairs. During this time, 1759-61, Livingston sat in the assembly.

In 1769 Livingston's supporters, split by the growing debate as to how to respond to British taxation of the colonies, lost control of the assembly. Not long thereafter, Livingston, who had also grown tired of legal practice, moved to the Elizabethtown (present Elizabeth), NJ, area, where he had purchased land in 1760. There, in 1772-73, he built the estate, Liberty Hall, continued to write verse, and planned to live the life of a gentleman farmer.

The Revolutionary upsurge, however, brought Livingston out of retirement. He soon became a member of the Essex County, NJ, committee of correspondence; in 1774 a representative in the First Continental Congress; and in 1775-76 a delegate to the Second Continental Congress. In June 1776 he left Congress to command the New Jersey militia as a brigadier general and held this post until he was elected later in the year as the first governor of the state.

Livingston held the position throughout and beyond the war- -in fact, for 14 consecutive years until his death in 1790. During his administration, the government was organized, the war won, and New Jersey launched on her path as a sovereign state. Although the pressure of affairs often prevented it, he enjoyed his estate whenever possible, conducted agricultural experiments, and became a member of the Philadelphia Society for Promoting Agriculture. He was also active in the antislavery movement.

In 1787 Livingston was selected as a delegate to the Constitutional Convention, though his gubernatorial duties prevented him from attending every session. He did not arrive until June 5 and missed several weeks in July, but he performed vital committee work, particularly as chairman of the one that reached a compromise on the issue of slavery. He also supported the New Jersey Plan. In addition, he spurred New Jersey's rapid ratification of the Constitution (1787). The next year, Yale awarded him an honorary doctor of laws degree.

Livingston died at Liberty Hall in his 67th year in 1790. He was originally buried at the local Presbyterian Churchyard, but a year later his remains were moved to a vault his son owned at Trinity Churchyard in Manhattan and in 1844 were again relocated, to Brooklyn's Greenwood Cemetery.

**William Paterson,** Presbyterian, New Jersey[17]

William Paterson (Patterson) was born in County Antrim, Ireland, in 1745. When he was almost 2 years of age, his family emigrated to America, disembarking at New Castle, DE. While the father traveled about the country, apparently selling tinware, the family lived in New London, other places in Connecticut, and in Trenton, NJ. In 1750 he settled in Princeton, NJ. There, he became a merchant and manufacturer of tin goods. His prosperity enabled William to attend local private schools and the College of New Jersey (later Princeton). He took a B.A. in 1763 and an M.A. 3 years later.

Meantime, Paterson had studied law in the city of Princeton under Richard Stockton, who later was to sign the Declaration of Independence, and near the end of the decade began practicing at New Bromley, in Hunterdon County. Before long, he moved to South Branch, in Somerset County, and then in 1779 relocated near New Brunswick at Raritan estate.

When the War for Independence broke out, Paterson joined the vanguard of the New Jersey patriots. He served in the provincial congress (1775-76), the constitutional convention (1776), legislative council (1776-77), and council of safety (1777). During the last year, he also held a militia commission. From 1776 to 1783 he was attorney general of New Jersey, a task that occupied so much of his time that it prevented him from accepting election to the Continental Congress in 1780. Meantime, the year before, he had married Cornelia Bell, by whom he had three children before her death in 1783. Two years later, he took a new bride, Euphemia White, but it is not known whether or not they had children.

From 1783, when he moved into the city of New Brunswick, until 1787, Paterson devoted his energies to the law and stayed out of the public limelight. Then he was chosen to represent New Jersey at the Constitutional Convention, which he attended only until late July. Until then, he took notes of the proceedings. More importantly, he figured prominently because of his advocacy and coauthorship of the New Jersey, or Paterson, Plan, which asserted the rights of the small states against the large. He apparently returned to the convention only to sign the final document. After supporting its ratification in New Jersey, he began a career in the new government.

In 1789 Paterson was elected to the U.S. Senate (1789-90), where he played a pivotal role in drafting the Judiciary Act of 1789. His next position was governor of his state (1790-93). During this time, he began work on the volume later published as Laws of the State of New Jersey (1800) and began to revise the rules and practices of the chancery and common law courts.

During the years 1793-1806, Paterson served as an associate justice of the U.S. Supreme Court. Riding the grueling circuit to which federal judges were subjected in those days and sitting with the full Court, he presided over a number of major trials.

In September 1806, his health failing, the 60-year-old Paterson embarked on a journey to Ballston Spa, NY, for a cure but died en route at Albany in the home of his daughter, who had married Stephen Van Rensselaer. Paterson was at first laid to rest in the nearby Van Rensselaer manor house family vault, but later his body was apparently moved to the Albany Rural Cemetery, Menands, NY.

# North Carolina

**William Blount,** Episcopalian, Presbyterian, North Carolina[18]

William Blount was the great-grandson of Thomas Blount, who came from England to Virginia soon after 1660 and settled on a North Carolina plantation. William, the eldest in a large family, was born in 1749 while his mother was visiting his grandfather's Rosefield estate, on the site of present Windsor near Pamlico Sound. The youth apparently received a good education.

Shortly after the War for Independence began, in 1776, Blount enlisted as a paymaster in the North Carolina forces. Two years later, he wed Mary Grainier (Granger); of their six children who reached adulthood, one son also became prominent in Tennessee politics.

Blount spent most of the remainder of his life in public office. He sat in the lower house of the North Carolina legislature (1780-84), including service as speaker, as well as in the upper (1788-90). In addition, he took part in national politics, serving in the Continental Congress in 1782-83 and 1786-87.

Appointed as a delegate to the Constitutional Convention at the age of 38, Blount was absent for more than a month because he chose to attend the Continental Congress on behalf of his state. He said almost nothing in the debates and signed the Constitution reluctantly--only, he said, to make it "the unanimous act of the States in Convention." Nonetheless, he favored his state's ratification of the completed document.

Blount hoped to be elected to the first U.S. Senate. When he failed to achieve that end, in 1790 he pushed westward beyond the Appalachians, where he held speculative land interests and had represented North Carolina in dealings with the Indians. He settled in what became Tennessee, to which he devoted the rest of his life. He resided first at Rocky Mount, a cabin near present Johnson City and in 1792 built a mansion in Knoxville.

Two years earlier, Washington had appointed Blount as Governor for the Territory South of the River Ohio (which included Tennessee) and also as Superintendent of Indian Affairs for the Southern Department, in which positions he increased his popularity with the frontiersmen. In 1796 he presided over the constitutional convention that transformed part of the territory into the State of Tennessee. He was elected as one of its first U.S. senators (1796-97).

During this period, Blount's affairs took a sharp turn for the worse. In 1797 his speculations in western lands led him into serious financial difficulties. That same year, he also apparently concocted a plan involving use of Indians, frontiersmen, and British naval forces to conquer for Britain the Spanish provinces of Florida and Louisiana. A letter he wrote alluding to the plan fell into the hands of President Adams, who turned it over to the Senate on July 3, 1797. Five days later, that body voted 25 to 1 to expel Blount. The House impeached him, but the Senate dropped the charges in 1799 on the grounds that no further action could be taken beyond his dismissal.

The episode did not hamper Blount's career in Tennessee. In 1798 he was elected to the senate and rose to the speakership. He died 2 years later at Knoxville in his early fifties. He is buried there in the cemetery of the First Presbyterian Church.

**William Richardson Davie\*,** Presbyterian, North Carolina[19]

One of the eight delegates born outside of the thirteen colonies, Davie was born in Egremont, Cumberlandshire, England, on June 20, 1756. In 1763 Archibald Davie brought his son William to Waxhaw, SC, where the boy's maternal uncle, William Richardson, a Presbyterian clergyman, adopted him. Davie attended Queen's Museum College in Charlotte, North Carolina, and graduated from the College of New Jersey (later Princeton) in 1776.

Davie's law studies in Salisbury, NC, were interrupted by military service, but he won his license to practice before county courts in 1779 and in the superior courts in 1780. When the War for Independence broke out, he helped raise a troop of cavalry near Salisbury and eventually achieved the rank of colonel. While attached to Pulaski's division, Davie was wounded leading a charge at Stono, near Charleston, on June 20, 1779. Early in 1780 he raised another troop and operated mainly in western North Carolina. In January 1781 Davie was appointed commissary general for the Carolina campaign. In this capacity he oversaw the collection of arms and supplies to Gen. Nathanael Greene's army and the state militia.

After the war, Davie embarked on his career as a lawyer, traveling the circuit in North Carolina. In 1782 he married Sarah Jones, the daughter of his former commander, Gen. Allen Jones, and settled in Halifax. His legal knowledge and ability won him great respect, and his presentation of arguments was admired. Between 1786 and 1798 Davie represented Halifax in the North Carolina legislature. There he was the principal agent behind that body's actions to revise and codify state laws, send representatives to the Annapolis and Philadelphia conventions, cede Tennessee to the Union, and fix disputed state boundaries.

During the Constitutional Convention Davie favored plans for a strong central government. He was a member of the committee that considered the question of representation in Congress and swung the North Carolina delegation's vote in favor of the Great Compromise. He favored election of senators and presidential electors by the legislature and insisted on counting slaves in determining representation. Though he left the convention on August 13, before its adjournment, Davie fought hard for the Constitution's ratification and took a prominent part in the North Carolina convention.

The political and military realms were not the only ones in which Davie left his mark. The University of North Carolina, of which he was the chief founder, stands as an enduring reminder of Davie's interest in education. Davie selected the location, instructors, and a curriculum that included the literary and social sciences as well as mathematics and classics. In 1810 the trustees conferred upon him the title of "Father of the University" and in the next year granted him the degree of Doctor of Laws.

Davie became Governor of North Carolina in 1798. His career also turned back briefly to the military when President John Adams appointed him a brigadier general in the U.S. Army that same year. Davie later served as a peace commissioner to France in 1799.

Davie stood as a candidate for Congress in 1803 but met defeat. In 1805, after the death of his wife, Davie retired from politics to his plantation, "Tivoli," in Chester County, South Carolina. In 1813 he declined an appointment as major-general from President Madison. Davie was 64 years old when he died on November 29, 1820, at "Tivoli," and he was buried in the Old Waxhaw Presbyterian Churchyard in northern Lancaster County.

**Alexander Martin\*,** Presbyterian, North Carolina[20]

Though he represented North Carolina at the Constitutional Convention, Alexander Martin was born in Hunterdon County, NJ, in 1740. His parents, Hugh and Jane Martin, moved first to Virginia, then to Guilford County, NC, when Alexander was very young. Martin attended the College of New Jersey (later Princeton), received his degree in 1756, and moved to Salisbury. There he started his career as a merchant but turned to public service as he became justice of the peace, deputy king's attorney, and, in 1774 and 1775, judge of Salisbury district.

At the September 1770 session of the superior court at Hillsboro, 150 Regulators armed with sticks, switches, and cudgels crowded into the courtroom. They had come to present a petition to the judge demanding unprejudiced juries and a public accounting of taxes by sheriffs. Violence erupted, and several, including Alexander Martin, were beaten. In 1771 Martin signed an agreement with the Regulators to refund all fees taken illegally and to arbitrate all differences.

From 1773 to 1774 Martin served in the North Carolina House of Commons and in the second and third provincial congresses in 1775. In September 1775 he was appointed a lieutenant colonel in the 2d North Carolina Continental Regiment. Martin saw military action in South Carolina and won promotion to a colonelcy. He joined Washington's army in 1777, but after the Battle of Germantown he was arrested for cowardice. A court-martial tried and acquitted Martin, but he resigned his commission on November 22, 1777.

Martin's misfortune in the army did not impede his political career. The year after his court-martial he entered the North Carolina Senate, where he served for 8 years (1778-82, 1785, and 1787-88). For every session except those of 1778-79, Martin served as speaker. From 1780 to 1781 he also sat on the Board of War and its successor, the Council Extraordinary. In 1781 Martin became acting governor of the state, and in 1782 through 1785 he was elected in his own right.

After his 1785 term in the North Carolina Senate, Martin represented his state in the Continental Congress, but he resigned in 1787. Of the five North Carolina delegates to the Constitutional Convention, Martin was the least strongly Federalist. He did not take an active part in the proceedings, and he left Philadelphia in late August 1787, before the Constitution was signed. Martin was considered a good politician but not suited to public debate. A colleague, Hugh Williamson, remarked that Martin needed time to recuperate after his great exertions as governor "to enable him again to exert his abilities to the advantage of the nation."

Under the new national government, Martin again served as Governor of North Carolina, from 1789 until 1792. After 1790 he moved away from the Federalists to the Republicans. In 1792 Martin, elected by the Republican legislature, entered the U.S. Senate. His vote in favor of the Alien and Sedition Acts cost him reelection. Back in North Carolina, Martin returned to the state senate in 1804 and 1805 to represent Rockingham County. In 1805 he once again served as speaker. From 1790 until 1807 he was a trustee of the University of North Carolina. Martin never married, and he died on November 2, 1807 at the age of 67 at his plantation, "Danbury," in Rockingham County and was buried on the estate.

**Richard Dobbs Spaight, Sr.,** Episcopalian, North Carolina[21]

Spaight was born at New Bern, NC of distinguished English-Irish parentage in 1758. When he was orphaned at 8 years of age, his guardians sent him to Ireland, where he obtained an excellent education. He apparently graduated from Scotland's Glasgow University before he returned to North Carolina in 1778.

At that time, the War for Independence was in full swing, and Spaight's superior attainments soon gained him a commission. He became an aide to the state militia commander and in 1780 took part in the Battle of Camden, SC. The year before, he had been elected to the lower house of the legislature.

In 1781 Spaight left the military service to devote full time to his legislative duties. He represented New Bern and Craven County (1781-83 and 1785-87); in 1785 he became speaker. Between terms, he also served in the Continental Congress (178385).

In 1787, at the age of 29, Spaight joined the North Carolina delegation to the Philadelphia convention. He was not a leader but spoke on several occasions and numbered among those who attended every session. After the convention, he worked in his home state for acceptance of the Constitution.

Spaight met defeat in bids for the governorship in 1787 and the U.S. Senate 2 years later. From then until 1792, illness forced his retirement from public life, during which time he visited the West Indies, but he captured the governorship in the latter year (1792-95). In 1793 he served as presidential elector. Two years later, he wed Mary Leach, who bore three children.

In 1798 Spaight entered the U.S. House of Representatives as a Democratic-Republican and remained in office until 1801. During this time, he advocated repeal of the Alien and Sedition Acts and voted for Jefferson in the contested election of 1800. The next year, Spaight was voted into the lower house of the North Carolina legislature; the following year, to the upper.

Only 44 years old in 1802, Spaight was struck down in a duel at New Bern with a political rival, Federalist John Stanly. So ended the promising career of one of the state's foremost leaders. He was buried in the family sepulcher at Clermont estate, near New Bern.

**Hugh Williamson,** Presbyterian, North Carolina[22]

The versatile Williamson was born of Scotch-Irish descent at West Nottingham, PA., in 1735. He was the eldest son in a large family, whose head was a clothier. Hoping he would become a Presbyterian minister, his parents oriented his education toward that calling. After attending preparatory schools at New London Cross Roads, DE, and Newark, DE, he entered the first class of the College of Philadelphia (later part of the University of Pennsylvania) and took his degree in 1757.

The next 2 years, at Shippensburg, PA, Williamson spent settling his father's estate. Then training in Connecticut for the ministry, he soon became a licensed Presbyterian preacher but was never ordained. Around this time, he also took a position as professor of mathematics at his alma mater.

In 1764 Williamson abandoned these pursuits and studied medicine at Edinburgh, London, and Utrecht, eventually obtaining a degree from the University of Utrecht. Returning to Philadelphia, he began to practice but found it to be emotionally exhausting. His pursuit of scientific interests continued, and in 1768 he became a member of the American Philosophical Society. The next year, he served on a commission that observed the transits of Venus and Mercury. In 1771 he wrote An Essay on Comets, in which he advanced several original ideas. As a result, the University of Leyden awarded him an LL.D. degree.

In 1773, to raise money for an academy in Newark, DE, Williamson made a trip to the West Indies and then to Europe. Sailing from Boston, he saw the Tea Party and carried news of it to London. When the British Privy Council called on him to testify as to what he had seen, he warned the councilors that the colonies would rebel if the British did not change their policies. While in England, he struck up a close friendship with fellow scientist Benjamin Franklin, and they cooperated in electrical experiments. Moreover, Williamson furnished to Franklin the letters of Massachusetts Royal Governor Thomas Hutchinson to his lieutenant governor that created a sensation and tended to further alienate the mother country and colonies. In 1775 a pamphlet Williamson had written while in England, called The Plea of the Colonies, was published. It solicited the support of the English Whigs for the American cause. When the United States proclaimed their independence the next year, Williamson was in the Netherlands. He soon sailed back to the United States, settling first in Charleston, SC, and then in Edenton, NC. There, he prospered in a mercantile business that traded with the French West Indies and once again took up the practice of medicine.

Williamson applied for a medical post with the patriot forces, but found all such positions filled. The governor of North Carolina, however, soon called on his specialized skills, and he became surgeon-general of state troops. After the Battle of Camden, SC, he frequently crossed British lines to tend to the wounded. He also prevented sickness among the troops by paying close attention to food, clothing, shelter, and hygiene.

After the war, Williamson began his political career. In 1782 he was elected to the lower house of the state legislature and to the Continental Congress. Three years later, he left Congress and returned to his legislative seat. In 1786 he was chosen to represent his state at the Annapolis Convention but arrived too late to take part. The next year, he again served in Congress (178789) and was chosen as a delegate to the Constitutional Convention. Attending faithfully and demonstrating keen debating skill, he served on five committees, notably on the Committee on Postponed Matters, and played a significant part in the proceedings, particularly the major compromise on representation.

After the convention, Williamson worked for ratification of the Constitution in North Carolina. In 1788 he was chosen to settle outstanding accounts between the state and the federal government. The next year, he was elected to the first U.S. House of Representatives, where he served two terms. In 1789 he married Maria Apthorpe, who bore at least two sons.

In 1793 Williamson moved to New York City to facilitate his literary and philanthropic pursuits. Over the years, he published many political, educational, economic, historical, and scientific works, but the last earned him the most praise. The University of

Leyden awarded him an honorary degree. In addition, he was an original trustee of the University of North Carolina and later held trusteeships at the College of Physicians and Surgeons and the University of the State of New York. He was also a founder of the Literary and Philosophical Society of New York and a prominent member of the New-York Historical Society.

# South Carolina

**Pierce Butler,** Episcopalian, South Carolina[23]

One of the most aristocratic delegates at the convention, Butler was born in 1744 in County Carlow, Ireland. His father was Sir Richard Butler, Member of Parliament and a baronet.

Like so many younger sons of the British aristocracy who could not inherit their fathers' estates because of primogeniture, Butler pursued a military career. He became a major in His Majesty's 29th Regiment and during the colonial unrest was posted to Boston in 1768 to quell disturbances there. In 1771 he married Mary Middleton, daughter of a wealthy South Carolinian, and before long resigned his commission to take up a planter's life in the Charleston area. The couple was to have at least one daughter.

When the Revolution broke out, Butler took up the Whig cause. He was elected to the assembly in 1778, and the next year he served as adjutant general in the South Carolina militia. While in the legislature through most of the 1780s, he took over leadership of the democratic upcountry faction in the state and refused to support his own planter group. The War for Independence cost him much of his property, and his finances were so precarious for a time that he was forced to travel to Amsterdam to seek a personal loan. In 1786 the assembly appointed him to a commission charged with settling a state boundary dispute.

The next year, Butler won election to both the Continental Congress (1787-88) and the Constitutional Convention. In the latter assembly, he was an outspoken nationalist who attended practically every session and was a key spokesman for the

Madison-Wilson caucus. Butler also supported the interests of southern slaveholders. He served on the Committee on Postponed Matters.

On his return to South Carolina Butler defended the Constitution but did not participate in the ratifying convention. Service in the U.S. Senate (1789-96) followed. Although nominally a Federalist, he often crossed party lines. He supported Hamilton's fiscal program but opposed Jay's Treaty and Federalist judiciary and tariff measures.

Out of the Senate and back in South Carolina from 1797 to 1802, Butler was considered for but did not attain the governorship. He sat briefly in the Senate again in 1803-4 to fill out an unexpired term, and he once again demonstrated party independence. But, for the most part, his later career was spent as a wealthy planter. In his last years, he moved to Philadelphia, apparently to be near a daughter who had married a local physician. Butler died there in 1822 at the age of 77 and was buried in the yard of Christ Church.

**Charles Pinckney,** Episcopalian, South Carolina[24]

Charles Pinckney, the second cousin of fellow-signer Charles Cotesworth Pinckney, was born at Charleston, SC, in 1757. His father, Col. Charles Pinckney, was a rich lawyer and planter, who on his death in 1782 was to bequeath Snee Farm, a country estate outside the city, to his son Charles. The latter apparently received all his education in the city of his birth, and he started to practice law there in 1779.

About that time, well after the War for Independence had begun, young Pinckney enlisted in the militia, though his father demonstrated ambivalence about the Revolution. He became a lieutenant, and served at the siege of Savannah (September-October 1779). When Charleston fell to the British the next year, the youth was captured and remained a prisoner until June 1781.

Pinckney had also begun a political career, serving in the Continental Congress (1777-78 and 1784-87) and in the state legislature (1779-80, 178689, and 1792-96). A nationalist, he worked hard in Congress to ensure that the United States would receive navigation rights to the Mississippi and to strengthen congressional power.

Pinckney's role in the Constitutional Convention is controversial. Although one of the youngest delegates, he later claimed to have been the most influential one and contended he had submitted a draft that was the basis of the final Constitution. Most historians have rejected this assertion. They do, however, recognize that he ranked among the leaders. He attended full time, spoke often and effectively, and contributed immensely to the final draft and to the resolution of problems that arose during the debates. He also worked for ratification in South Carolina (1788). That same year, he married Mary Eleanor Laurens, daughter of a wealthy and politically powerful South Carolina merchant; she was to bear at least three children.

Subsequently, Pinckney's career blossomed. From 1789 to 1792 he held the governorship of South Carolina, and in 1790 chaired the state constitutional convention. During this period, he became associated with the Federalist Party, in which he and his cousin Charles Cotesworth Pinckney were leaders. But, with the passage of time, the former's views began to change. In 1795 he attacked the Federalist backed Jay's Treaty and increasingly began to cast his lot with Carolina back-country Democratic-Republicans against his own eastern aristocracy. In 1796 he became governor once again, and in 1798 his Democratic-Republican supporters helped him win a seat in the U.S. Senate. There, he bitterly opposed his former party, and in the presidential election of 1800 served as Thomas Jefferson's campaign manager in South Carolina.

The victorious Jefferson appointed Pinckney as Minister to Spain (1801-5), in which capacity he struggled valiantly but unsuccessfully to win cession of the Floridas to the United States and facilitated Spanish acquiescence in the transfer of Louisiana from France to the United States in 1803.

Upon completion of his diplomatic mission, his ideas moving ever closer to democracy, Pinckney headed back to Charleston and to leadership of the state Democratic-Republican Party. He sat in the legislature in 18056 and then was again elected as governor (1806-8). In this position, he favored legislative reapportionment, giving better representation to backcountry districts, and advocated universal white manhood suffrage. He served again in the legislature from 1810 to 1814 and then temporarily withdrew from politics. In 1818 he won election to the U.S. House of Representatives, where he fought against the Missouri Compromise.

In 1821, Pinckney's health beginning to fail, he retired for the last time from politics. He died in 1824, just 3 days after his 67th birthday. He was laid to rest in Charleston at St. Philip's Episcopal Churchyard.

**Charles Cotesworth Pinckney,** Episcopalian, South Carolina[25]

The eldest son of a politically prominent planter and a remarkable mother who introduced and promoted indigo culture in South Carolina, Charles Cotesworth Pinckney was born in 1746 at Charleston. Only 7 years later, he accompanied his father, who had been appointed colonial agent for South Carolina, to England. As a result, the youth enjoyed a European education.

Pinckney received tutoring in London, attended several preparatory schools, and went on to Christ Church College, Oxford, where he heard the lectures of the legal authority Sir William Blackstone and graduated in 1764. Pinckney next pursued legal training at London's Middle Temple and was accepted for admission into the English bar in 1769. He then spent part of a year touring Europe and studying chemistry, military science, and botany under leading authorities.

Late in 1769, Pinckney sailed home and the next year entered practice in South Carolina. His political career began in 1769, when he was elected to the provincial assembly. In 1773 he acted as attorney general for several towns in the colony. By 1775 he had identified with the patriot cause and that year sat in the provincial congress. Then, the next year, he was elected to the local committee of safety and made chairman of a committee that drew up a plan for the interim government of South Carolina.

When hostilities broke out, Pinckney, who had been a royal militia officer since 1769, pursued a full-time military calling. When South Carolina organized its forces in 1775, he joined the First South Carolina Regiment as a captain. He soon rose to the rank of colonel and fought in the South in defense of Charleston and in the North at the Battles of Brandywine, PA, and Germantown, PA. He commanded a regiment in the campaign against the British in the Floridas in 1778 and at the siege of Savannah. When Charleston fell in 1780, he was taken prisoner and held until 1782. The following year, he was discharged as a brevet brigadier general.

After the war, Pinckney resumed his legal practice and the management of estates in the Charleston area but found time to continue his public service, which during the war had included tours in the lower house of the state legislature (1778 and 1782) and the senate (1779).

Pinckney was one of the leaders at the Constitutional Convention. Present at all the sessions, he strongly advocated a powerful national government. His proposal that senators should serve without pay was not adopted, but he exerted influence in such matters as the power of the Senate to ratify treaties and the compromise that was reached concerning abolition of the international slave trade. After the convention, he defended the Constitution in South Carolina.

Under the new government, Pinckney became a devoted Federalist. Between 1789 and 1795 he declined presidential offers to command the U.S. Army and to serve on the Supreme Court and as Secretary of War and Secretary of State. In 1796, however, he accepted the post of Minister to France, but the revolutionary regime there refused to receive him and he was forced to proceed to the Netherlands. The next year, though, he returned to France when he was appointed to a special mission to restore relations with that country. During the ensuing XYZ affair, refusing to pay a bribe suggested by a French agent to facilitate negotiations, he was said to have replied "No! No! Not a sixpence!"

When Pinckney arrived back in the United States in 1798, he found the country preparing for war with France. That year, he was appointed as a major general in command of American forces in the South and served in that capacity until 1800, when the threat of war ended. That year, he represented the Federalists as Vice-Presidential candidate, and in 1804 and 1808 as the Presidential nominee. But he met defeat on all three occasions.

For the rest of his life, Pinckney engaged in legal practice, served at times in the legislature, and engaged in philanthropic activities. He was a charter member of the board of trustees of South Carolina College (later the University of South Carolina), first president of the Charleston Bible Society, and chief executive of the Charleston Library Society. He also gained prominence in the Society of the Cincinnati, an organization of former officers of the War for Independence.

During the later period of his life, Pinckney enjoyed his Belmont estate and Charleston high society. He was twice married; first to Sarah Middleton in 1773 and after her death to Mary Stead in 1786. Survived by three daughters, he died in Charleston in 1825 at the age of 79. He was interred there in the cemetery at St. Michael's Episcopal Church.

**John Rutledge,** Episcopalian, South Carolina[26]

John Rutledge, elder brother of Edward Rutledge, signer of the Declaration of Independence, was born into a large family at or near Charleston, SC, in 1739. He received his early education from his father, an Irish immigrant and physician, and from an Anglican minister and a tutor. After studying law at London's Middle Temple in 1760, he was admitted to English practice. But, almost at once, he sailed back to Charleston to begin a fruitful legal career and to amass a fortune in plantations and slaves. Three years later, he married Elizabeth Grimke, who eventually bore him 10 children, and moved into a townhouse, where he resided most of the remainder of his life.

In 1761 Rutledge became politically active. That year, on behalf of Christ Church Parish, he was elected to the provincial assembly and held his seat until the War for Independence. For 10 months in 1764 he temporarily held the post of provincial attorney general. When the troubles with Great Britain intensified about the time of the Stamp Act in 1765, Rutledge, who hoped to ensure continued self-government for the colonies, sought to avoid severance from the British and maintained a restrained stance. He did, however, chair a committee of the Stamp Act Congress that drew up a petition to the House of Lords.

In 1774 Rutledge was sent to the First Continental Congress, where he pursued a moderate course. After spending the next year in the Second Continental Congress, he returned to South Carolina and helped reorganize its government. In 1776 he served on the committee of safety and took part in the writing of the state constitution. That year, he also became president of the lower house of the legislature, a post he held until 1778. During this period, the new government met many stern tests.

In 1778 the conservative Rutledge, disapproving of democratic revisions in the state constitution, resigned his position. The next year, however, he was elected as governor. It was a difficult time. The British were invading South Carolina, and the military situation was desperate. Early in 1780, by which time the legislature had adjourned, Charleston was besieged. In May it fell, the American army was captured, and the British confiscated Rutledge's property. He ultimately escaped to North Carolina and set about attempting to rally forces to recover South Carolina. In 1781, aided by Gen. Nathanael Greene and a new Continental Army force, he reestablished the government. In January 1782 he resigned the governorship and took a seat in the lower house of the legislature. He never recouped the financial losses he suffered during the war.

In 1782-83 Rutledge was a delegate to the Continental Congress. He next sat on the state chancery court (1784) and again in the lower house of the legislature (1784-90). One of the most influential delegates at the Constitutional Convention, where he maintained a moderate nationalist stance and chaired the Committee of Detail, he attended all the sessions, spoke often and effectively, and served on five committees. Like his fellow South Carolina delegates, he vigorously advocated southern interests.

The new government under the Constitution soon lured Rutledge. He was a Presidential elector in 1789 and Washington then appointed him as Associate Justice of the U.S. Supreme Court, but for some reason he apparently served only a short time. In 1791 he became chief justice of the South Carolina supreme court. Four years later, Washington again appointed him to the U.S. Supreme Court, this time as Chief Justice to replace John Jay. But Rutledge's outspoken opposition to Jay's Treaty (1794), and the intermittent mental illness he had suffered from since the death of his wife in 1792, caused the Federalist-dominated Senate to reject his appointment and end his public career. Meantime, however, he had presided over one term of the Court.

Rutledge died in 1800 at the age of 60 and was interred at St. Michael's Episcopal Church in Charleston.

# Virginia

**John Blair**, Presbyterian, Episcopalian, Virginia[27]

Scion of a prominent Virginia family, Blair was born at Williamsburg in 1732. He was the son of John Blair, a colonial official and nephew of James Blair, founder and first president of the College of William and Mary. Signer Blair graduated from that institution and studied law at London's Middle Temple. Thereafter, he practiced at Williamsburg. In the years 1766-70 he sat in the Virginia House of Burgesses as the representative of William and Mary. From 1770 to 1775 he held the position of clerk of the colony's council.

An active patriot, Blair signed the Virginia Association of June 22, 1770, which pledged to abandon importation of British goods until the Townshend Duties were repealed. He also underwrote the Association of May 27, 1774, calling for a meeting of the colonies in a Continental Congress and supporting the Bostonians. He took part in the Virginia constitutional convention (1776), at which he sat on the committee that framed a declaration of rights as well as the plan for a new government. He next served on the Privy Council (1776-78). In the latter year, the legislature elected him as a judge of the General Court, and he soon took over the chief justiceship. In 1780 he won election to Virginia's high chancery court, where his colleague was George Wythe.

Blair attended the Constitutional Convention religiously but never spoke or served on a committee. He usually sided with the position of the Virginia delegation. And, in the commonwealth ratifying convention, Blair helped win backing for the new framework of government.

In 1789 Washington named Blair as an associate justice of the U.S. Supreme Court, where he helped decide many important cases. Resigning that post in 1796, he spent his remaining years in Williamsburg. A widower, his wife (born Jean Balfour) having died in 1792, he lived quietly until he succumbed in 1800. He was 68 years old. His tomb is in the graveyard of Bruton Parish Church.

**James Madison,** Christian, Episcopalian, Virginia[28]

The oldest of 10 children and a scion of the planter aristocracy, Madison was born in 1751 at Port Conway, King George County, VA, while his mother was visiting her parents. In a few weeks she journeyed back with her newborn son to Montpelier estate, in Orange County, which became his lifelong home. He received his early education from his mother, from tutors, and at a private school. An excellent scholar though frail and sickly in his youth, in 1771 he graduated from the College of New Jersey (later Princeton), where he demonstrated special interest in government and the law. But, considering the ministry for a career, he stayed on for a year of postgraduate study in theology.

Back at Montpelier, still undecided on a profession, Madison soon embraced the patriot cause, and state and local politics absorbed much of his time. In 1775 he served on the Orange County committee of safety; the next year at the Virginia convention, which, besides advocating various Revolutionary steps, framed the Virginia constitution; in 1776-77 in the House of Delegates; and in 1778-80 in the Council of State. His ill health precluded any military service.

In 1780 Madison was chosen to represent Virginia in the Continental Congress (1780-83 and 1786-88). Although originally the youngest delegate, he played a major role in the deliberations of that body. Meantime, in the years 1784-86, he had again sat in the Virginia House of Delegates. He was a guiding force behind the Mount Vernon Conference (1785), attended the Annapolis Convention (1786), and was otherwise highly instrumental in the convening of the Constitutional Convention in 1787. He had also written extensively about deficiencies in the Articles of Confederation.

Madison was clearly the preeminent figure at the convention. Some of the delegates favored an authoritarian central government; others, retention of state sovereignty; and most occupied positions in the middle of the two extremes. Madison, who was rarely absent and whose Virginia Plan was in large part the basis of the Constitution, tirelessly advocated a strong government, though many of his proposals were rejected. Despite his poor speaking capabilities, he took the floor more than 150 times, third only after Gouverneur Morris and James Wilson. Madison was also a member of numerous committees, the most important of which were those on postponed matters and style. His journal of the convention is the best single record of the event. He also played a key part in guiding the Constitution through the Continental Congress.

Playing a lead in the ratification process in Virginia, too, Madison defended the document against such powerful opponents as Patrick Henry, George Mason, and Richard Henry Lee. In New York, where Madison was serving in the Continental Congress, he collaborated with Alexander Hamilton and John Jay in a series of essays that in 1787-88 appeared in the newspapers and were soon published in book form as The Federalist (1788). This set of essays is a classic of political theory and a lucid exposition of the republican principles that dominated the framing of the Constitution.

In the U.S. House of Representatives (1789-97), Madison helped frame and ensure passage of the Bill of Rights. He also assisted in organizing the executive department and creating a system of federal taxation. As leaders of the opposition to Hamilton's policies, he and Jefferson founded the Democratic-Republican Party.

In 1794 Madison married a vivacious widow who was 16 years his junior, Dolly Payne Todd, who had a son; they were to raise no children of their own. Madison spent the period 1797-1801 in semiretirement, but in 1798 he wrote the Virginia Resolutions, which attacked the Alien and Sedition Acts. While he served as Secretary of State (1801-9), his wife often served as President Jefferson's hostess.

In 1809 Madison succeeded Jefferson. Like the first three Presidents, Madison was enmeshed in the ramifications of European wars. Diplomacy had failed to prevent the seizure of U.S. ships, goods, and men on the high seas, and a depression wracked the country. Madison continued to apply diplomatic techniques and economic sanctions, eventually effective to some degree against France. But continued British interference with shipping, as well as other grievances, led to the War of 1812.

The war, for which the young nation was ill prepared, ended in stalemate in December 1814 when the inconclusive Treaty of Ghent which nearly restored prewar conditions, was signed. But, thanks mainly to Andrew Jackson's spectacular victory at the Battle of New Orleans (Chalmette) in January 1815, most Americans believed they had won. Twice tested, independence had survived, and an ebullient nationalism marked Madison's last years in office, during which period the Democratic-Republicans held virtually uncontested sway.

In retirement after his second term, Madison managed Montpelier but continued to be active in public affairs. He devoted long hours to editing his journal of the Constitutional Convention, which the government was to publish 4 years after his death. He served as co-chairman of the Virginia constitutional convention of 1829-30 and as rector of the University of Virginia during the period 1826-36. Writing newspaper articles defending the administration of Monroe, he also acted as his foreign policy adviser.

Madison spoke out, too, against the emerging sectional controversy that threatened the existence of the Union. Although a slaveholder all his life, he was active during his later years in the American Colonization Society, whose mission was the resettlement of slaves in Africa.

Madison died at the age of 85 in 1836, survived by his wife and stepson.

**George Mason\*,** Episcopalian, Virginia[29]

In 1725 George Mason was born to George and Ann Thomson Mason. When the boy was 10 years old his father died, and young George's upbringing was left in the care of his uncle, John Mercer. The future jurist's education was profoundly shaped by the contents of his uncle's 1500-volume library, one-third of which concerned the law.

Mason established himself as an important figure in his community. As owner of Gunston Hall he was one of the richest planters in Virginia. In 1750 he married Anne Eilbeck, and in 23 years of marriage they had five sons and four daughters. In 1752 he acquired an interest in the Ohio Company, an organization that speculated in western lands. When the crown revoked the company's rights in 1773, Mason, the company's treasurer, wrote his first major state paper, *Extracts from the Virginia Charters, with Some Remarks upon Them.*

During these years Mason also pursued his political interests. He was a justice of the Fairfax County court, and between 1754 and 1779 Mason was a trustee of the city of Alexandria. In 1759 he was elected to the Virginia House of Burgesses. When the Stamp Act of 1765 aroused outrage in the colonies, George Mason wrote an open letter explaining the colonists' position to a committee of London merchants to enlist their support.

In 1774 Mason again was in the forefront of political events when he assisted in drawing up the Fairfax Resolves, a document that outlined the colonists' constitutional grounds for their objections to the Boston Port Act. Virginia's Declaration of Rights, framed by Mason in 1776, was widely copied in other colonies, served as a model for Jefferson in the first part of the Declaration of Independence, and was the basis for the federal Constitution's Bill of Rights.

The years between 1776 and 1780 were filled with great legislative activity. The establishment of a government independent of Great Britain required the abilities of persons such as George Mason. He supported the disestablishment of the church and was active in the organization of military affairs, especially in the West. The influence of his early work, Extracts from the Virginia Charters, is seen in the 1783 peace treaty with Great Britain, which fixed the Anglo-American boundary at the Great Lakes instead of the Ohio River. After independence, Mason drew up the plan for Virginia's cession of its western lands to the United States.

By the early 1780s, however, Mason grew disgusted with the conduct of public affairs and retired. He married his second wife, Sarah Brent, in 1780. In 1785 he attended the Mount Vernon meeting that was a prelude to the Annapolis convention of 1786, but, though appointed, he did not go to Annapolis.

At Philadelphia in 1787 Mason was one of the five most frequent speakers at the Constitutional Convention. He exerted great influence, but during the last 2 weeks of the convention he decided not to sign the document.

Mason's refusal prompts some surprise, especially since his name is so closely linked with constitutionalism. He explained his reasons at length, citing the absence of a declaration of rights as his primary concern. He then discussed the provisions of the Constitution point by point, beginning with the House of Representatives. The House he criticized as not truly representative of the nation, the Senate as too powerful. He also claimed that the power of the federal judiciary would destroy the state judiciaries, render justice unattainable, and enable the rich to oppress and ruin the poor. These fears led Mason to conclude that the new government was destined to either become a monarchy or fall into the hands of a corrupt, oppressive aristocracy.

Two of Mason's greatest concerns were incorporated into the Constitution. The Bill of Rights answered his primary objection, and the 11th amendment addressed his call for strictures on the judiciary.

Throughout his career Mason was guided by his belief in the rule of reason and in the centrality of the natural rights of man. He approached problems coolly, rationally, and impersonally. In recognition of his accomplishments and dedication to the principles of the Age of Reason, Mason has been called the American manifestation of the Enlightenment.

Mason died on October 7, 1792, and was buried on the grounds of Gunston Hall.

**James McClurg***, Presbyterian, Virginia[30]

James McClurg was born near Hampton, VA, in 1746. He attended the College of William and Mary and graduated in 1762. McClurg then studied medicine at the University of Edinburgh and received his degree in 1770. He pursued postgraduate medical studies in Paris and London and published Experiments upon the Human Bile and Reflections on the Biliary Secretions (1772) in London. His work and writings were well-received and respected by the medical community, and his article was translated into several languages. In 1773 McClurg returned to Virginia and served as a surgeon in the state militia during the Revolution.

Before the end of the war the College of William and Mary appointed McClurg its professor of anatomy and medicine. The same year, 1779, he married Elizabeth Seldon. James McClurg's reputation continued to grow, and he was regarded as one of the most eminent physicians in Virginia. In 1820 and 1821 he was president of the state medical society.

In addition to his medical practice, McClurg pursued politics. In 1782 James Madison advocated McClurg's appointment as secretary of foreign affairs for the United States but was unsuccessful. When Richard Henry Lee and Patrick Henry declined to serve as representatives to the Constitutional Convention in 1787, McClurg was asked to join Virginia's delegation. In Philadelphia McClurg advocated a life tenure for the President and argued for the ability of the federal government to override state laws. Even as some at the convention expressed apprehension of the powers allotted to the presidency, McClurg championed greater independence of the executive from the legislative branch. He left the convention in early August, however, and did not sign the Constitution.

James McClurg's political service did not end with the convention. During George Washington's administration McClurg served on Virginia's executive council. He died in Richmond, VA, on July 9, 1823.

**Edmund Randolph\*,** Episcopalian, Virginia[31]

On August 10, 1753, Edmund Randolph was born in Tazewell Hall, Williamsburg, VA. His parents were Ariana Jenings and John Randolph. Edmund attended the College of William and Mary and continued his education by studying the law under his father's tutelage.

When the Revolution broke out, father and son followed different paths. John Randolph, a Loyalist, followed the royal governor, Lord Dunmore, to England, in 1775. Edmund then lived with his uncle Peyton Randolph, a prominent figure in Virginia politics. During the war Edmund served as an aide-de-camp to General Washington and also attended the convention that adopted Virginia's first state constitution in 1776. He was the convention's youngest member at age 23. Randolph married Elizabeth Nicholas in 1776.

Randolph continued to advance in the political world. He became mayor of Williamsburg and Virginia's attorney-general. In 1779 he was elected to the Continental Congress, and in November 1786 Randolph became Governor of Virginia. In 1786 he was a delegate to the Annapolis Convention.

Four days after the opening of the federal convention in Philadelphia, on May 29, 1787, Edmund Randolph presented the Virginia Plan for creating a new government. This plan proposed a strong central government composed of three branches, legislative, executive, and judicial, and enabled the legislative to veto state laws and use force against states that failed to fulfill their duties. After many debates and revisions, including striking the section permitting force against a state, the Virginia Plan became in large part the basis of the Constitution.

Though Randolph introduced the highly centralized Virginia Plan, he fluctuated between the Federalist and Antifederalist points of view. He sat on the Committee of Detail that prepared a draft of the Constitution, but by the time the document was adopted, Randolph declined to sign. He felt it was not sufficiently republican, and he was especially wary of creating a oneman executive. He preferred a three-man council since he regarded "a unity in the Executive" to be the "foetus of monarchy." In a Letter... on the Federal Constitution, dated October 10, 1787, Randolph explained at length his objections to the Constitution. The old Articles of Confederation were inadequate, he agreed, but the proposed new plan of union contained too many flaws. Randolph was a strong advocate of the process of amendment. He feared that if the Constitution were submitted for ratification without leaving the states the opportunity to amend it, the document might be rejected and thus close off any hope of another plan of union. However, he hoped that amendments would be permitted and second convention called to incorporate the changes.

By the time of the Virginia convention for ratification, Randolph supported the Constitution and worked to win his state's approval of it. He stated his reason for his switch: "The accession of eight states reduced our deliberations to the single question of Union or no Union."

Under President Washington, Edmund Randolph became Attorney General of the United States. After Thomas Jefferson resigned as Secretary of State, Randolph assumed that post for the years 1794-95. During the Jefferson-Hamilton conflict he tried to remain unaligned. After retiring from politics in 1795, Randolph resumed his law practice and was regarded as a leading figure in the legal community. During his retirement he wrote a history of Virginia. When Aaron Burr went on trial for treason in 1807, Edmund Randolph acted as his senior counsel. In 1813, at age 60 and suffering from paralysis, Randolph died while visiting Nathaniel Burwell at Carter Hall. His body is buried in the graveyard of the nearby chapel.

**George Washington,** Episcopalian, Virginia[32]

The eldest of six children from his father's second marriage, George Washington was born into the landed gentry in 1732 at Wakefield Plantation, VA. Until reaching 16 years of age, he lived there and at other plantations along the Potomac and Rappahannock Rivers, including the one that later became known as Mount Vernon. His education was rudimentary, probably being obtained from tutors but possibly also from private schools, and he learned surveying. After he lost his father when he was 11 years old, his half-brother Lawrence, who had served in the Royal Navy, acted as his mentor. As a result, the youth acquired an interest in pursuing a naval career, but his mother discouraged him from doing so.

At the age of 16, in 1748, Washington joined a surveying party sent out to the Shenandoah Valley by Lord Fairfax, a land baron. For the next few years, Washington conducted surveys in Virginia and present West Virginia and gained a lifetime interest in the West. In 1751-52 he also accompanied Lawrence on a visit he made to Barbados, West Indies, for health reasons just before his death.

The next year, Washington began his military career when the royal governor appointed him to an adjutantship in the militia, as a major. That same year, as a gubernatorial emissary, accompanied by a guide, he traveled to Fort Le Boeuf, PA, in the Ohio River Valley, and delivered to French authorities an ultimatum to cease fortification and settlement in English territory. During the trip, he tried to better British relations with various Indian tribes.

In 1754, winning the rank of lieutenant colonel and then colonel in the militia, Washington led a force that sought to challenge French control of the Ohio River Valley, but met defeat at Fort Necessity, PA - an event that helped trigger the French and Indian War (1754-63). Late in 1754, irked by the dilution of his rank because of the pending arrival of British regulars, he resigned his commission. That same year, he leased Mount Vernon, which he was to inherit in 1761.

In 1755 Washington reentered military service with the courtesy title of colonel, as an aide to Gen. Edward Braddock, and barely escaped death when the French defeated the general's forces in the Battle of the Monongahela, PA. As a reward for his bravery, Washington rewon his colonelcy and command of the Virginia militia forces, charged with defending the colony's frontier. Because of the shortage of men and equipment, he found the assignment challenging. Late in 1758 or early in 1759, disillusioned over governmental neglect of the militia and irritated at not rising in rank, he resigned and headed back to Mount Vernon.

Washington then wed Martha Dandridge Custis, a wealthy widow and mother of two children. The marriage produced no offspring, but Washington reared those of his wife as his own. During the period 1759-74, he managed his plantations and sat in the Virginia House of Burgesses. He supported the initial protests against British policies; took an active part in the nonimportation movement in Virginia; and, in time, particularly because of his military experience, became a Whig leader.

By the 1770s, relations of the colony with the mother country had become strained. Measured in his behavior but strongly sympathetic to the Whig position and resentful of British restrictions and commercial exploitation, Washington represented Virginia at the First and Second Continental Congresses. In 1775, after the bloodshed at Lexington and Concord, Congress appointed him as commander in chief of the Continental Army. Overcoming severe obstacles, especially in supply, he eventually fashioned a well-trained and disciplined fighting force.

The strategy Washington evolved consisted of continual harassment of British forces while avoiding general actions. Although his troops yielded much ground and lost a number of battles, they persevered even during the dark winters at Valley Forge, PA, and Morristown, NJ. Finally, with the aid of the French fleet and army, he won a climactic victory at the Battle of Yorktown, VA, in 1781.

During the next 2 years, while still commanding the agitated Continental Army, which was underpaid and poorly supplied, Washington denounced proposals that the military take over the government, including one that planned to appoint him as king, but supported army petitions to the Continental Congress for proper compensation. Once the Treaty of Paris (1783) was signed, he resigned his commission and returned once again to Mount Vernon. His wartime financial sacrifices and long absence, as well as generous loans to friends, had severely impaired his extensive fortune, which consisted mainly of his plantations, slaves, and landholdings in the West. At this point, however, he was to have little time to repair his finances, for his retirement was brief.

Dissatisfied with national progress under the Articles of Confederation, Washington advocated a stronger central government. He hosted the Mount Vernon Conference (1785) at his estate after its initial meetings in Alexandria, though he apparently did not directly participate in the discussions. Despite his sympathy with the goals of the Annapolis Convention (1786), he did not attend. But, the following year, encouraged by many of his friends, he presided over the Constitutional Convention, whose success was immeasurably influenced by his presence and dignity. Following ratification of the new instrument of government in 1788, the electoral college unanimously chose him as the first President.

The next year, after a triumphal journey from Mount Vernon to New York City, Washington took the oath of office at Federal Hall. During his two precedent-setting terms, he governed with dignity as well as restraint. He also provided the stability and authority the emergent nation so sorely needed, gave substance to the Constitution, and reconciled competing factions and divergent policies within the government and his administration. Although not averse to exercising presidential power, he respected the role of Congress and did not infringe upon its prerogatives. He also tried to maintain harmony between his Secretary of State Thomas Jefferson and Secretary of the Treasury Alexander Hamilton, whose differences typified evolving party divisions from which Washington kept aloof.

Yet, usually leaning upon Hamilton for advice, Washington supported his plan for the assumption of state debts, concurred in the constitutionality of the bill establishing the Bank of the United States, and favored enactment of tariffs by Congress to provide federal revenue and protect domestic manufacturers.

Washington took various other steps to strengthen governmental authority, including suppression of the Whisky Rebellion (1794). To unify the country, he toured the Northeast in 1789 and the South in 1791. During his tenure, the government moved from New York to Philadelphia in 1790, he superintended planning for relocation to the District of Columbia, and he laid the cornerstone of the Capitol (1793).

In foreign affairs, despite opposition from the Senate, Washington exerted dominance. He fostered United States interests on the North American continent by treaties with Britain and Spain. Yet, until the nation was stronger, he insisted on the maintenance of neutrality. For example, when the French Revolution created war between France and Britain, he ignored the remonstrances of pro-French Jefferson and pro-English Hamilton.

Although many people encouraged Washington to seek a third term, he was weary of politics and refused to do so. In his "Farewell Address" (1796), he urged his countrymen to forswear party spirit and sectional differences and to avoid entanglement in the wars and domestic policies of other nations.

Washington enjoyed only a few years of retirement at Mount Vernon. Even then, demonstrating his continued willingness to make sacrifices for his country in 1798 when the nation was on the verge of war with France he agreed to command the army, though his services were not ultimately required. He died at the age of 67 in 1799. In his will, he emancipated his slaves.

**George Wythe\***, Episcopalian, Virginia[33]

George Wythe, the second of Thomas and Margaret Wythe's three children, was born in 1726 on his family's plantation on the Back River in Elizabeth City County, VA. Both parents died when Wythe was young, and he grew up under the guardianship of his older brother, Thomas. Though Wythe was to become an eminent jurist and teacher, he received very little formal education. He learned Latin and Greek from his well-educated mother, and he probably attended for a time a grammar school operated by the College of William and Mary.

Wythe's brother later sent him to Prince George County to read law under an uncle. In 1746, at age 20, he joined the bar, moved to Spotsylvania County, and became associated with a lawyer there. In 1747 he married his partner's sister, Ann Lewis, but she died the next year. In 1754 Lt. Gov. Robert Dinwiddie appointed him as acting colonial attorney general, a position that he held for only a few months. The next year, Wythe's brother died and he inherited the family estate. He chose, however, to live in Williamsburg in the house that his new father-in-law, an architect, designed and built for him and his wife, Elizabeth Taliaferro. They married in 1755, and their only child died in infancy.

At Williamsburg, Wythe immersed himself in further study of the classics and the law and achieved accreditation by the colonial supreme court. He served in the House of Burgesses from the mid-1750s until 1775, first as delegate and after 1769 as clerk. In 1768 he became mayor of Williamsburg, and the next year he sat on the board of visitors of the College of William and Mary. During these years he also directed the legal studies of young scholars, notably Thomas Jefferson. Wythe and Jefferson maintained a lifelong friendship, first as mentor and pupil and later as political allies.

Wythe first exhibited revolutionary leanings in 1764 when Parliament hinted to the colonies that it might impose a stamp tax. By then an experienced legislator, he drafted for the House of Burgesses a remonstrance to Parliament so strident that his fellow delegates modified it before adoption. Wythe was one of the first to express the concept of separate nationhood for the colonies within the British empire.

When war broke out, Wythe volunteered for the army but was sent to the Continental Congress. Although present from 1775 through 1776, Wythe exerted little influence and signed the Declaration of Independence after the formal signing in August 1776. That same year, Wythe, Jefferson, and Edmund Pendleton undertook a 3-year project to revise Virginia's legal code. In 1777 Wythe also presided as speaker of the Virginia House of Delegates.

An appointment as one of the three judges of the newly created Virginia high court of chancery followed in 1778. For 28 years, during 13 of which he was the only chancellor, Wythe charted the course of Virginia jurisprudence. In addition, he was an ex officio member of the state superior court.

Wythe's real love was teaching. In 1779 Jefferson and other officials of the College of William and Mary created the first chair of law in a U.S. institution of higher learning and appointed Wythe to fill it. In that position, he educated America's earliest college-trained lawyers, among them John Marshall and James Monroe. In 1787 he attended the Constitutional Convention but played an insignificant role. He left the proceedings early and did not sign the Constitution. The following year, however, he was one of the Federalist leaders at the Virginia ratifying convention. There he presided over the Committee of the Whole and offered the resolution for ratification.

In 1791, the year after Wythe resigned his professorship, his chancery duties caused him to move to Richmond, the state capital. He was reluctant to give up his teaching, however, and opened a private law school. One of his last and most promising pupils was young Henry Clay.

In 1806, in his eightieth year, Wythe died at Richmond under mysterious circumstances, probably of poison administered by his grandnephew and heir, George Wythe Sweeney. Reflecting a lifelong aversion to slavery, Wythe emancipated his slaves in his will. His grave is in the yard of St. John's Episcopal Church in Richmond.

# Delaware

### Richard Bassett, Methodist, Delaware[34]

Bassett (Basset) was born in Cecil County, MD., in April 1745. After his tavern-keeper father deserted his mother, he was reared by a relative, Peter Lawson, from whom he later inherited Bohemia Manor (MD.) estate. He read for the law at Philadelphia and in 1770 received a license to practice in Dover, DE. He prospered as a lawyer and planter, and eventually came to own not only Bohemia Manor, but homes in Dover and Wilmington as well.

During the Revolution, Bassett captained a troop of Dover cavalry militia and served on the Delaware council of safety. Subsequently, he participated in Delaware's constitutional convention and sat in both the upper and lower houses of the legislature. In 1786 he represented his state in the Annapolis Convention.

At the U.S. Constitutional Convention the next year, Bassett attended diligently but made no speeches, served on no committees, and cast no critical votes. Like several other delegates of estimable reputation and talent, he allowed others to make the major steps.

Bassett subsequently went on to a bright career in the state and federal governments. In the Delaware ratifying convention, he joined in the 30-0 vote for the Constitution. Subsequently, in the years 1789-93, he served in the U.S. Senate. In that capacity, he voted in favor of the power of the President to remove governmental officers and against Hamilton's plan for the federal assumption of state debts.

From 1793 until 1799 Bassett held the chief justiceship of the court of common pleas. He espoused the Federalist cause in the 1790s, and served as a Presidential elector on behalf of John Adams in 1797. Two years later, Bassett was elected Governor of Delaware and continued in that post until 1801. That year, he became one of President Adams' "midnight" appointments as a judge of the U.S. Circuit Court. Subsequently, the Jeffersonian Republicans abolished his judgeship, and he spent the rest of his life in retirement.

Twice married, to Ann Ennals and a woman named Bruff, Bassett fathered several children. He was a devout Methodist, held religious meetings at Bohemia Manor, and supported the church financially. He died in 1815 at the age of 70 and is interred at the Wilmington and Brandywine Cemetery, Wilmington, DE.

### Gunning Bedford, Jr., Presbyterian, Delaware[35]

Bedford was born in 1747 at Philadelphia and reared there. The fifth of seven children, he was descended from a distinguished family that originally settled in Jamestown, VA. He usually referred to himself as Gunning Bedford, Jr., to avoid confusion with his cousin and contemporary Delaware statesman and soldier, Col. Gunning Bedford.

In 1771 signer Bedford graduated with honors from the College of New Jersey (later Princeton), where he was a classmate of James Madison. Apparently while still in school, Bedford wed Jane B. Parker, who bore at least one daughter. After reading law with Joseph Read in Philadelphia, Bedford won admittance to the bar and set up a practice. Subsequently, he moved to Dover and then to Wilmington. He apparently served in the Continental Army, possibly as an aide to General Washington.

Following the war, Bedford figured prominently in the politics of his state and nation. He sat in the legislature, on the state council, and in the Continental Congress (1783-85). In the latter year, he was chosen as a delegate to the Annapolis Convention but for some reason did not attend. From 1784 to 1789 he was attorney general of Delaware.

Bedford numbered among the more active members of the Constitutional Convention, and he missed few sessions. A large and forceful man, he spoke on several occasions and was a member of the committee that drafted the Great Compromise.

An ardent small-state advocate, he attacked the pretensions of the large states over the small and warned that the latter might be forced to seek foreign alliances unless their interests were accommodated. He attended the Delaware ratifying convention.

For another 2 years, Bedford continued as Delaware's attorney general. In 1789 Washington designated him as a federal district judge for his state, an office he was to occupy for the rest of his life. His only other ventures into national politics came in 1789 and 1793, as a Federalist presidential elector. In the main, however, he spent his later years in judicial pursuits, in aiding Wilmington Academy, in fostering abolitionism, and in enjoying his Lombardy Hall farm.

Bedford died at the age of 65 in 1812 and was buried in the First Presbyterian Churchyard in Wilmington. Later, when the cemetery was abandoned, his body was transferred to the Masonic Home, on the Lancaster Turnpike in Christiana Hundred, DE.

**Jacob Broom,** Lutheran, Delaware[36]

Broom was born in 1752 at Wilmington, DE, the eldest son of a blacksmith who prospered in farming. The youth was educated at home and probably at the local Old Academy. Although he followed his father into farming and also studied surveying, he was to make his career primarily in mercantile pursuits, including shipping and the import trade, and in real estate. In 1773 he married Rachel Pierce, who bore eight children.

Broom was not a distinguished patriot. His only recorded service was the preparation of maps for George Washington before the Battle of Brandywine, PA. In 1776, at 24 years of age, Broom became assistant burgess of Wilmington. Over the next several decades, he held that office six times and that of chief burgess four times, as well as those of borough assessor, president of the city "street regulators," and justice of the peace for New Castle County.

Broom sat in the state legislature in the years 1784-86 and 1788, during which time he was chosen as a delegate to the Annapolis Convention, but he did not attend. At the Constitutional

Convention, he never missed a session and spoke on several occasions, but his role was only a minor one.

After the convention, Broom returned to Wilmington, where in 1795 he erected a home near the Brandywine River on the outskirts of the city. He was its first postmaster (1790-92) and continued to hold various local offices and to participate in a variety of economic endeavors. For many years, he chaired the board of directors of Wilmington's Delaware Bank. He also operated a cotton mill, as well as a machine shop that produced and repaired mill machinery. He was involved, too, in an unsuccessful scheme to mine bog iron ore. A further interest was internal improvements: toll roads, canals, and bridges.

Broom also found time for philanthropic and religious activities. He served on the board of trustees of the College of Wilmington and as a lay leader at Old Swedes Church. He died at the age of 58 in 1810 while in Philadelphia on business and was buried there at Christ Church Burial Ground.

**John Dickinson,** Quaker – Episcopalian, Delaware[37]

Dickinson, "Penman of the Revolution," was born in 1732 at Crosiadore estate, near the village of Trappe in Talbot County, MD. He was the second son of Samuel Dickinson, the prosperous farmer, and his second wife, Mary (Cadwalader) Dickinson. In 1740 the family moved to Kent County near Dover, DE, where private tutors educated the youth. In 1750 he began to study law with John Moland in Philadelphia. In 1753 Dickinson went to England to continue his studies at London's Middle Temple. Four years later, he returned to Philadelphia and became a prominent lawyer there. In 1770 he married Mary Norris, daughter of a wealthy merchant. The couple had at least one daughter.

By that time, Dickinson's superior education and talents had propelled him into politics. In 1760 he had served in the assembly of the Three Lower Counties (Delaware), where he held the speakership. Combining his Pennsylvania and Delaware careers in 1762, he won a seat as a Philadelphia member in the Pennsylvania assembly and sat there again in 1764. He became the leader of the conservative side in the colony's political battles. His defense of the proprietary governor against the faction led by Benjamin Franklin hurt his popularity but earned him respect for his integrity. Nevertheless, as an immediate consequence, he lost his legislative seat in 1764.

Meantime, the struggle between the colonies and the mother country had waxed strong and Dickinson had emerged in the forefront of Revolutionary thinkers. In the debates over the Stamp Act (1765), he played a key part. That year, he wrote The Late Regulations Respecting the British Colonies... Considered, an influential pamphlet that urged Americans to seek repeal of the act by pressuring British merchants. Accordingly, the Pennsylvania legislature appointed him as a delegate to the Stamp Act Congress, whose resolutions he drafted.

In 1767-68 Dickinson wrote a series of newspaper articles in the Pennsylvania Chronicle that came to be known collectively as Letters from a Farmer in Pennsylvania. They attacked British taxation policy and urged resistance to unjust laws, but also emphasized the possibility of a peaceful resolution. So popular were the Letters in the colonies that Dickinson received an honorary LL.D. from the College of New Jersey (later Princeton) and public thanks from a meeting in Boston. In 1768, responding to the Townshend Duties, he championed rigorous colonial resistance in the form of nonimportation and non-exportation agreements.

In 1771, Dickinson returned to the Pennsylvania legislature and drafted a petition to the king that was unanimously approved. Because of his continued opposition to the use of force, however, he lost much of his popularity by 1774. He particularly resented the tactics of New England leaders in that year and refused to support aid requested by Boston in the wake of the Intolerable Acts, though he sympathized with the city's plight. Reluctantly, Dickinson was drawn into the Revolutionary fray. In 1774 he chaired the Philadelphia committee of correspondence and briefly sat in the First Continental Congress as a representative from Pennsylvania.

Throughout 1775, Dickinson supported the Whig cause, but continued to work for peace. He drew up petitions asking the king for redress of grievances. At the same time, he chaired a Philadelphia committee of safety and defense and held a colonelcy in the first battalion recruited in Philadelphia to defend the city.

After Lexington and Concord, Dickinson continued to hope for a peaceful solution. In the Second Continental Congress (1775-76), still a representative of Pennsylvania, he drew up them> Declaration of the Causes of Taking Up Arms. In the Pennsylvania assembly, he drafted an authorization to send delegates to Congress in 1776. It directed them to seek redress of grievances, but ordered them to oppose separation of the colonies from Britain.

By that time, Dickinson's moderate position had left him in the minority. In Congress he voted against the Declaration of Independence (1776) and refused to sign it. Nevertheless, he then became one of only two contemporary congressional members (with Thomas McKean) who entered the military. When he was not reelected he resigned his brigadier general's commission and withdrew to his estate in Delaware. Later in 1776, though reelected to Congress by his new constituency, he declined to serve and also resigned from the Pennsylvania Assembly. He may have taken part in the Battle of Brandywine, PA (September 11, 1777), as a private in a special Delaware force but otherwise saw no further military action.

Dickinson came out of retirement to take a seat in the Continental Congress (1779-80), where he signed the Articles of Confederation; earlier he had headed the committee that had drafted them. In 1781 he became president of Delaware's Supreme Executive Council. Shortly thereafter, he moved back to Philadelphia. There, he became president of Pennsylvania (178285). In 1786, representing Delaware, he attended and chaired the Annapolis Convention.

The next year, Delaware sent Dickinson to the Constitutional Convention. He missed a number of sessions and left early because of illness, but he made worthwhile contributions, including service on the Committee on Postponed Matters. Although he resented the forcefulness of Madison and the other nationalists, he helped engineer the Great Compromise and wrote public letters supporting constitutional ratification. Because of his premature departure from the convention, he did not actually sign the Constitution but authorized his friend and fellow-delegate George Read to do so for him.

Dickinson lived for two decades more but held no public offices. Instead, he devoted himself to writing on politics and in 1801 published two volumes of his collected works. He died at Wilmington in 1808 at the age of 75 and was entombed in the Friends Burial Ground.

### George Read, Episcopalian, Delaware[38]

Read's mother was the daughter of a Welsh planter, and his Dublin born father a landholder of means. Soon after George's birth in 1733 near the village of North East in Cecil County, MD, his family moved to New Castle, DE, where the youth, who was one of six sons, grew up. He attended school at Chester, PA, and Rev. Francis Alison's academy at New London, PA, and about the age of 15 he began reading with a Philadelphia lawyer.

In 1753 Read was admitted to the bar and began to practice. The next year, he journeyed back to New Castle, hung out his shingle, and before long enlisted a clientele that extended into Maryland. During this period he resided in New Castle but maintained Stonum a country retreat near the city. In 1763 he wed Gertrude Ross Till, the widowed sister of George Ross, like Read a future signer of the Declaration of Independence. She bore four sons and a daughter.

While crown attorney general (1763-74) for the Three Lower Counties (present Delaware), Read protested against the Stamp Act. In 1765 he began a career in the colonial legislature that lasted more than a decade. A moderate Whig, he supported nonimportation measures and dignified protests. His attendance at the Continental Congress (1774-77) was irregular. Like his friend John Dickinson, he was willing to protect colonial rights but was wary of extremism. He voted against independence on July 2,

1776, the only signer of the Declaration to do so, apparently either bowing to the strong Tory sentiment in Delaware, or believing reconciliation with Britain was still possible.

That same year, Read gave priority to state responsibilities. He presided over the Delaware constitutional convention, in which he chaired the drafting committee, and began a term as speaker of the legislative council, which in effect made him vice president of the state. When the British took Wilmington the next fall, they captured the president, a resident of the city. At first, because Read was away in Congress, Thomas McKean, speaker of the lower house, took over as acting president. But in November, after barely escaping from the British himself while he and his family were en route to Dover from Philadelphia, newly occupied by the redcoats, Read assumed the office and held it until the spring of 1778. Back in the legislative council, in 1779 he drafted the act directing Delaware congressional delegates to sign the Articles of Confederation.

During 1779, in poor health, Read resigned from the legislative council, refused reelection to Congress, and began a period of inactivity. During the years 1782-88, he again sat on the council and concurrently held the position of judge of the court of appeals in admiralty cases.

Meantime, in 1784, Read had served on a commission that adjusted New York Massachusetts land claims. In 1786 he attended the Annapolis Convention. The next year, he participated in the Constitutional Convention, where he missed few if any sessions and championed the rights of the small states. Otherwise, he adopted a Hamiltonian stance, favoring a strong executive. He later led the ratification movement in Delaware, the first state to ratify.

In the U.S. Senate (1789-93), Read's attendance was again erratic, but when present he allied with the Federalists. He resigned to accept the post of chief justice of Delaware. He held it until his death at New Castle 5 years later, just 3 days after he celebrated his 65th birthday. His grave is there in the Immanuel Episcopal Churchyard.

# Maryland

**Daniel Carroll**, Catholic, Maryland[39]

Daniel Carroll was member of a prominent Maryland family of Irish descent. A collateral branch was led by Charles Carroll of Carrollton, signer of the Declaration of Independence. Daniel's older brother was John Carroll, the first Roman Catholic bishop in the United States.

Daniel was born in 1730 at Upper Marlboro, MD. Befitting the son of a wealthy Roman Catholic family, he studied for 6 years (1742-48) under the Jesuits at St. Omer's in Flanders. Then, after a tour of Europe, he sailed home and soon married Eleanor Carroll, apparently a first cousin of Charles Carroll of Carrollton. Not much is known about the next two decades of his life except that he backed the War for Independence reluctantly and remained out of the public eye. No doubt he lived the life of a gentleman planter.

In 1781 Carroll entered the political arena. Elected to the Continental Congress that year, he carried to Philadelphia the news that Maryland was at last ready to accede to the Articles of Confederation, to which he soon penned his name. During the decade, he also began a tour in the Maryland senate that was to span his lifetime and helped George Washington promote the Patowmack Company, a scheme to canalize the Potomac River so as to provide a transportation link between the East and the trans-Appalachian West.

Carroll did not arrive at the Constitutional Convention until July 9, but thereafter he attended quite regularly. He spoke about 20 times during the debates and served on the Committee on Postponed Matters. Returning to Maryland after the convention, he campaigned for ratification of the Constitution but was not a delegate to the state convention.

In 1789 Carroll won a seat in the U.S. House of Representatives, where he voted for locating the Nation's Capital on the banks of the Potomac and for Hamilton's program for the federal assumption of state debts. In 1791 George Washington named his friend Carroll as one of three commissioners to survey and define the District of

Columbia, where Carroll owned much land. Ill health caused him to resign this post 4 years later, and the next year at the age of 65 he died at his home near Rock Creek in Forest Glen, MD. He was buried there in St. John's Catholic Cemetery.

**Daniel of St. Thomas Jennifer,** Episcopalian, Maryland[40]

Jenifer was born in 1723 of Swedish and English descent at Coates Retirement (now Ellerslie) estate, near Port Tobacco in Charles County, MD. Little is known about his childhood or education, but as an adult he came into possession of a large estate near Annapolis, called Stepney, where he lived most of his life. He never married. The web of his far-reaching friendships included such illustrious personages as George Washington.

As a young man, Jenifer served as agent and receiver general for the last two proprietors of Maryland. He also filled the post of justice of the peace in Charles County and later for the western circuit of Maryland. In 1760 he sat on a boundary commission that settled disputes between Pennsylvania and Delaware. Six years later, he became a member of the provincial court and from 1773 to 1776 sat on the Maryland royal governor's council.

Despite his association with conservative proprietary politics, Jenifer supported the Revolutionary movement, albeit at first reluctantly. He served as president of the Maryland council of safety (1775-77), then as president of the first state senate (177780). He sat in the Continental Congress (1778-82) and held the position of state revenue and financial manager (1782-85).

A conservative nationalist, Jenifer favored a strong and permanent union of the states and a Congress with taxation power. In 1785 he represented Maryland at the Mount Vernon Conference. Although he was one of 29 delegates who attended nearly every session of the Constitutional Convention, he did not speak often but backed Madison and the nationalist element.

Jenifer lived only 3 more years and never again held public office. He died at the age of 66 or 67 at Annapolis in 1790. The exact location of his grave, possibly at Ellerslie estate, is unknown.

**Luther Martin\***, Episcopalian, Maryland[41]

Like many of the delegates to the Constitutional Convention, Luther Martin attended the College of New Jersey (later Princeton), from which he graduated with honors in 1766. Though born in Brunswick, NJ, in 1748, Martin moved to Maryland after receiving his degree and taught there for 3 years. He then began to study the law and was admitted to the Virginia bar in 1771.

Martin was an early advocate of American independence from Great Britain. In the fall of 1774 he served on the patriot committee of Somerset County, and in December he attended a convention of the Province of Maryland in Annapolis, which had been called to consider the recommendations of the Continental Congress. Maryland appointed Luther Martin its attorney general in early 1778. In this capacity, Martin vigorously prosecuted Loyalists, whose numbers were strong in many areas. Tensions had even led to insurrection and open warfare in some counties. While still attorney general, Martin joined the Baltimore Light Dragoons. In July 1781 his unit joined Lafayette's forces near Fredericksburg, VA., but Martin was recalled by the governor to prosecute a treason trial.

Martin married Maria Cresap on Christmas Day 1783. Of their five children, three daughters lived to adulthood. His postwar law practice grew to become one of the largest and most successful in the country. In 1785 Martin was elected to the Continental Congress, but this appointment was purely honorary. His numerous public and private duties prevented him from traveling to Philadelphia.

At the Constitutional Convention Martin opposed the idea of a strong central government. When he arrived on June 9, 1787, he expressed suspicion of the secrecy rule imposed on the proceedings. He consistently sided with the small states and voted against the Virginia Plan. On June 27 Martin spoke for more than 3 hours in opposition to the Virginia Plan's proposal for proportionate representation in both houses of the legislature. Martin served on the committee formed to seek a compromise on representation, where he supported the case for equal numbers of delegates in at least one house. Before the convention closed, he and another Maryland delegate, John Francis Mercer, walked out.

In an address to the Maryland House of Delegates in 1787 and in numerous newspaper articles, Martin attacked the proposed new form of government and continued to fight ratification of the Constitution through 1788. He lamented the ascension of the national government over the states and condemned what he saw as unequal representation in Congress. Martin opposed including slaves in determining representation and believed that the absence of a jury in the Supreme Court gravely endangered freedom. At the convention, Martin complained, the aggrandizement of particular states and individuals often had been pursued more avidly than the welfare of the country. The assumption of the term "federal" by those who favored a national government also irritated Martin. Around 1791, however, Martin turned to the Federalist party because of his animosity toward Thomas Jefferson.

The first years of the 1800s saw Martin as defense counsel in two controversial national cases. In the first Martin won an acquittal for his close friend, Supreme Court Justice Samuel Chase, in his impeachment trial in 1805. Two years later Martin was one of Aaron Burr's defense lawyers when Burr stood trial for treason in 1807.

After a record 28 consecutive years as state attorney general, Luther Martin resigned in December 1805. In 1813 Martin became chief judge of the court of oyer and terminer for the City and County of Baltimore. He was reappointed attorney general of Maryland in 1818, and in 1819 he argued Maryland's position in the landmark Supreme Court case McCulloch v. Maryland. The plaintiff, represented by Daniel Webster, William Pinckney, and William Wirt, won the decision, which determined that states could not tax federal institutions.

Martin's fortunes declined dramatically in his last years. Heavy drinking, illness, and poverty all took their toll. Paralysis, which had struck in 1819, forced him to retire as Maryland's attorney general in 1822. In 1826, at the age of 78, Luther Martin died in Aaron Burr's home in New York City and was buried in an unmarked grave in St. John's churchyard.

**James McHenry,** Presbyterian, Maryland[42]

McHenry was born at Ballymena, County Antrim, Ireland, in 1753. He enjoyed a classical education at Dublin, and emigrated to Philadelphia in 1771. The following year, the rest of his family came to the colonies, and his brother and father established an import business at Baltimore. During that year, James continued schooling at Newark Academy in Delaware and then studied medicine for 2 years under the well-known Dr. Benjamin Rush in Philadelphia.

During the War for Independence, McHenry served as a military surgeon. Late in 1776, while he was on the staff of the 5th Pennsylvania Battalion, the British captured him at Fort Washington, NY. He was paroled early the next year and exchanged in March 1778. Returning immediately to duty, he was assigned to Valley Forge, PA, and in May became secretary to George Washington. About this time, McHenry apparently quit the practice of medicine to devote himself to politics and administration; he apparently never needed to return to it after the war because of his excellent financial circumstances.

McHenry stayed on Washington's staff until 1780, when he joined that of the Marquis de Lafayette, and he remained in that assignment until he entered the Maryland Senate (1781-86). During part of this period, he served concurrently in the Continental Congress (1783-86). In 1784 he married Margaret Allison Caldwell.

McHenry missed many of the proceedings at the Philadelphia convention, in part because of the illness of his brother, and played an insubstantial part in the debates when he was present. He did, however, maintain a private journal that has been useful to posterity. He campaigned strenuously for the Constitution in Maryland and attended the state ratifying convention.

From 1789 to 1791, McHenry sat in the state assembly and in the years 1791-96 again in the senate. A staunch Federalist, he then accepted Washington's offer of the post of Secretary of War and held it into the administration of John Adams. McHenry looked to Hamilton rather than to Adams for leadership. As time passed, the latter became increasingly dissatisfied with McHenry's performance and distrustful of his political motives and in 1800 forced him to resign. Subsequently, the Democratic-Republicans accused him of maladministration, but a congressional committee vindicated him.

McHenry returned to his estate near Baltimore and to semiretirement. He remained a loyal Federalist and opposed the War of 1812. He also held the office of president of a Bible society. He died in 1816 at the age of 62, survived by two of his three children. His grave is in Baltimore's Westminster Presbyterian Cemetery.

**John Francis Mercer\***, Episcopalian, Maryland[43]

John Francis Mercer, born on May 17, 1759, was the fifth of nine children born to John and Ann Mercer of Stafford County, VA. He attended the College of William and Mary, and in early 1776 he joined the 3d Virginia Regiment. Mercer became Gen. Charles Lee's aide-decamp in 1778, but after General Lee's court martial in October 1779, Mercer resigned his commission. He spent the next year studying law at the College of William and Mary and then rejoined the army, where he served briefly under Lafayette.

In 1782 Mercer was elected to the Virginia House of Delegates. That December he became one of Virginia's representatives to the Continental Congress. He later returned to the House of Delegates in 1785 and 1786.

Mercer married Sophia Sprigg in 1785 and soon after moved to Anne Arundel County, MD. He attended the Constitutional Convention as part of Maryland's delegation when he was only 28 years old, the second youngest delegate in Philadelphia. Mercer was strongly opposed to centralization, and both spoke and voted against the Constitution. He and fellow Marylander Luther Martin left the proceedings before they ended. After the convention,

Mercer continued in public service. He allied himself with the Republicans and served in the Maryland House of Delegates in 1778-89, 1791-92, 1800-1801, and 1803-6. Between 1791 and 1794 he also sat in the U.S. House of Representatives for Maryland and was chosen governor of the state for two terms, 1801-3. During Thomas Jefferson's term as President, Mercer broke with the Republicans and joined the Federalist camp.

Illness plagued him during his last years. In 1821 Mercer traveled to Philadelphia to seek medical attention, and he died there on August 30. His remains lay temporarily in a vault in St. Peter's Church in Philadelphia and were reinterred on his estate, "Cedar Park" in Maryland.

# New Hampshire

**Nicholas Gilman,** Congregationalist, New Hampshire[44]

Member of a distinguished New Hampshire family and second son in a family of eight, Nicholas Gilman was born at Exeter in 1755. He received his education in local schools and worked at his father's general store. When the War for Independence began, he enlisted in the New Hampshire element of the Continental Army, soon won a captaincy, and served throughout the war.

Gilman returned home, again helped his father in the store, and immersed himself in politics. In the period 1786-88 he sat in the Continental Congress, though his attendance record was poor. In 1787 he represented New Hampshire at the Constitutional Convention. He did not arrive at Philadelphia until July 21, by which time much major business had already occurred. Never much of a debater, he made no speeches and played only a minor part in the deliberations. He did, however, serve on the Committee on Postponed Matters. He was also active in obtaining New Hampshire's acceptance of the Constitution and in shepherding it through the Continental Congress.

Gilman later became a prominent Federalist politician. He served in the U.S. House of Representatives from 1789 until 1797;

and in 1793 and 1797 was a presidential elector. He also sat in the New Hampshire legislature in 1795, 1802, and 1804, and in the years 1805-8 and 1811-14 he held the office of state treasurer.

Meantime, Gilman's political philosophy had begun to drift toward the Democratic-Republicans. In 1802, when he was defeated for the U.S. Senate, President Jefferson appointed him as a bankruptcy commissioner, and 2 years later as a Democratic-Republican he won election to the U.S. Senate. He was still serving there when he passed away at Philadelphia, while on his way home from Washington, DC, in 1814 at the age of 58. He is interred at the Winter Street Cemetery at Exeter.

**John Langdon,** Congregationalist, New Hampshire[45]

Langdon was born in 1741 at or near Portsmouth, NH. His father, whose family had emigrated to America before 1660, was a prosperous farmer who sired a large family. The youth's education was intermittent. He attended a local grammar school, worked as an apprentice clerk, and spent some time at sea. Eventually he went into the mercantile business for himself and prospered.

Langdon, a vigorous supporter of the Revolution, sat on the New Hampshire committee of correspondence and a nonimportation committee. He also attended various patriot assemblies. In 1774 he participated in the seizure and confiscation of British munitions from the Portsmouth fort.

The next year, Langdon served as speaker of the New Hampshire assembly and also sat in the Continental Congress (1775-76). During the latter year, he accepted a colonelcy in the militia of his state and became its agent for British prizes on behalf of the Continental Congress, a post he held throughout the war. In addition, he built privateers for operations against the British--a lucrative occupation.

Langdon also actively took part in the land war. In 1777 he organized and paid for Gen. John Stark's expedition from New Hampshire against British Gen. John Burgoyne and was present in command of a militia unit at Saratoga, NY, when the latter surrendered. Langdon later led a detachment of troops during the

Rhode Island campaign, but found his major outlet in politics. He was speaker of the New Hampshire legislature from 1777 to 1781. In 1777, meantime, he had married Elizabeth Sherburne, who was to give birth to one daughter.

In 1783 Langdon was elected to the Continental Congress; the next year, to the state senate; and the following year, as president, or chief executive, of New Hampshire. In 1784 he built a home at Portsmouth. In 1786-87 he was back again as speaker of the legislature and during the latter year for the third time in the Continental Congress.

Langdon was forced to pay his own expenses and those of Nicholas Gilman to the Constitutional Convention because New Hampshire was unable or unwilling to pay them. The pair did not arrive at Philadelphia until late July, by which time much business had already been consummated. Thereafter, Langdon made a significant mark. He spoke more than 20 times during the debates and was a member of the committee that struck a compromise on the issue of slavery. For the most part, his sympathies lay on the side of strengthening the national government. In 1788, once again as state president (1788-89), he took part in the ratifying convention.

From 1789 to 1801 Langdon sat in the U.S. Senate, including service as the first President pro tem for several sessions. During these years, his political affiliations changed. As a supporter of a strong central government, he had been a member of the Federalist Party, but by the time of Jay's Treaty (1794) he was opposing its policies. By 1801 he was firmly backing the Democratic-Republicans.

That year, Langdon declined Jefferson's offer of the Secretaryship of the Navy. Between then and 1812, he kept active in New Hampshire politics. He sat again in the legislature (1801-5), twice holding the position of speaker. After several unsuccessful attempts, in 1805 he was elected as governor and continued in that post until 1811 except for a year's hiatus in 1809. Meanwhile, in 1805, Dartmouth College had awarded him an honorary doctor of laws degree.

In 1812 Langdon refused the Democratic-Republican Vice Presidential nomination on the grounds of age and health. He enjoyed retirement for another 7 years before he died at the age of 78. His grave is at Old North Cemetery in Portsmouth.

# New York

**Alexander Hamilton,** Huguenot – Presbyterian – Episcopalian, New York[46]

Hamilton was born in 1757 on the island of Nevis, in the Leeward group, British West Indies. He was the illegitimate son of a common-law marriage between a poor itinerant Scottish merchant of aristocratic descent and an English-French Huguenot mother who was a planter's daughter. In 1766, after the father had moved his family elsewhere in the Leewards to St. Croix in the Danish (now United States) Virgin Islands, he returned to St. Kitts while his wife and two sons remained on St. Croix.

The mother, who opened a small store to make ends meet, and a Presbyterian clergyman provided Hamilton with a basic education, and he learned to speak fluent French. About the time of his mother's death in 1768, he became an apprentice clerk at Christiansted in a mercantile establishment, whose proprietor became one of his benefactors. Recognizing his ambition and superior intelligence, they raised a fund for his education.

In 1772, bearing letters of introduction, Hamilton traveled to New York City. Patrons he met there arranged for him to attend Barber's Academy at Elizabethtown (present Elizabeth), NJ. During this time, he met and stayed for a while at the home of William Livingston, who would one day be a fellow signer of the Constitution. Late the next year, 1773, Hamilton entered King's College (later Columbia College and University) in New York City, but the Revolution interrupted his studies.

Although not yet 20 years of age, in 1774-75 Hamilton wrote several widely read pro-Whig pamphlets. Right after the war broke out, he accepted an artillery captaincy and fought in the principal campaigns of 1776-77. In the latter year, winning the rank of lieutenant colonel, he joined the staff of General Washington as secretary and aide-de-camp and soon became his close confidant as well.

In 1780 Hamilton wed New Yorker Elizabeth Schuyler, whose family was rich and politically powerful; they were to have eight children. In 1781, after some disagreements with Washington, he took a command position under Lafayette in the Yorktown, VA, campaign (1781). He resigned his commission that November.

Hamilton then read law at Albany and quickly entered practice, but public service soon attracted him. He was elected to the Continental Congress in 1782-83. In the latter year, he established a law office in New York City. Because of his interest in strengthening the central government, he represented his state at the Annapolis Convention in 1786, where he urged the calling of the Constitutional Convention.

In 1787 Hamilton served in the legislature, which appointed him as a delegate to the convention. He played a surprisingly small part in the debates, apparently because he was frequently absent on legal business, his extreme nationalism put him at odds with most of the delegates, and he was frustrated by the conservative views of his two fellow delegates from New York. He did, however, sit on the Committee of Style, and he was the only one of the three delegates from his state who signed the finished document. Hamilton's part in New York's ratification the next year was substantial, though he felt the Constitution was deficient in many respects. Against determined opposition, he waged a strenuous and successful campaign, including collaboration with John Jay and James Madison in writing The Federalist. In 1787 Hamilton was again elected to the Continental Congress.

When the new government got under way in 1789, Hamilton won the position of Secretary of the Treasury. He began at once to place the nation's disorganized finances on a sound footing. In a series of reports (1790-91), he presented a program not only to stabilize national finances but also to shape the future of the country as a powerful, industrial nation. He proposed establishment of a national bank, funding of the national debt, assumption of state war debts, and the encouragement of manufacturing.

Hamilton's policies soon brought him into conflict with Jefferson and Madison. Their disputes with him over his pro-business economic program, sympathies for Great Britain, disdain for the common man, and opposition to the principles and excesses of the French revolution contributed to the formation of the first U.S. party system. It pitted Hamilton and the Federalists against Jefferson and Madison and the Democratic-Republicans.

During most of the Washington administration, Hamilton's views usually prevailed with the President, especially after 1793 when Jefferson left the government. In 1795 family and financial needs forced Hamilton to resign from the Treasury Department and resume his law practice in New York City. Except for a stint as inspector-general of the Army (1798-1800) during the undeclared war with France, he never again held public office.

While gaining stature in the law, Hamilton continued to exert a powerful impact on New York and national politics. Always an opponent of fellow-Federalist John Adams, he sought to prevent his election to the presidency in 1796. When that failed, he continued to use his influence secretly within Adams' cabinet. The bitterness between the two men became public knowledge in 1800 when Hamilton denounced Adams in a letter that was published through the efforts of the Democratic-Republicans.

In 1802 Hamilton and his family moved into The Grange, a country home he had built in a rural part of Manhattan not far north of New York City. But the expenses involved and investments in northern land speculations seriously strained his finances.

Meanwhile, when Jefferson and Aaron Burr tied in Presidential electoral votes in 1800, Hamilton threw valuable support to Jefferson. In 1804, when Burr sought the governorship of New York, Hamilton again managed to defeat him. That same year, Burr, taking offense at remarks he believed to have originated with Hamilton, challenged him to a duel, which took place at present Weehawken, NJ, on July 11. Mortally wounded, Hamilton died the next day. He was in his late forties at death. He was buried in Trinity Churchyard in New York City.

**John Lansing\*,** Dutch Reformed, New York[47]

On January 30, 1754, John Lansing was born in Albany, NY, to Gerrit Jacob and Jannetje Lansing. At age 21 Lansing had completed his study of the law and was admitted to practice. In 1781 he married Cornelia Ray. They had 10 children, 5 of whom died in infancy. Lansing was quite wealthy; he owned a large estate at Lansingburg and had a lucrative law practice.

From 1776 to 1777 Lansing acted as military secretary to Gen. Philip Schuyler. From the military world Lansing turned to the political and served six terms in the New York Assembly-1780-84, 1786, and 1788. During the last two terms he was speaker of the assembly. In the 2-year gap between his first four terms in the assembly and the fifth, Lansing sat in the Confederation Congress. He rounded out his public service by serving as Albany's mayor between 1786 and 1790.

Lansing went to Philadelphia as part of the New York delegation to the Constitutional Convention. As the convention progressed, Lansing became disillusioned because he believed it was exceeding its instructions.

Lansing believed the delegates had gathered together simply to amend the Articles of Confederation and was dismayed at the movement to write an entirely new constitution. After 6 weeks, John Lansing and fellow New York delegate Robert Yates left the convention and explained their departure in a joint letter to New York Governor George Clinton. They stated that they opposed any system that would consolidate the United States into one government, and they had understood that the convention would not consider any such consolidation. Furthermore, warned Lansing and Yates, the kind of government recommended by the convention could not "afford that security to equal and permanent liberty which we wished to make an invariable object of our pursuit." In 1788, as a member of the New York ratifying convention, Lansing again vigorously opposed the Constitution.

Under the new federal government Lansing pursued a long judicial career. In 1790 he began an 11-year term on the supreme court of New York; from 1798 until 1801 he served as its chief justice. Between 1801 and 1814 Lansing was chancellor of the state. Retirement from that post did not slow him down; in 1817 he accepted an appointment as a regent of the University of the State of New York.

Lansing's death was the most mysterious of all the delegates to the Constitutional Convention. While on a visit to New York City in 1829, he left his hotel to post some letters. No trace of him was ever found, and it was supposed that he had been murdered.

**Robert Yates\*,** Dutch Reformed, New York[48]

The son of Joseph and Maria Yates, Robert Yates was born in Schenectady, NY, on January 27, 1738. He received a classical education in New York City and later studied law with William Livingston. Yates was admitted to the New York bar in 1760 and thereafter resided in Albany.

Between 1771 and 1775 Yates sat on the Albany board of aldermen. During the pre-Revolution years Yates counted himself among the Radical Whigs, whose vigilance against corruption and emphasis on the protection of liberty in England appealed to many in the colonies. Once the Revolution broke out, Yates served on the Albany committee of safety and represented his county in four provincial congresses and in the convention of 1775-77. At the convention he sat on various committees, including the one that drafted the first constitution for New York State.

On May 8, 1777, Yates was appointed to New York's supreme court and presided as its chief justice from 1790 through 1798. While on the bench he attracted criticism for his fair treatment of Loyalists. Other duties included serving on commissions that were called to settle boundary disputes with Massachusetts and Vermont.

In the 1780s Robert Yates stood as a recognized leader of the Antifederalists. He opposed any concessions to the federal congress, such as the right to collect impost duties, that might diminish the sovereignty of the states. When he travelled to Philadelphia in May 1787 for the federal convention, he expected that the delegates would simply discuss revising the existing Articles. Yates was on the committee that debated the question of representation in the legislature, and it soon became apparent that the convention intended much more than modification of the current plan of union. On July 5, the day the committee presented its report, Yates and John Lansing (to whom Yates was related by marriage) left the proceedings. In a joint letter to Gov. George Clinton of New York, they spelled out the reasons for their early departure. They warned against the dangers of centralizing power and urged opposition to adopting the Constitution. Yates continued to attack the Constitution in a series of letters signed "Brutus" and "Sydney" and voted against ratification at the Poughkeepsie convention.

In 1789 Yates ran for governor of New York but lost the election. Three years after his retirement from the state supreme court, on September 9, 1801, he died, leaving his wife, Jannetje Van Ness Yates, and four of his six children. Though he had enjoyed a comfortable income at the start of his career, his capital had dwindled away until very little was left. In 1821 his notes from the Constitutional Convention were published under the title Secret Proceedings and Debates of the Convention Assembled... for the Purpose of Forming the Constitution of the United States.

# Pennsylvania

**George Clymer,** Quaker, Episcopalian, Pennsylvania[49]

Clymer was orphaned in 1740, only a year after his birth in Philadelphia. A wealthy uncle reared and informally educated him and advanced him from clerk to full-fledged partner in his mercantile firm, which on his death he bequeathed to his ward. Later Clymer merged operations with the Merediths, a prominent business family, and cemented the relationship by marrying his senior partner's daughter, Elizabeth, in 1765.

Motivated at least partly by the impact of British economic restrictions on his business, Clymer early adopted the Revolutionary cause and was one of the first to recommend independence. He attended patriotic meetings, served on the Pennsylvania council of safety, and in 1773 headed a committee that forced the resignation of Philadelphia tea consignees appointed by Britain under the Tea Act. Inevitably, in light of his economic background, he channeled his energies into financial matters. In 1775-76 he acted as one of the first two Continental treasurers, even personally underwriting the war by exchanging all his own specie for Continental currency.

In the Continental Congress (1776-77 and 1780-82) the quiet and unassuming Clymer rarely spoke in debate but made his mark in committee efforts, especially those pertaining to commerce, finance, and military affairs. During the War for Independence, he also served on a series of commissions that conducted important field investigations. In December 1776, when Congress fled from Philadelphia to Baltimore, he and George Walton and Robert Morris remained behind to carry on congressional business. Within a year, after their victory at the Battle of Brandywine, Pa. (September 11, 1777), British troops advancing on Philadelphia detoured for the purpose of vandalizing Clymer's home in Chester County about 25 miles outside the city. His wife and children hid nearby in the woods.

After a brief retirement following his last term in the Continental Congress, Clymer was reelected for the years 1784-88 to the Pennsylvania legislature, where he had also served part time in 1780-82 while still in Congress. As a state legislator, he advocated a bicameral legislature and reform of the penal code and opposed capital punishment. At the Constitutional Convention, where he rarely missed a meeting, he spoke seldom but effectively and played a modest role in shaping the final document.

The next phase of Clymer's career consisted of service in the U.S. House of Representatives in the First Congress (1789-91), followed by appointment as collector of excise taxes on alcoholic beverages in Pennsylvania (1791-94). In 1795-96 he sat on a Presidential commission that negotiated a treaty with the Cherokee and Creek Indians in Georgia. During his retirement, Clymer advanced various community projects, including the Philadelphia Society for Promoting Agriculture and the Pennsylvania Academy of the Fine Arts, and served as the first president of the Philadelphia Bank. At the age of 73, in 1813, he died at Summerseat, an estate a few miles outside Philadelphia at Morrisville that he had purchased and moved to in 1806. His grave is in the Friends Meeting House Cemetery at Trenton, NJ.

**Thomas Fitzsimons,** Catholic, Pennsylvania[50]

Fitzsimons (FitzSimons; Fitzsimmons) was born in Ireland in 1741. Coming to America about 1760, he pursued a mercantile career in Philadelphia. The next year, he married Catherine Meade, the daughter of a prominent local merchant, Robert Meade, and not long afterward went into business with one of his brothers-in-law. The firm of George Meade and Company soon became one of the leading commercial houses in the city and specialized in the West India trade.

When the Revolution erupted, Fitzsimons enthusiastically endorsed the Whig position. During the war, he commanded a company of militia (1776-77). He also sat on the Philadelphia committee of correspondence, council of safety, and navy board. His firm provided supplies and "fire" ships to the military forces and, toward the end of the war, donated £: 5,000 to the Continental Army.

In 1782-83 Fitzsimons entered politics as a delegate to the Continental Congress. In the latter year, he became a member of the Pennsylvania council of censors and served as a legislator (1786-89). His attendance at the Constitutional Convention was regular, but he did not make any outstanding contributions to the proceedings. He was, however, a strong nationalist.

After the convention, Fitzsimons continued to demonstrate his nationalistic proclivities as a three-term U.S. representative (1789-95). He allied himself closely with the program of Hamilton and the emerging Federalist Party. Once again demonstrating his commercial orientation, he advocated a protective tariff and retirement of the national debt.

Fitzsimons spent most of the remainder of his life in private business, though he retained an interest in public affairs. His views remained essentially Federalist. During the maritime difficulties in the late 1790s, he urged retaliation against British and French interference with American shipping. In the first decade of the 19th century, he vigorously opposed Jefferson's embargo of 1807-9. In 1810, again clashing with the Jeffersonians, he championed the re-charter of the First United States Bank.

But Fitzsimons's prominence stemmed from his business leadership. In 1781 he had been one of the founders of the Bank of North America. He also helped organize and held a directorship in the Insurance Company of North America and several times acted as president of the Philadelphia Chamber of Commerce. His financial affairs, like those somewhat earlier of his associate and fellow-signer Robert Morris, took a disastrous turn in 1805. He later regained some of his affluence, but his reputation suffered.

Despite these troubles, Fitzsimons never ceased his philanthropy. He was an outstanding supporter of Philadelphia's St. Augustine's Roman Catholic Church. He also strived to improve public education in the commonwealth and served as trustee of the University of Pennsylvania.

Fitzsimons died at Philadelphia in 1811 after seven decades of life. His tomb is there in the graveyard at St. Mary's Roman Catholic Church, which is in present Independence National Historical Park.

**Benjamin Franklin,** Episcopalian, Deist, Pennsylvania[51]

Franklin was born in 1706 at Boston. He was the tenth son of a soap and candlemaker. He received some formal education but was principally self-taught. After serving an apprenticeship to his father between the ages of 10 and 12, he went to work for his half-brother James, a printer. In 1721 the latter founded the New England Courant, the fourth newspaper in the colonies. Benjamin secretly contributed 14 essays to it, his first published writings.

In 1723, because of dissension with his half-brother, Franklin moved to Philadelphia, where he obtained employment as a printer. He spent only a year there and then sailed to London for 2 more years. Back in Philadelphia, he rose rapidly in the printing industry. He published The Pennsylvania Gazette (173048), which had been founded by another man in 1728, but his most successful literary venture was the annual Poor Richard's Almanac (1733-58). It won a popularity in the colonies second only to the Bible, and its fame eventually spread to Europe.

Meantime, in 1730 Franklin had taken a common-law wife, Deborah Read, who was to bear him a son and daughter, and he also apparently had children with another nameless woman out of wedlock. By 1748 he had achieved financial independence and gained recognition for his philanthropy and the stimulus he provided to such civic causes as libraries, educational institutions, and hospitals. Energetic and tireless, he also found time to pursue his interest in science, as well as to enter politics.

Franklin served as clerk (1736-51) and member (1751-64) of the colonial legislature and as deputy postmaster of Philadelphia (1737-53) and deputy postmaster general of the colonies (1753-74). In addition, he represented Pennsylvania at the Albany Congress (1754), called to unite the colonies during the French and Indian War. The congress adopted his "Plan of Union," but the colonial assemblies rejected it because it encroached on their powers.

During the years 1757-62 and 1764-75, Franklin resided in England, originally in the capacity of agent for Pennsylvania and later for Georgia, New Jersey, and Massachusetts. During the latter period, which coincided with the growth of colonial unrest, he underwent a political metamorphosis. Until then a contented Englishman in outlook, primarily concerned with Pennsylvania provincial politics, he distrusted popular movements and saw little purpose to be served in carrying principle to extremes. Until the issue of parliamentary taxation undermined the old alliances, he led the Quaker party attack on the Anglican proprietary party and its Presbyterian frontier allies. His purpose throughout the years at London in fact had been displacement of the Penn family administration by royal authority-the conversion of the province from a proprietary to a royal colony.

It was during the Stamp Act crisis that Franklin evolved from leader of a shattered provincial party's faction to celebrated spokesman at London for American rights. Although as agent for Pennsylvania he opposed by every conceivable means the enactment of the bill in 1765, he did not at first realize the depth of colonial hostility. He regarded passage as unavoidable and preferred to submit to it while actually working for its repeal.

Franklin's nomination of a friend and political ally as stamp distributor for Pennsylvania, coupled with his apparent acceptance of the legislation, armed his proprietary opponents with explosive issues. Their energetic exploitation of them endangered his reputation at home until reliable information was published demonstrating his unabated opposition to the act. For a time, mob resentment threatened his family and new home in Philadelphia until his tradesmen supporters rallied. Subsequently, Franklin's defense of the American position in the House of Commons during the debates over the Stamp Act's repeal restored his prestige at home.

Franklin returned to Philadelphia in May 1775 and immediately became a distinguished member of the Continental Congress. Thirteen months later, he served on the committee that drafted the Declaration of Independence. He subsequently contributed to the government in other important ways, including service as postmaster general, and took over the duties of president of the Pennsylvania constitutional convention.

But, within less than a year and a half after his return, the aged statesman set sail once again for Europe, beginning a career as diplomat that would occupy him for most of the rest of his life. In the years 1776-79, as one of three commissioners, he directed the negotiations that led to treaties of commerce and alliance with France, where the people adulated him, but he and the other commissioners squabbled constantly. While he was sole commissioner to France (1779-85), he and John Jay and John

Adams negotiated the Treaty of Paris (1783), which ended the War for Independence.

Back in the United States, in 1785 Franklin became president of the Supreme Executive Council of Pennsylvania. At the Constitutional Convention, though he did not approve of many aspects of the finished document and was hampered by his age and ill-health, he missed few if any sessions, lent his prestige, soothed passions, and compromised disputes.

In his twilight years, working on his Autobiography, Franklin could look back on a fruitful life as the toast of two continents. Energetic nearly to the last, in 1787 he was elected as first president of the Pennsylvania Society for Promoting the Abolition of Slavery-a cause to which he had committed himself as early as the 1730s. His final public act was signing a memorial to Congress recommending dissolution of the slavery system. Shortly thereafter, in 1790 at the age of 84, Franklin passed away in Philadelphia and was laid to rest in Christ Church Burial Ground.

**Jared Ingersoll,** Presbyterian, Pennsylvania[52]

The son of Jared Ingersoll, Sr., a British colonial official and later prominent Loyalist, Ingersoll was born at New Haven, CT, in 1749. He received an excellent education and graduated from Yale in 1766. He then oversaw the financial affairs of his father, who had relocated from New Haven to Philadelphia. Later, the youth joined him, took up the study of law, and won admittance to the Pennsylvania bar.

In the midst of the Revolutionary fervor, which neither father nor son shared, in 1773, on the advice of the elder Ingersoll, Jared, Jr., sailed to London and studied law at the Middle Temple. Completing his work in 1776, he made a 2-year tour of the Continent, during which time for some reason he shed his Loyalist sympathies.

Returning to Philadelphia and entering the legal profession, Ingersoll attended to the clients of one of the city's leading lawyers and a family friend, Joseph Reed, who was then occupied with the affairs of the Supreme Executive Council of Pennsylvania. In 1781 Ingersoll married Elizabeth Pettit (Petit). The year before, he had entered politics by winning election to the Continental Congress (1780-81).

Although Ingersoll missed no sessions at the Constitutional Convention, had long favored revision of the Articles of Confederation, and as a lawyer was used to debate, he seldom spoke during the proceedings.

Subsequently, Ingersoll held a variety of public positions: member of the Philadelphia common council (1789); attorney general of Pennsylvania (1790-99 and 1811-17); Philadelphia city solicitor (1798-1801); U.S. District Attorney for Pennsylvania (1800-01); and presiding judge of the Philadelphia District Court (1821-22). Meantime, in 1812, he had been the Federalist Vice Presidential candidate, but failed to win election.

While pursuing his public activities, Ingersoll attained distinction in his legal practice. For many years, he handled the affairs of Stephen Girard, one of the nation's leading businessmen. In 1791 Ingersoll began to practice before the U.S. Supreme Court and took part in some memorable cases. Although in both Chisholm v. Georgia (1792) and Hylton v. United States (1796) he represented the losing side, his arguments helped to clarify difficult constitutional issues. He also represented fellowsigner William Blount, a senator, when he was threatened with impeachment in the late 1790s.

Ingersoll's long career ended in 1822, when he died less than a week after his 73d birthday. Survived by three children, he was buried in the cemetery of Philadelphia's First Presbyterian Church.

**Thomas Mifflin,** Quaker, Presbyterian, Pennsylvania[53]

A member of the fourth generation of a Pennsylvania Quaker family who had emigrated from England, Mifflin was born at Philadelphia in 1744, the son of a rich merchant and local politician. He studied at a Quaker school and then at the College of Philadelphia (later part of the University of Pennsylvania), from which he won a diploma at the age of 16 and whose interests he advanced for the rest of his life.

Mifflin then worked for 4 years in a Philadelphia counting house. In 1764 he visited Europe, and the next year entered the mercantile business in Philadelphia with his brother.

In 1767 he wed Sarah Morris. Although he prospered in business, politics enticed him.

In the Pennsylvania legislature (1772-76), Mifflin championed the colonial position against the crown. In 1774 he attended the Continental Congress (1774-76). Meanwhile, he had helped to raise troops and in May 1775 won appointment as a major in the Continental Army, which caused him to be expelled from his Quaker faith. In the summer of 1775 he first became an aide-de-camp to Washington and then Quartermaster General of the Continental Army. Late in 1775 he became a colonel and in May 1776 a brigadier general. Preferring action to administration, after a time he began to perform his quartermaster duties perfunctorily. Nevertheless, he participated directly in the war effort. He took part in the Battles of Long Island, NY, Trenton, NJ, and Princeton, NJ. Furthermore, through his persuasive oratory, he apparently convinced many men not to leave the military service.

In 1777 Mifflin attained the rank of major general but, restive at criticism of his quartermaster activities, he resigned. About the same time, though he later became a friend of Washington, he became involved in the cabal that advanced Gen. Horatio Gates to replace him in command of the Continental Army. In 1777-78 Mifflin sat on the Congressional Board of War. In the latter year, he briefly reentered the military, but continuing attacks on his earlier conduct of the quartermastership soon led him to resign once more.

Mifflin returned immediately to politics. He sat in the state assembly (1778-79) and again in the Continental Congress (1782-84), from December 1783 to the following June as its president. In 1787 he was chosen to take part in the Constitutional Convention. He attended regularly, but made no speeches and did not play a substantial role.

Mifflin continued in the legislature (1785-88 and 17991800); succeeded Franklin as president of the Supreme Executive Council (1788-90); chaired the constitutional convention (178990); and held the governorship (1790-99), during which time he affiliated himself with the emerging Democratic-Republican Party.

Although wealthy most of his life, Mifflin was a lavish spender. Pressure from his creditors forced him to leave Philadelphia in 1799, and he died at Lancaster the next year, aged 56. The Commonwealth of Pennsylvania paid his burial expenses at the local Trinity Lutheran Church.

**Gouverneur Morris,** Episcopalian, Pennsylvania[54]

Gouverneur Morris was born at Morrisania estate, in Westchester (present Bronx) County, NY, in 1752. His family was wealthy and enjoyed a long record of public service. His elder half-brother, Lewis, signed the Declaration of Independence.

Gouverneur was educated by private tutors and at a Huguenot school in New Rochelle. In early life, he lost a leg in a carriage accident. He attended King's College (later Columbia College and University) in New York City, graduating in 1768 at the age of 16. Three years later, after reading law in the city, he gained admission to the bar.

When the Revolution loomed on the horizon, Morris became interested in political affairs. Because of his conservatism, however, he at first feared the movement, which he believed would bring mob rule. Furthermore, some of his family and many of his friends were Loyalists. But, beginning in 1775, for some reason he sided with the Whigs. That same year, representing Westchester County, he took a seat in New York's Revolutionary provincial congress (1775-77). In 1776, when he also served in the militia, along with John Jay and Robert R. Livingston he drafted the first constitution of the state. Subsequently he joined its council of safety (1777).

In 1777-78 Morris sat in the legislature and in 1778-79 in the Continental Congress, where he numbered among the youngest and most brilliant members. During this period, he signed the

Articles of Confederation and drafted instructions for Benjamin Franklin, in Paris, as well as those that provided a partial basis for the treaty ending the War for Independence.

Morris was also a close friend of Washington and one of his strongest congressional supporters.

Defeated in his bid for reelection to Congress in 1779 because of the opposition of Gov. George Clinton's faction, Morris relocated to Philadelphia and resumed the practice of law. This temporarily removed him from the political scene, but in 1781 he resumed his public career when he became the principal assistant to Robert Morris, Superintendent of Finance for the United States, to whom he was unrelated. Gouverneur held this position for 4 years.

Morris emerged as one of the leading figures at the Constitutional Convention. His speeches, more frequent than those by anyone else, numbered 173. Although sometimes presented in a light vein, they were usually substantive. A strong advocate of nationalism and aristocratic rule, he served on many committees, including those on postponed matters and style, and stood in the thick of the decision-making process. Above all, it was apparently he who actually drafted the Constitution. Morris subsequently left public life for a time to devote his attention to business. Having purchased the family home from his halfbrother, Lewis, he moved back to New York. Afterward, in 1789, Gouverneur joined in a business venture with Robert Morris, and traveled to France, where he witnessed the beginnings of the French Revolution.

Morris was to remain in Europe for about a decade. In 1790-91 he undertook a diplomatic mission to London to try to negotiate some of the outstanding problems between the United States and Great Britain. The mission failed, but in 1792 Washington appointed him as Minister to France, to replace Thomas Jefferson. Morris was recalled 2 years later but did not come home. Instead, he traveled extensively in Europe for more than 4 years, during which time he handled his complicated business affairs and contemplated the complex political situation.

Morris returned to the United States in 1799. The next year, he was elected to finish an unexpired term in the U.S. Senate. An ardent Federalist, he was defeated in his bid for reelection in 1802 and left office the following year.

Morris retired to a glittering life at Morrisania, where he had built a new residence. In 1809 he married Anne Cary (Carey) Randolph of Virginia, and they had one son. During his last years, he continued to speak out against the Democratic-Republicans and violently opposed the War of 1812. In the years 1810-13 he served as chairman of the Erie Canal Commission.

Morris died at Morrisania in 1816 at the age of 64 and was buried at St. Anne's Episcopal Churchyard, in the Bronx, New York City.

**Robert Morris,** Episcopalian, Pennsylvania[55]

Robert Morris was born at or near Liverpool, England, in 1734. When he reached 13 years of age, he emigrated to Maryland to join his father, a tobacco exporter at Oxford, Md. After brief schooling at Philadelphia, the youth obtained employment with Thomas and Charles Willing's well-known shipping-banking firm. In 1754 he became a partner and for almost four decades was one of the company's directors as well as an influential Philadelphia citizen. Wedding Mary White at the age of 35, he fathered five sons and two daughters.

During the Stamp Act turmoil in 1765, Morris joined other merchants in protest, but not until the outbreak of hostilities a decade later did he fully commit himself to the Revolution. In 1775 the Continental Congress contracted with his firm to import arms and ammunition, and he was elected to the Pennsylvania council of safety (1775-76), the committee of correspondence, the provincial assembly (1775-76), the legislature (177678), and the Continental Congress (1775-78). In the last body, on July 1, 1776, he voted against independence, which he personally considered premature, but the next day he purposely absented himself to facilitate an affirmative ballot by his delegation.

Morris, a key congressman, specialized in financial affairs and military procurement. Although he and his firm profited handsomely, had it not been for his assiduous labors the Continental

Army would probably have been forced to demobilize. He worked closely with General Washington, wheedled money and supplies from the states, borrowed money in the face of overwhelming difficulties, and on occasion even obtained personal loans to further the war cause.

Immediately following his congressional service, Morris sat for two more terms in the Pennsylvania legislature (1778-81). During this time, Thomas Paine and others attacked him for profiteering in Congress, which investigated his accounts and vindicated him. Nevertheless, his reputation suffered.

Morris embarked on the most dramatic phase of his career by accepting the office of Superintendent of Finance (1781-84) under the Articles of Confederation. Congress, recognizing the perilous state of the nation's finances and its impotence to provide remedies, granted him dictatorial powers and acquiesced to his condition that he be allowed to continue his private commercial enterprises. He slashed all governmental and military expenditures, personally purchased army and navy supplies, tightened accounting procedures, prodded the states to fulfill quotas of money and supplies, and when necessary strained his personal credit by issuing notes over his own signature or borrowing from friends.

To finance Washington's Yorktown campaign in 1781, in addition to the above techniques, Morris obtained a sizable loan from France. He used part of it, along with some of his own fortune, to organize the Bank of North America, chartered that December. The first government-incorporated bank in the United States, it aided war financing.

Although Morris was reelected to the Pennsylvania legislature for 1785-86, his private ventures consumed most of his time. In the latter year, he attended the Annapolis Convention, and the following year the Constitutional Convention, where he sympathized with the Federalists but was, for a man of his eminence, strangely silent. Although in attendance at practically every meeting, he spoke only twice in debates and did not serve on any committees. In 1789, declining Washington's offer of appointment as the first Secretary of the Treasury, he took instead a U.S. Senate seat (178995).

During the later years of his public life, Morris speculated wildly, often on overextended credit, in lands in the West and at the site of Washington, DC. To compound his difficulties, in 1794 he began constructing on Philadelphia's Chestnut Street a mansion designed by Maj. Pierre Charles L'Enfant. Not long thereafter, Morris attempted to escape creditors by retreating to The Hills, the country estate along the Schuylkill River on the edge of Philadelphia that he had acquired in 1770.

Arrested at the behest of creditors in 1798 and forced to abandon completion of the mansion, thereafter known in its unfinished state as "Morris' Folly," Morris was thrown into the Philadelphia debtor's prison, where he was nevertheless well treated. By the time he was released in 1801, under a federal bankruptcy law, however, his property and fortune had vanished, his health had deteriorated, and his spirit had been broken. He lingered on in poverty and obscurity, living in a simple Philadelphia home on an annuity obtained for his wife by fellow-signer Gouverneur Morris.

Robert Morris died in 1806 in his 73d year and was buried in the yard of Christ Church.


**James Wilson,** Episcopalian, Presbyterian, Pennsylvania[56]

Wilson was born in 1741 or 1742 at Carskerdo, near St. Andrews, Scotland, and educated at the universities of St. Andrews, Glasgow, and Edinburgh. He then emigrated to America, arriving in the midst of the Stamp Act agitations in 1765. Early the next year, he accepted a position as Latin tutor at the College of Philadelphia (later part of the University of Pennsylvania) but almost immediately abandoned it to study law under John Dickinson.

In 1768, the year after his admission to the Philadelphia bar, Wilson set up practice at Reading, Pa. Two years later, he moved westward to the Scotch-Irish settlement of Carlisle, and the following year he took a bride, Rachel Bird. He specialized in land law and built up a broad clientele. On borrowed capital, he also began to speculate in land. In some way he managed, too, to lecture on English literature at the College of Philadelphia, which had awarded him an honorary master of arts degree in 1766.

Wilson became involved in Revolutionary politics. In 1774 he took over chairmanship of the Carlisle committee of correspondence, attended the first provincial assembly, and completed preparation of Considerations on the Nature and Extent of the Legislative Authority of the British Parliament. This tract circulated widely in England and America and established him as a Whig leader.

The next year, Wilson was elected to both the provincial assembly and the Continental Congress, where he sat mainly on military and Indian affairs committees. In 1776, reflecting the wishes of his constituents, he joined the moderates in Congress voting for a 3-week delay in considering Richard Henry Lee's resolution of June 7 for independence. On the July 1 and 2 ballots on the issue, however, he voted in the affirmative and signed the Declaration of Independence on August 2.

Wilson's strenuous opposition to the republican Pennsylvania constitution of 1776, besides indicating a switch to conservatism on his part, led to his removal from Congress the following year. To avoid the clamor among his frontier constituents, he repaired to Annapolis during the winter of 177778 and then took up residence in Philadelphia.

Wilson affirmed his newly assumed political stance by closely identifying with the aristocratic and conservative republican groups, multiplying his business interests, and accelerating his land speculation. He also took a position as Advocate General for France in America (1779-83), dealing with commercial and maritime matters, and legally defended Loyalists and their sympathizers.

In the fall of 1779, during a period of inflation and food shortages, a mob which included many militiamen and was led by radical constitutionalists, set out to attack the republican leadership. Wilson was a prime target. He and some 35 of his colleagues barricaded themselves in his home at Third and Walnut Streets, thereafter known as "Fort Wilson." During a brief skirmish, several people on both sides were killed or wounded. The shock cooled sentiments and pardons were issued all around, though major political battles over the commonwealth constitution still lay ahead.

During 1781 Congress appointed Wilson as one of the directors of the Bank of North America, newly founded by his close associate and legal client Robert Morris. In 1782, by which time the conservatives had regained some of their power, the former was reelected to Congress, and he also served in the period 1785-87.

Wilson reached the apex of his career in the Constitutional Convention (1787), where his influence was probably second only to that of Madison. Rarely missing a session, he sat on the Committee of Detail and in many other ways applied his excellent knowledge of political theory to convention problems. Only Gouverneur Morris delivered more speeches.

That same year, overcoming powerful opposition, Wilson led the drive for ratification in Pennsylvania, the second state to endorse the instrument. The new commonwealth constitution, drafted in 1789-90 along the lines of the U.S. Constitution, was primarily Wilson's work and represented the climax of his 14-year fight against the constitution of 1776.

For his services in the formation of the federal government, though Wilson expected to be appointed Chief Justice of the Supreme Court, in 1789 President Washington named him as an associate justice. He was chosen that same year as the first law professor at the College of Philadelphia. Two years later he began an official digest of the laws of Pennsylvania, a project he never completed, though he carried on for a while after funds ran out.

Wilson, who wrote only a few opinions, did not achieve the success on the Supreme Court that his capabilities and experience promised. Indeed, during those years he was the object of much criticism and barely escaped impeachment. For one thing, he tried to influence the enactment of legislation in Pennsylvania favorable to land speculators. Between 1792 and 1795 he also made huge but unwise land investments in western New York and Pennsylvania, as well as in Georgia. This did not stop him from conceiving a grandiose but ill-fated scheme, involving vast sums of European capital, for the recruitment of European colonists and their settlement in the West. Meantime, in 1793, as a widower with six children, he remarried to Hannah Gray; their one son died in infancy.

Four years later, to avoid arrest for debt, the distraught Wilson moved from Philadelphia to Burlington, NJ. The next year, apparently while on federal circuit court business, he arrived at Edenton, NC, in a state of acute mental stress and was taken into the home of James Iredell, a fellow Supreme Court justice. He died there within a few months. Although first buried at Hayes Plantation near Edenton, his remains were later reinterred in the yard of Christ Church at Philadelphia.

# Rhode Island

*Rhode Island did not send any delegates to the Constitutional Convention*

## Religious Affiliation of the Delegates to the Continental Convention[8]

Like the 55 delegates who attended the Constitutional Convention, the 39 signers as a whole were a distinguished body of men who represented an excellent cross section of 18th-century American leadership. Almost all of them were well-educated men of means who were dominant in their communities and States, and many were also prominent in national affairs. Virtually every one had taken part in the Revolution; at least 23 had served in the Continental forces, most of them in positions of command.

# The Signers of the Constitution

| Religious Affiliation | Number of Delegates |
|---|---|
| Episcopalian/Anglicans | 23 |
| Presbyterians | 12 |
| Congregationalist | 6 |
| Quaker | 3 |
| Catholic | 2 |
| Methodist | 2 |
| Lutheran | 2 |
| Total | 39* |

*Total religions listed are actually 50, since some listed two religious affiliations.

# The Non-Signers of the Constitution

| Religious Affiliation | Number of Delegates |
|---|---|
| Episcopalian/Anglicans | 8 |
| Presbyterians | 4 |
| Congregationalist | 2 |
| Dutch Reformed | 2 |
| Total | 16 |
| Total Delegates | 55 |

http://thomaslegion.net/listofsignersoftheunitedstatesconstitution.html#sthash.b18nmXlr.dpuf

There are many books on the Constitution available. Excellent sources for such material can be found at David Barton's www.WallBuilders.com and William Federer's www.americanminute.com. You will be interested in Federer's "America's God and Country, Encyclopedia of Quotations" (FAME Publishing, Inc. Coppell, TX. 1994). See Appendix B for some of the available materials from WallBuilders and American Minute.

In addition, there are several excellent lectures available on-line from Hillsdale College. All course lectures are archived and available to view at your convenience at Appendix C: https://online.hillsdale. edu/login.

# CHAPTER 7

## The Bill of Rights[1]

The call for a bill of rights had been the anti-Federalists' most powerful weapon. Attacking the proposed Constitution for its vagueness and lack of specific protection against tyranny, Patrick Henry asked the Virginia convention, "What can avail your specious, imaginary balances, your rope dancing, chain rattling, ridiculous ideal checks and contrivances." The anti-Federalists, demanding a more concise, unequivocal Constitution, one that laid out for all to see the right of the people and limitations of the power of government, claimed that the brevity of the document only revealed its inferior nature. Richard Henry Lee despaired at the lack of provisions to protect "those essential rights of mankind without which liberty cannot exist." Trading the old government for the new without such a bill of rights, Lee argued, would be trading Scylla for Charybdis.

A bill of rights had been barely mentioned in the Philadelphia convention, most delegates holding that the fundamental rights of individuals had been secured in the state constitutions. James Wilson maintained that a bill of rights was superfluous because all power not expressly delegated to the new government was reserved to the people. It was clear, however, that in this argument the anti-Federalists held the upper hand. Even Thomas Jefferson, generally in favor of the new government, wrote to Madison that a bill of rights was "what the people are entitled to against every government on earth."

By the fall of 1788 Madison had been convinced that not only was a bill of rights necessary to ensure acceptance of the Constitution but that it would have positive effects. He wrote, on October 17, that such "fundamental maxims of free Government" would be "a good ground for an appeal to the sense of community" against potential oppression and would "counteract the impulses of interest and passion."

Madison's support of the bill of rights was of critical significance. One of the new representatives from Virginia to the First Federal Congress, as established by the new Constitution, he worked tirelessly to persuade the House to enact amendments.

Defusing the anti-Federalists' objections to the Constitution, Madison was able to shepherd through 17 amendments in the early months of the Congress, a list that was later trimmed to 12 in the Senate. On October 2, 1789, President Washington sent to each of the states a copy of the 12 amendments adopted by the Congress in September. By December 15, 1791, three-fourths of the states had ratified the 10 amendments now so familiar to Americans as the "Bill of Rights."

Benjamin Franklin told a French correspondent in 1788 that the formation of the new government had been like a game of dice, with many players of diverse prejudices and interests unable to make any uncontested moves. Madison wrote to Jefferson that the welding of these clashing interests was "a task more difficult than can be well conceived by those who were not concerned in the execution of it." When the delegates left Philadelphia after the convention, few, if any, were convinced that the Constitution they had approved outlined the ideal form of government for the country. But late in his life James Madison scrawled out another letter, one never addressed. In it he declared that no government can be perfect, and "that which is the least imperfect is therefore the best government."

# CHAPTER 8

---◆--- ••◆•• ---◆---

## *The Individual States' Constitutions*[1]

The Government In The United States Before The U.s. Constitution Was the Articles of Confederation and Perpetual Union, ratified by the States, March 1, 1781.

Signed by such statesmen as John Hancock and Samuel Adams, it was an attempt to loosely knit the thirteen States together, leaving most of the authority under each individual State's Constitution.

Lincoln referred to "The Articles of Confederation and Perpetual Union" in his First Inaugural Address:

> "Union...thirteen States expressly plighted and engaged that it should be perpetual, by The Articles of Confederation."

The Articles declared: "Whereas the delegates of the United States of America in Congress assembled did on the fifteenth day of November in the **Year of Our Lord** 1777, and in the second year of the independence of America agree on certain Articles of Confederation and Perpetual Union between the States.... The said states hereby severally enter into a firm **league of friendship** with each other, for their common defense, the security of their liberties, and their mutual and general welfare, binding themselves to assist each other, against all force...or attacks made upon them...on account of **religion**, sovereignty, trade, or any other pretense."

The Articles end with the line: "It has pleased **the Great Governor of the World** to incline the hearts of the Legislatures we respectively represent in Congress, to approve of and to authorize us to ratify the said Articles of Confederation."

The Articles of Confederation were ratified by the States.

**Virginia** was the first to ratify.

1776, CONSTITUTION OF VIRGINIA, "BILL OF RIGHTS, SECTION 16: That **religion**, or the duty which we owe to our **Creator**, and the manner of discharging it, can be directed only by reason and conviction, not by force or violence; and therefore all men are equally entitled to the free exercise of **religion**, according to the dictates of conscience; and that it is the mutual duty of all to practice **Christian forbearance**, love, and charity towards each other."

**South Carolina** was the 2nd to ratify.

1778, CONSTITUTION OF SOUTH CAROLINA, "PREAMBLE. We, the people of the State of South Carolina...grateful to **God** for our liberties, do ordain and establish this Constitution... ARTICLE 3...Senate and House... shall... choose...a governor and commander-in-chief, a lieutenant-governor...and a privy council, all of the **Protestant religion**... ARTICLE 12. No person shall be eligible to a seat in the said Senate unless he be of the **Protestant religion**... 13...No person shall be eligible to sit in the House of Representatives unless he be of the **Protestant religion**... 38. All persons and **religious societies** who acknowledge that there is one **God**, and a future state of rewards and punishments, and that **God** is publicly to be worshipped, shall be freely tolerated. The **Christian Protestant religion** shall be deemed...the established religion of this State. That all denominations of **Christian Protestants** in this State...shall enjoy equal **religious** and civil privileges... And that whenever fifteen or more male persons, not under twenty-one years of age, professing the **Christian Protestant religion**, and agreeing to unite themselves in a society for the purposes of **religious worship**, they shall...be constituted a **Church**... That every **society of Christians**...so petitioning shall have agreed to and subscribed in a book the following five articles... (See Locke's Constitution, Article 97-100): 1. That there is **one eternal God**, and a future state of rewards and punishments. 2. That **God** is publicly to be worshipped. 3. That the **Christian religion is the true religion** 4. That the **Holy Scriptures of the Old and New Testaments** are of Divine inspiration, and are the rule of faith and practice. 5. That it is lawful and the duty of every man being thereunto called by those that govern, to bear witness to the truth...No person shall officiate as minister of any established **Church**...until the minister...shall have made and subscribed to the following declaration, over and above the aforesaid five articles, viz: That he is determined by **God's grace** out of the **Holy Scriptures**, to instruct the people committed to his charge, and to teach nothing as required of necessity to **eternal salvation** but that which he shall be persuaded may be concluded and proved from the **Scripture**; That he will use both public and private admonitions, as well to the sick as to the whole within his cure, as need shall require and occasion shall be given, and that he will be diligent in prayers, and in reading of the same; That he will be diligent to frame and fashion his own self and his family according to the **doctrine of Christ,** and to make both himself and them, as much as in him lieth, wholesome examples and patterns to the **flock of Christ.**

**New York** was the 3rd to ratify.

1777, CONSTITUTION OF NEW YORK: "Whereas the Delegates of the United American States...solemnly... declare, in the words following; viz: '...Laws of nature and of nature's **God** entitle them...All men are created equal; that they are endowed by their **Creator** with certain unalienable rights...Appealing to the **Supreme Judge of the world** for the rectitude of our intentions...with a firm reliance on the protection of **Divine Providence...'** 7...Every person who now is a freeman...on or before the fourteenth day of October, in the **Year of Our Lord** one thousand seven hundred and seventy-five...shall be entitled to vote... 38. This convention doth further...declare, that the free exercise and enjoyment of **religious profession and worship**, without discrimination or preference, shall forever hereafter be allowed, within this State, to all mankind: Provided, That the liberty of conscience, hereby granted, shall not be so construed as to excuse **acts of licentiousness."**

**Rhode Island** was the 4ᵗʰ to ratify.

1663 CHARTER OF RHODE ISLAND AND PROVIDENCE PLANTATIONS (served as the State's Constitution till 1842) "That they, pursuing...**religious** intentions, of **Godly edifying** themselves, and one another, in the **Holy Christian faith and worship**...Together with the gaining over and **conversion of the poor ignorant Indian natives**, in those parts of America, to the sincere profession and obedience of the same **faith and worship**... by the good **Providence of God**, from whom the Plantations have taken their name...there may, in due time, by the **blessing of God** upon their endeavors, be laid a sure foundation of happiness to all America...that among our English subjects, with a full liberty in **religious concernements**; and that **true piety** rightly grounded upon **Gospel principles**, will give the best and greatest security... to secure them in the free exercise and enjoyment of all their civil and **religious rights**, appertaining to them, as our loving subjects; and to preserve unto them that liberty, in the **true Christian faith** and **worship of** God...and because some of the people and inhabitants of the same colony cannot, in their private opinions, conform to the...ceremonies of the Church of England...our royal will and pleasure is, that no person within the said colony...shall be any wise molested, punished, disquieted, or called in question, for any differences in opinion in **matters of religion**...not using this liberty to **licentiousness and profaneness**...that they may be in the better capacity to defend themselves, in their just rights and liberties against **all the enemies of the Christian faith**...and...

by their good life and orderly conversations, they may win and invite the native Indians of the country to the knowledge and obedience of the **only true God, and Savior of mankind."** Connecticut was the 5th to ratify.

**Connecticut** was the 5th to ratify:

1662 CHARTER OF CONNECTICUT (served as the State's Constitution till 1818) "Our said people inhabitants there, may be so **religiously,** peaceably and civilly governed, as their good life and orderly **conversation may win and invite the natives** of the country to the knowledge and obedience of the **only true GOD, and the Savior of Mankind,** and the **Christian Faith,** which...is the only and principal End of this Plantation."

**Georgia** was the 6th to ratify.

1777, CONSTITUTION OF GEORGIA, "ARTICLE 6: The representatives shall be chosen out of the residents in each county...and they shall be of the **Protestant religion...** ARTICLE 14. Every person entitled to vote shall take the following oath...'I, A B. do voluntarily and solemnly swear (or affirm, as the case may be) that I do owe true allegiance to this State, and will support the constitution thereof; So Help Me **God.**'"

**New Hampshire** was the 7th to ratify.

1784, NEW HAMPSHIRE CONSTITUTION, "PART 1, ARTICLE 6: "As **morality and piety,** rightly grounded on **evangelical principles** will give the best and greatest security to government...the people of this state...empower the legislature to...make adequate provision...for the support and maintenance of **public Protestant teachers of piety, religion and morality...**Every denomination of **Christians** demeaning themselves quietly, and as good subjects of the state, shall be equally under the protection of the law... PART 2-THE FORM OF GOVERNMENT, SENATE: That no person shall be capable of being elected a senator who is not of the **Protestant religion...** HOUSE OF REPRESENTATIVES...Every member of the house of representatives... shall be of the **Protestant religion**. EXECUTIVE POWER-PRESIDENT. The President shall be chosen annually; and no person shall be eligible to this office, less.. he shall be of the **Protestant religion**."

**Pennsylvania** was the 8th to ratify.

1776, CONSTITUTION OF PENNSYLVANIA: "Government ought to...enable the individuals...to enjoy their natural rights, and the other blessings which the **Author of Existence** has bestowed upon man... A DECLARATION OF THE RIGHTS 2. That all men have a natural and unalienable right to **worship Almighty God** according to the dictates of their own consciences...Nor can any man, who acknowledges the being of a **God**, be justly deprived or abridged of any civil right... FRAME OF GOVERNMENT, SECTION 10. Each member, before he takes his seat, shall make... the following declaration, viz: I do believe in **one God, the Creator and Governor of the Universe, the Rewarder of the good and the Punisher of the wicked**. And I do acknowledge the **Scriptures of the Old and New Testament to be given by Divine Inspiration**. And no further or other **religious test** shall ever hereafter be required... SECTION 45. Laws for the **encouragement of virtue, and prevention of vice and immorality**, shall be made and constantly kept in force...All religious societies...shall be encouraged."

**Massachusetts** was the 9th to ratify.

1780, CONSTITUTION OF MASSACHUSETTS: "We, therefore, the people of Massachusetts, acknowledging, with grateful hearts, the goodness of the **Great Legislator of the Universe**, in affording us, in the course of **His Providence**, an opportunity, deliberately and peaceably... of forming a new constitution of civil government... PART THE FIRST-A DECLARATION OF RIGHTS, ARTICLE 2. It is the right as well as the duty of all men in society, publicly, and at stated seasons to worship the **Supreme Being, the great Creator and Preserver of the Universe**... ARTICLE 3...Civil government, essentially depend upon **piety, religion and morality**; and as these cannot be generally diffused through a community, but by the institution of the Public **worship of God**... The people of this commonwealth... authorize...the public **worship of God**, and for the support and maintenance of **public Protestant teachers of piety, religion and morality**...And every denomination of **Christians**, demeaning themselves peaceably, and as good subjects of the commonwealth, shall be equally under the protection of the law... PART THE SECOND-THE FRAME OF GOVERNMENT, CHAPTER 2, EXECUTIVE POWER, SECTION 1, THE GOVERNOR, ARTICLE 2: The governor shall be chosen annually; and no person shall be eligible to this office, unless...he shall declare himself to be of the **Christian religion**... CHAPTER 6, OATHS...ARTICLE 1. "Any person chosen governor, lieutenant governor, counselor, senator or representative, and accepting the trust, shall...make...the following declaration, viz.- 'I, A. B., do declare, that I believe the **Christian religion**, and have a firm persuasion of its truth.'"

**North Carolina** was the 10ᵗʰ to ratify.

1776, CONSTITUTION OF NORTH CAROLINA, "DECLARATION OF RIGHTS, ARTICLE 19. That all men have a natural and unalienable right to **worship Almighty God** according to the dictates of their own consciences. FORM OF GOVERNMENT, ARTICLE 32. That no person, who shall deny the being of **God** or the **truth of the Protestant religion**, or the **Divine authority either of the Old or New Testaments**, or who shall hold **religious principles** incompatible with the freedom and safety of the State, shall be capable of holding any office... ARTICLE 34. That there shall be no establishment of any One **religious Church or denomination** in this State, in preference to any other."

**New Jersey** was the 11ᵗʰ to ratify.

1776, CONSTITUTION OF NEW JERSEY, "ARTICLE 18: That no person shall ever...be deprived of the inestimable privilege of

**worshipping Almighty God** in a manner agreeable to the dictates of his own conscience... ARTICLE 19...No **Protestant** inhabitant of this Colony shall be denied the enjoyment of any civil right...but that all persons, professing a belief in the faith of **any Protestant sect**, who shall demean themselves peaceably under the government...shall be capable of being elected into any office."

**Delaware** was the 12ᵗʰ to ratify.

1776, CONSTITUTION OF DELAWARE, "ARTICLE 22. Every... member of either house...before taking his seat...shall... make...the following declaration, to wit: 'I...do profess faith in **God the Father, and in Jesus Christ His only Son, and in the Holy Ghost, one God, blessed for evermore**; and I do acknowledge the **Holy Scriptures of the Old and New Testament to be given by Divine inspiration**.' ARTICLE 29. There shall be no establishment of any **religious sect** in this State in preference to another... DECLARATION OF RIGHTS, ARTICLE 2.

That all Men have a natural and unalienable Right to **worship Almighty God** according to the Dictates of their own Consciences... ARTICLE 3. That all Persons professing the **Christian Religion** ought forever to enjoy equal Rights and Privileges in this State."

**Maryland** was the 13ᵗʰ to ratify.

1776, CONSTITUTION OF MARYLAND, "ARTICLE 33: It is the duty of every man to **worship God** in such manner as he thinks most acceptable to him; all persons, professing the **Christian religion**, are equally entitled to protection in their **religious liberty**...yet the Legislature may, in their discretion, lay a general and equal tax for the support of the **Christian religion**; leaving to each individual the power of appointing the payment...to the support of...his own denomination... ARTICLE 35. That no other test or qualification ought to be required, on admission to any office...than such oath of...fidelity to this State...

and a declaration of a belief in the **Christian religion**. ARTICLE 55. That every person, appointed to any office...shall...take the following oath; to wit: 'I, A. B., do swear, that I do not hold myself bound in allegiance to the King of Great Britain, and that I will be faithful, and bear true allegiance to the State of Maryland;' and shall also subscribe a declaration of his belief in the **Christian religion**."

**Vermont** was its own republic in 1777, till it became the *14th State* in 1791, approved by President George Washington.

1777, CONSTITUTION OF VERMONT: "Whereas, all government ought...to enable the individuals...to enjoy their natural rights, and the other blessings which the **Author of Existence** has bestowed upon man... CHAPTER 1, A DECLARATION OF RIGHTS: 3. That all men have a natural and unalienable right to **worship ALMIGHTY GOD**, according to the dictates of their own consciences and understanding, regulated by the **word of GOD**... Nor can any man who professes the **Protestant religion**, be justly deprived or abridged of any civil right...nevertheless, every sect or denomination of people ought to **observe the Sabbath, or the Lord's Day**, and keep up, and support, some sort of **religious worship**, which to them shall seem most agreeable to the revealed **Will of GOD**... CHAPTER 2, PLAN OR FRAME OF GOVERN-MENT, SECTION 9: And each member, before he takes his seat, shall make...the following declaration, viz. 'I _____ do believe in **one God, the Creator and Governor of the Universe, the Rewarder of the good and Punisher of the wicked.** And I do acknowledge the **Scriptures of the Old and New Testament to be given by Divine inspiration**, and own and profess the Protestant religion.' And no further or other **religious test** shall ever, hereafter, be required of any civil officer or magistrate in this State."

# CHAPTER 9

## *So, what now?*

Of the thirteen colonies, all thirteen recognized the Supreme Being, eleven stated they were based on 'Christian Religion' and five required candidates for office be Protestant Christians.

Almost all of the Founding Fathers recognized "Morality, Religion and Knowledge" to be the keystone of the American experience, which is reflected in the individual state Constitutions.

For one last time, you are urged: *"A nation which does not remember what it was yesterday, does not know what it is today, nor what it is trying to do. We are trying to do a futile thing if we don't know where we have come from or what we have been about"* (President Woodrow Wilson). Now that you have had a glimpse into the structure of who and what went into the foundation of the united States of America, two simple questions remain: 1) Which doctor would you entrust your family member to?, and 2) Do you understand the reasons why you must be fully aware of the functioning of this country, before you commit your vote to just any candidate?

So, does your one vote really count? Let's take a look at what the late Paul Harvey said regarding one vote:

"Over 200 million Americans are eligible to vote this year. Less than half will. Plato said it: The penalty good men pay for indifference to public affairs is to be ruled by evil men. So your vote is important. Historically, you use it...or you lose it. If you're not sure for whom you should vote, turn to a newspaper you can trust. Because everything we've won in ten wars at the point of a gun can be taken away one vote at a time. Edmund Burke said it another way: 'All that is necessary for the forces of evil to win in this world is for enough good men to do nothing.'"

While it may be difficult to find a reputable newspaper today, there are numerous sources where you can find both sides of an issue. For example, Barton states in his book, *Keys to Good Government; According to the Founding Fathers*, "Always examine the values of **each** candidate running, regardless of party affiliation."[1] He also includes that on *www.WallBuilders. com*, where you will find several links to "help identify the specific beliefs of candidates on numbers of important issues, especially those linked to Biblical values."

The main point is to study and learn the standards of our republic as established in The Declaration of Independence, The Constitution and the Bill of Rights. Then study the candidates to determine whether their positions agree with those standards, work for the selected candidate and vote. It really is that simple.

The most difficult part will be the study of what the Founding Fathers intended. To assist you a list of books and DVDs is included as Appendix B, to make the job easier.

In the same book, *Keys to Good Government*, Barton quotes Rev. Charles Finney,

"The time has come that Christians must vote for honest men and take consistent ground in politics... God cannot sustain this free and blessed country which we love and pray for unless the Church will take right ground... Christians seem to act as if they

think God does not see what they do in politics. But
I tell you He does see it, and He will bless or curse
this nation according to the course [Christians]
take."[2]

<u>You</u> are creating the future of the United States by your
action, or inaction. Which doctor did you say you wanted your
child and grandchild to have? The 'doctor' and their future is in
**your** hands. So, what now?

This compendium of information was collected to show the
reader several points

1. The Founding Fathers were real people who lived, sacrificed
   and died for their beliefs; not simply names scratched into
   history's log of humanity.
2. They used the Bible as the basis for the creation of the United
   States.
3. It was not numbers, but dedication and adherence to the
   Scriptures that allowed them to create the most unique form
   of government in history.
4. God will provide the 'miracles' when He is obeyed.

What is the future for this amazing creation, the United States
of America?

The condition of the colonies, as colonies, has been presented.
The travail which occurred as the delegates strove to create the
Declaration of Independence is made available. A copy of the
Declaration, with the reasons for declaring independence, as
listed by historian B. J. Lossing (1813 – 1891) is included. The
reasons Lossing gives are from a historian who lived during the
period following the Declaration, not a modern adaptation. The
background of the signers is listed. The cost to the signers for
standing against Britain are also listed.

Since there are so many excellent sources for the explanation
of what the Constitution means, only the references, rather than
the explanation, are shown. The background of those signing

approval of the Constitution is listed, as well as those who were involved with its creation who did not sign it.

Portions of the original thirteen colonies' Constitutions (plus Vermont in 1777) are shown to show their acknowledgement and dependence on Christianity as the basis for their 'rule of law'.

Finally, there is a test to allow the reader to quantify their knowledge of the United States format.

This work is not an end-in-all work. It is similar to giving one a sample of a product in a supermarket, with the hope the receiver will buy the product. In this case, the product to be bought is a desire of the reader to learn more about what the original intent of the Founding Fathers was in the creation of what the US Supreme Court would later say (the United States) ".... is a Christian nation."

The finding stated, in part;

"There is no dissonance in these declarations. There is a universal language pervading them all, having one meaning.

"They affirm and reaffirm that **this is a religious nation**. These are not individual sayings, declarations of private persons. They are organic utterances. They speak the voice of the entire people. While because of a general recognition of this truth the question has seldom been presented to the courts, yet we find that in Updegraph v. Com., 11 Serg. & R. 394, 400, it was decided that, **'Christianity, general Christianity, is, and always has been, a part of the common law of Pennsylvania."**[3] *(Emphasis added)*

So, what now?

In Judges 6 & 7, the story of Gideon is told. 32,000 men heeded Gideon's call to do battle against Israel's enemies. God told Gideon to let those who were afraid go home and 22,000 left, leaving 10,000. God said that was still too many and had Gideon reduce the number to 300. God told Gideon, if a large number went against the enemy, His (God's) hand in the results would not be recognized.

The enemy numbered 135,000. Following God's leading, 120,000 of the enemy were killed and the other 15,000 were disbanded. (300 divided by 120,000 = 2%).

Fast forward to the War for Independence. The census for 1790 listed approximately 3,900,000. The leadership of those seeking independence from Britain numbered under 1,000.

(1,000 divided by 3,900,000 = 2.6%). It would appear that the leadership of under 1,000 determined the fate of 3,900,000 colonists in the creation of an independent nation. Quite a feat. As an aside, Great Britain's census figures for 1790 was approximate 8,000,000.

(http://www.thepotteries.org/dates/census.htm).

In spite of error after error in battles by the 'Yankee Doodlers', their side prevailed and liberty was achieved. Why? How?

Many contend their reliance on God played a major part in the creation of the unique new nation. They point to the numerous times of prayer, fasting and 'humiliation' the colonists incorporated into their lives. This supplication to God has appeared time and time again with God answering their prayers

Also not to be overlooked is 'The Great Awakening' (1730's – 1740's):

"Not all American ministers were swept up by the Age of Reason. In the 1730s, a religious revival swept through the British American colonies. Jonathan Edwards, the Yale minister who refused to convert to the Church of England, became concerned that New Englanders were becoming far too concerned with worldly matters. It seemed to him that people found the pursuit of wealth to be more important than John Calvin's religious principles. Some were even beginning to suggest that predestination was wrong and that good works might save a soul. Edwards barked out from the pulpit against these notions. "God was an angry judge, and humans were sinners!" he declared. He spoke with such fury and conviction that people flocked to listen. This sparked what became known as the GREAT AWAKENING in the American colonies.

"George Whitefield was a minister from Britain who toured the American colonies. An actor by training, he would shout the word of God, weep with sorrow, and tremble with passion as he delivered his sermons. Colonists flocked by the thousands to hear him speak. He converted slaves and even a few Native Americans. Even religious skeptic Benjamin Franklin emptied his coin purse after hearing him speak in Philadelphia.

"Soon much of America became divided. Awakening, or **NEW LIGHT**, preachers set up their own schools and churches throughout the colonies. Princeton University was one such school. The **OLD LIGHT** ministers refused to accept this new style of worship. Despite the conflict, one surprising result was greater religious toleration. With so many new denominations, it was clear that no one religion would dominate any region.

"Although the Great Awakening was a reaction against the Enlightenment, it was also a long term cause of the Revolution. Before, ministers represented an upper class of sorts. Awakening ministers were not always ordained, breaking down respect for betters. The new faiths that emerged were much more democratic in their approach. The overall message was one of greater equality. The Great Awakening was also a "national" occurrence. It was the first major event that all the colonies could share, helping to break down differences between them. There was no such episode in England, further highlighting variances between Americans and their cousins across the sea. Indeed this religious upheaval had marked political consequences."[2]

The nation has fallen away from their reliance on God and the original commitment to Him. Listing all of those separations is unnecessary. The adherence to Christianity, low level morality, inadequate education and slow destruction of 'The American Way of Life' must be apparent to any objectively thinking person.

What will be the result of this rejection of "Religion, Morality, Knowledge"? One only has to look at what happened when Moses came down from the Mount with the Ten Commandments. That cycle has been repeated time after time in the history of mankind:

The 'Godly' people sin, are rejected by God, repent and return into His grace.

Reading the news and examining our communities, is there any question as to the point in that cycle where we are at this time?

So, what now? As was said, <u>you</u> are creating the future of the United States by your action, or inaction. Which doctor did you say you wanted your child and grandchild to have? The 'doctor' and your offspring's future is in **your** hands.

# APPENDIX A

---◆---

## *Intercollegiate Studies Institute's American Civic Literacy Test American History*

1. **Jamestown, Virginia, was first settled by Europeans during which period?**
   a) 1301-1400
   b) 1401-1500
   c) 1501-1600
   d) 1601-1700
   e) 1701-1800

2. **The Puritans:**
   a) opposed all wars on moral grounds.
   b) stressed the sinfulness of all humanity.
   c) believed in complete religious freedom.
   d) colonized Utah under the leadership of Brigham Young.
   e) e) were Catholic missionaries escaping religious persecution.

3. **The Constitution of the United States established what form of government?**
   a) Direct democracy
   b) Populism
   c) Indirect democracy
   d) Oligarchy

e) Aristocracy

4. **George Washington's role in America's founding is best characterized as:**
   a) prudent general and statesman.
   b) influential writer on constitutional principles.
   c) leader of the Massachusetts delegation to the Constitutional Congress.
   d) strong advocate for states' rights.
   e) social compact theorist.

5. **Which battle brought the American Revolution to an end?**
   a) Saratoga
   b) Gettysburg
   c) The Alamo
   d) Yorktown
   e) New Orleans

6. **Which of the following are the unalienable rights referred to in the Declaration of Independence?**
   a) Life, liberty, and property
   b) Honor, liberty, and peace
   c) Liberty, health, and community
   d) Life, respect, and equal protection
   e) Life, liberty, and the pursuit of happiness

7. **Which of the following are in correct chronological order?**
   a) The Constitution, the Declaration of Independence, the Articles of Confederation
   b) Fort Sumter, Gettysburg, Appomattox
   c) Cuban Missile Crisis, Sputnik, Bay of Pigs
   d) Mexican-American War, Louisiana Purchase, Spanish-American War
   e) Prohibition, Boston Tea Party, Reconstruction

8. **The phrase that in America there should be a "wall of separation" between church and state appears in:**
   a) George Washington's Farewell Address.
   b) the Mayflower Compact.
   c) the Constitution.
   d) the Declaration of Independence.
   e) Thomas Jefferson's letters.

9. **The War of 1812:**
   a) was a decisive victory for the United States over Spain.
   b) was a stalemate.
   c) established America as the leading power in the world.
   d) enhanced Robert E. Lee's reputation as America's most talented general.
   e) was confined only to sea battles.

10. **The dominant theme in the Lincoln-Douglas debates was:**
   a) treatment of Native Americans.
   b) westward expansion.
   c) whether Illinois should become a state.
   d) prohibition.
   e) slavery and its expansion.

11. **Abraham Lincoln was elected President during which period?**
   a) 1800-1825
   b) 1826-1850
   c) 1851-1875
   d) 1876-1900
   e) 1901-1925

12. **In 1933 Franklin Delano Roosevelt proposed a series of government programs that became known as:**
   a) The Great Society.
   b) The Square Deal.
   c) The New Deal.

d) The New Frontier.

e) supply-side economics.

**13. The struggle between President Andrew Johnson and the Radical Republicans was mainly over:**

a) United States alliances with European nations.

b) the nature and control of Reconstruction.

c) the purchase of Alaska.

d) whether or not to have a tariff.

e) whether slavery should be allowed in the Federal Territories.

**14. During which period was the American Constitution amended to guarantee women the right to vote?**

a) 1850-1875

b) 1876-1900

c) 1901-1925

d) 1926-1950

e) 1951-1975

**15. Which of the following statements is true about abortion?**

a) It was legal in most states in the 1960s.

b) The Supreme Court struck down most legal restrictions on it in Roe v. Wade.

c) The Supreme Court ruled in Plessy v. Ferguson that underage women must notify their parents of an impending abortion.

d) The National Organization for Women has lobbied for legal restrictions on it.

e) It is currently legal only in cases of rape or incest, or to protect the life of the mother.

**16. The end of legal racial segregation in United States schools was most directly the result of:**

a) the Civil War.

b) the Declaration of Independence.

c) the affirmative action policies of the 1980s.

d) Brown v. Board of Education of Topeka.

e) Miranda v. the State of Arizona.

**17. The Manhattan Project developed:**
   a) urban enterprise zones.
   b) equipment to decipher enemy codes.
   c) fighter planes.
   d) the Apollo lunar module.
   e) the atomic bomb.

**18. The line "We hold these truths to be self-evident, that all men are created equal..." is from:**
   a) The Federalist.
   b) the Preamble to the Constitution.
   c) The Communist Manifesto.
   d) the Declaration of Independence.
   e) an inscription on the Statue of Liberty.

**19. In *The Republic*, Plato points to the desirability of:**
   a) tyranny.
   b) democracy.
   c) philosopher kings.
   d) commercial republics.
   e) world government.

**20. A "representative democracy" is a form of government in which:**
   a) all or most citizens govern directly.
   b) a monarch is elected to represent a people.
   c) citizens exhibit wide ethnic and cultural diversity.
   d) a president's cabinet is popularly elected.
   e) those elected by the people govern on their behalf.

**21. The Federalist (or The Federalist Papers) was written to:**
a) support ratification of the U.S. Constitution.
b) oppose ratification of the U.S. Constitution.
c) support America's independence from Britain.
d) oppose America's independence from Britain.
e) support the Missouri Compromise.

**22. The principle of the "separation of powers" suggests that:**
a) legislative, executive, and judicial powers should be dispersed.
b) government becomes more efficient with division of labor.
c) there should always be at least two global superpowers.
d) no single political party should dominate any legislature.
e) courts should formulate policy during periods of Congressional gridlock.

**23. The power of judicial review was established in:**
a) the Constitution.
b) Marbury v. Madison.
c) McCulloch v. Maryland.
d) the Bill of Rights.
e) a Presidential executive order.

**24. What is federalism?**
a) A political party at the time of the Founding
b) A set of essays defending the Constitution
c) A political system where the national government has ultimate power
d) A political system where state and national governments share power
e) The belief that America should be unified with a transcontinental railroad

25. **The common law:**
   a) was ruled unconstitutional by the United States Supreme Court.
   b) is based upon past custom and emerging case law.
   c) was the fundamental law for the Nazis and the Soviets.
   d) is a new form of jurisprudence being tested in Louisiana.
   e) consists of only those statutes approved by popular referendum.

26. **The Declaration of Independence relies most obviously on the political thought of:**
   a) Plato.
   b) Niccolo Machiavelli.
   c) David Hume.
   d) John Locke.
   e) Georg Hegel.

27. **Which statement is a common argument against the claim that "man cannot know things"?**
   a) Professors teach opinion not knowledge.
   b) Appellate judges do not comprehend social justice.
   c) Consensus belief in a democracy always contains error.
   d) Man trusts his ability to know in order to reject his ability to know.
   e) Social scientists cannot objectively rank cultures.

28. **In his "I Have a Dream" speech, Dr. Martin Luther King, Jr.:**
   a) argued for the abolition of slavery.
   b) advocated black separatism.
   c) morally defended affirmative action.
   d) expressed his hopes for racial justice and brotherhood.
   e) proposed that several of America's founding ideas were discriminatory.

29. **Socrates, Plato, Aristotle, and Aquinas would concur that:**
   a) all moral and political truth is relative to one's time and place.
   b) moral ideas are best explained as material accidents or byproducts of evolution.
   c) values originating in one's conscience cannot be judged by others.
   d) Christianity is the only true religion and should rule the state.
   e) certain permanent moral and political truths are accessible to human reason.

30. **The Bill of Rights explicitly prohibits:**
   a) prayer in public school.
   b) discrimination based on race, sex, or religion.
   c) the ownership of guns by private individuals.
   d) establishing an official religion for the United States.
   e) the President from vetoing a line item in a spending bill.

31. **Which author's view of society is presented correctly?**
   a) Edmund Burke argued that society consists of a union of past, present, and future generations.
   b) Adam Smith argued that the division of labor decreases the wealth of nations.
   c) Alexis de Tocqueville argued that voluntary associations are usually dangerous to society.
   d) Max Weber argued that the Jewish work ethic is central to American capitalism.
   e) John Locke defended the divine right of kings.

32. **In 1776, Thomas Paine argued for colonial independence from Britain in:**
   a) the Declaration of Independence.
   b) Common Sense.
   c) Novanglus.

d) A View of the Controversy between Great Britain and Her Colonies.

e) Letter from Birmingham Jail.

**33. Which of the following is NOT among the official powers of Congress?**

a) To declare war

b) To regulate commerce with foreign nations

c) To receive ambassadors

d) To create courts lower than the Supreme Court

e) To approve treaties with foreign nations

**34. The warning to the American people to avoid entangling alliances and involvement in Europe's wars is found in:**

a) President Eisenhower's Farewell Address.

b) President Washington's Farewell Address.

c) Woodrow Wilson's Fourteen Points.

d) The League of Nations Covenant.

e) The Treaty of Versailles of 1919.

**35. The Monroe Doctrine:**

a) discouraged new colonies in the Western hemisphere.

b) proclaimed America's "Manifest Destiny."

c) was the earliest recorded agreement between the United States and France.

d) was America's response to Aleksandra Solzhenitsyn's Gulag Archipelago.

e) resolved border disputes among the thirteen colonies.

**36. According to just-war theory, a just war requires which of the following?**

a) Approval by the International Court of Justice

b) Endorsement by democratic vote

c) A threatening shift in the balance of powers

d) The authority of a legitimate sovereign

e) That no civilian casualties occur

37. **Which of the following was an alliance to resist Soviet expansion:**
a) United Nations.
b) League of Nations.
c) North Atlantic Treaty Organization.
d) Warsaw Pact.
e) Asian Tigers.

38. **What kind of government is a junta?**
a) Military
b) Religious
c) Populist
d) Social democratic
e) Parliamentarian

39. **The question of why democracy leads to well-ordered government in America when disorder prevails in Europe is central to:**
a) Thomas Jefferson's Notes on the State of Virginia.
b) Walt Whitman's Democratic Vistas.
c) John Adams's "Thoughts on Government."
d) Alexis de Tocqueville's Democracy in America.
e) Charles Beard's An Economic Interpretation of the Constitution of the United States.

40. **The United Nations was organized in:**
a) 1953 to combat the power of American corporations.
b) 1945 to promote "international organization."
c) 1937 to deter the spread of Nazism.
d) 1968 to pursue nuclear disarmament.
e) 1961 to curtail global warming.

41. **The major powers at odds with each other in the "Cold War" were the United States and:**
a) Germany.
b) Iran.

c) Vietnam.

d) the Soviet Union.

e) Poland.

**42. How did President Kennedy respond to the Cuban Missile Crisis?**

a) He imposed a naval blockade on Cuba.

b) He landed Cuban exiles at the Bay of Pigs.

c) He sent troops to Cuba to destroy nuclear weapons.

d) He went to Havana to meet with Fidel Castro.

e) He ended all diplomatic communications with the Soviets.

**43. "Balance of power" refers to:**

a) a state that seeks to expand its power generates resistance by other states.

b) states that are militarily powerful tend to acquire strong allies.

c) weaker states tend to "join the winner" in most international conflicts.

d) land and sea powers have tended to balance one another.

e) terrorists conceal their demands and affiliations.

**44. The Gulf of Tonkin Resolution (1964) was significant because it:**

a) ended the war in Korea.

b) gave President Johnson the authority to expand the scope of the Vietnam War.

c) was an attempt to take foreign policy power away from the President.

d) allowed China to become a member of the United Nations.

e) allowed for oil exploration in Southeast Asia.

45. **Which wall was President Reagan referring to when he said, "Mr. Gorbachev, tear down this wall"?**
   a) Kremlin Wall
   b) Wailing Wall
   c) Hadrian's Wall
   d) Great Wall of China
   e) Berlin Wall

46. **Among which of these groups would Saddam Hussein have found his most reliable supporters?**
   a) Islamic Brotherhood
   b) Baath Party
   c) Communist Party
   d) Hamas
   e) Israelis

47. **The stated United States objective of the 1991 Persian Gulf War was to:**
   a) block Soviet expansion in the Middle East.
   b) defend Israel.
   c) overthrow the Iraqi government.
   d) expel Iraqi forces from Kuwait.
   e) recover control of the Suez Canal.

48. **Inflation:**
   a) results from an over-abundance of goods and services.
   b) has not been a problem since the Great Depression.
   c) reduces money's purchasing power even when some prices decrease.
   d) is monitored daily by the Dow Jones Industrial Average.
   e) remains beyond the influence of central banks due to oil price fluctuations.

**49. Free enterprise or capitalism exists insofar as:**

a) experts managing the nation's commerce are appointed by elected officials.

b) individual citizens create, exchange, and control goods and resources.

c) charity, philanthropy, and volunteering decrease.

d) demand and supply are decided through majority vote.

e) Government implements policies that favor businesses over consumers.

**50. Free markets typically secure more economic prosperity than government's centralized planning because:**

a) the price system utilizes more local knowledge of means and ends.

b) markets rely upon coercion, whereas government relies upon voluntary compliance with the law.

c) more tax revenue can be generated from free enterprise.

d) property rights and contracts are best enforced by the market system.

e) government planners are too cautious in spending taxpayers' money.

**51. Which of the following is the best measure of production or output of an economy?**

a) Gross Domestic Product

b) Consumer Price Index

c) Unemployment Rate

d) Prime Rate

e) Exchange Rate

**52. Business profit is:**

a) cost minus revenue.

b) assets minus liabilities.

c) revenue minus expenses.

d) selling price of a stock minus its purchase price.

e) earnings minus assets.

**53. National defense is considered a public good because:**
a) a majority of citizens value it.
b) a resident can benefit from it without directly paying for it.
c) military contracts increase employment opportunities.
d) a majority of citizens support the military during war.
e) airport security personnel are members of the Federal civil service.

**54. Keynesian economists conclude that the recession phase of a business cycle:**
a) involves a lower unemployment rate.
b) occurs when investment spending crowds out consumer spending.
c) can be eliminated by government taxing more than it spends.
d) can be reversed by government spending more than it taxes.
e) can be reversed with higher interest rates.

**55. Over the past forty years, real income among American households has:**
a) remained the same when averaged over all households.
b) involved the rich getting richer and the poor getting poorer.
c) involved the poor getting richer and the rich getting poorer.
d) decreased for the middle class and increased for the upper class.
e) increased for the lower and middle classes and increased most for the upper class.

56. **Why are businesses in two different countries most likely to trade with each other?**
   a) They know that although one business will be hurt from trading, the other will be better off, and they both hope to be the winner.
   b) Businesses are unable to sell their products in their own countries.
   c) Each business expects to be better off as a result of the trade.
   d) Their respective governments require them to do so.
   e) The natural resources of both countries are similar.

57. **The price of movie tickets has increased. According to the law of demand, what is likely to be the result?**
   a) Theaters will sell fewer tickets.
   b) Theaters' revenues will increase.
   c) The quality of movie theaters will improve.
   d) The number of videos rented will decrease.
   e) Popcorn purchases at theaters will increase.

58. **What is a major effect of a purchase of bonds by the Federal Reserve?**
   a) A reduction in the supply of common stock
   b) An increase in the volume of commercial bank loans
   c) A decrease in the supply of money
   d) An increase in interest rates
   e) A decrease in investment spending by businesses

59. **A progressive tax:**
   a) encourages more investment from those with higher incomes.
   b) is illustrated by a 6% sales tax.
   c) requires those with higher incomes to pay a higher ratio of taxes to income.
   d) requires every income class to pay the same ratio of taxes to income.
   e) earmarks revenues for poverty reduction.

**60.** The Federal government's largest pay out over the past twenty years has been for:
   a)  military.
   b)  social security.
   c)  interest on the national debt.
   d)  education.
   e)  foreign aid.

What was your score? Are you more knowledgeable than the average citizen? The average score for all 2,508 Americans taking the following test was 49%; college educators scored 55%. Can you do better? Questions were drawn from past Intercollegiate Student Institute (ISI) surveys, at http:///www.americancivicliteracy. org/as well as other nationally recognized exams. The inclusion of this copyrighted test is included with the permission of ISI.

# APPENDIX B

## Declaration of Independence Accusations

The history behind the accusations in the Declaration from historian Benson J. Lossing, (February 12, 1813 – June 3, 1891)

**I. He has refused his assent to laws the most wholesome and necessary for the public good.**

After the conclusion of a general peace in 1763, between Great Britain and the states of Europe with which she had been at war for seven long years, the conduct of the government toward its American colonies was very materially altered. Whether it arose from avarice, or from a jealousy of the *power* of the colonies so signally displayed during the war just closed, or a fear that a knowledge of that power would make the colonists aspire to political independence, it is not easy to determine. It is probable that these several causes combined engendered those acts of direct and indirect oppression, which finally impelled the colonies to open rebellion.

The growing commercial importance of the colonies, and their rapidly accumulating wealth and more rapid increase of population, required new laws to be enacted, from time to time, to meet the exigencies which these natural increments produced. The colonial assemblies made several enactments touching their commercial operations, the emission of a colonial currency, and colonial representation in the imperial parliament, all of which would have been highly beneficial to the colonies, and not at all prejudicial to the best interests of Great Britain. But the jealousies of weak or wicked ministers, excited by the still stronger jealousies of colonial governors, interposed between the King and his American subjects, and to these laws, so wholesome and necessary for the public good," he refused his royal assent. When the excitements produced by the Stamp Act" resulted in popular tumults, and public property was destroyed, and royal authority was defied, the home government, through Secretary Conway, informed the Americans that these things should be overlooked, provided the assemblies should, by appropriations, make full compensation for all losses thus sustained. This requisition the assemblies complied with; but in Massachusetts, where most of the indemnification was to be made, the legislature, in authorizing the payment thereof, granted free pardon to all concerned in the tumults, desiring thus to test the sincerity of the proposition of the Crown to forgive the offenders. This act was "wholesome and necessary for the public good," for it would have produced quiet, and a return of confidence in the promises of the King. But the King and his council disallowed the act—he "refused his assent." http://colonialhall.com/histdocs/declaration/declaration analysis01.php

*II. He has forbidden his governors to pass laws of immediate and pressing importance, unless suspended in their operation till his assent should be obtained; and, when so suspended, he has utterly neglected to attend to them.*

In 1764, the assembly of New York were desirous of taking measures to conciliate the Indian tribes, particularly the Six Nations, and to attach them firmly to the British colonies. To this measure Governor Colden lent his cheerful assent, privately; but representations having been made to the King, by an agent of Lord Bute, then travelling in the colonies, that the ulterior design was to add new strength to the physical power of the colonists for some future action inimical to their dependence upon Great Britain, the monarch sent instructions to all his governors to desist from such alliances, or to suspend their operations until his assent should be given. With this order, the matter rested, for then (as was doubtless his intention) he "utterly neglected to attend to them."

The assembly of Massachusetts, in 1770, passed a law for taxing the commissioners of customs and other officers of the Crown, the same as other citizens. Of this they complained to the King, and he sent instructions to Governor Hutchinson to assent to no tax bill of this kind, without first obtaining the royal consent. These instructions were in violation of the expressed power of the charter of Massachusetts; and the assembly, by resolution, declared "that for the Governor to withhold his assent to bills, merely by force of his instructions, is vacating the charter, giving *instructions* the force of *law* within the province." Neither the assembly nor the Governor would yield, and no tax *bill* was passed that session. The assembly was prorogued until September, and then again until April, 1772; and all that while laws of pressing importance were virtually annulled—the King "utterly neglected to attend to them."

*III.   He has refused to pass other laws for the accommodation of large districts of people unless those people would relinquish the right of representation in the legislature, a right inestimable to them and formidable to tyrants only.*

In the spring of 1774, Parliament passed a bill, by which the free system of English government in Canada, or, as it was called, the "province of Quebec," was radically changed. Instead of the popular representative system by a colonial assembly, as obtained in the other Anglo-American colonies, the government was vested in a Legislative council, having all power, except that of levying taxes. The members of the council were appointed by the crown, the tenure of their office depending upon the will of the King. Thus the people were deprived of the representative privilege. A large majority of the inhabitants were French Roman Catholics, and as the same act, established that religion in the province, they consided this a sufficient equivalent for the political privilege that had been taken away from them. But "large districts" of people of English descent bordering on Nova Scotia, tell this act to be a grievous burden, for they had ever been taught that the right of representation was the dearest prerogative conferred by the Magna Charta of Great Britain. They therefore sent strong remonstrances to parliament, and humble petitions to the King, to restore them this right. But not only were their remonstrances and petitions unheeded, but their efforts to procure the passage of laws by the Legislative Council touching their commercial regulations with Nova Scotia, were fruitless, and they were plainly told by Governor Carleton (under instructions from the Secretary for Foreign Affairs) that no such laws should be passed until they should cease their clamors for representation, and quietly submit to the administration of the new laws. But, like their more southern neighbors, they could not consent to sacrifice a principle, even upon the stern demands of hard necessity, and they were obliged to forego the advantages which asked-for enactments would have given. The right which they claimed, was a right guarantied by the British constitution, and was "inestimable to them." But as the right was "formidable to tyrants," and as the King, by his sanction of the destruction of free English laws in Canada had dared to become such, they were oblied for submit, or else "relinquish the right of representation in the Legislature."

About the same time, a bill was passed "For the better regulating the government in the province of Massachusetts Bay." This bill provided for an alteration in the constitution of that province, as it stood upon the charter of William III to do away with the popular elections which decided everything in that colony; to take away the executive power out of the hands of the growing democratic party; and to vest the nominations of the council, of the judges, and of magistrates of all kinds, including sheriffs, in the Crown, and in some cases in the King's governor. This act deprived the people of free "representation in the legislature;" and when in the exercise of their rights, and on the refusal of the Governor to issue warrants for the election of members of Assembly, in accordance with the provisions of their charter before altered, they called a convention, their expressed wishes, for the passage of "laws for the accommodation of large districts of people" were entirely disregarded. They were refused the passage of necessary laws, unless they would quietly "relinquish the right of representation in the legislature,—a right inestimable to them, and formidable to tyrants only."

**IV. He has called together legislative bodies at places unusual, uncomfortable, and distant from the repository of their public records, for the sole purpose of fatiguing them into compliance with his measures.**

The inhabitants of Boston became the special objects of ministerial vengeance, after the news of the destruction of tea in that harbor reached England. That event occurred on the evening of the sixteenth of December, 1773, and in February following the matter was laid before Parliament. It was at once determined to punish severely the people of that refractory town; and accordingly Lord North, then prime minister, presented a bill which provided for the total annihilation of the trade and commerce of Boston, and the removal of the courts, officers of customs, &c., therefrom. This was the famous "Boston Port Bill," and it went into effect on the first of June following.

General Gage, who had been appointed governor of the province, arrived at Boston about the last of May, and at once proceeded, according to his instructions, to remove the courts, &c., from that town. He also adjourned the assembly, on the thirty-first of May, to meet on the seventh of June, at Salem. But he retained all the public records in Boston, so that if the members of the assembly had been so disposed they could not have referred to them. Military power ruled there—two regiments of British troops being encamped upon the Commons. The patriotic assembly, although "distant from the repository of the public records," and in a place extremely "uncomfortable," were *not* "fatigued into compliance with his measures," but, in spite of the Governor, they elected delegates to a general Congress. They adopted various other measures for the public good, and then adjourned.

### V. He has dissolved, representative houses repeatedly, for opposing with manly firmness his invasions on the rights of the people.

In January, 1768, the assembly of Massachusetts addressed a circular to all the other colonies, asking their co-operation with them in asserting and maintaining the principle that Great Britain had no right to tax the colonies without their consent. This was a bold measure, and more than all others displeased the British ministry. As soon as intelligence of this proceeding reached the ministry, Lord Hillsborough, the secretary for foreign affairs, was directed to send a letter to Bernard, the Governor of Massachusetts, in which it was declared, that "his majesty considers this step as evidently tending to create unwarrantable combinations, to excite unjustifiable opposition to the constitutional authority of parliament;" and then he added, "It is the King's pleasure, that as soon as the general court is again assembled, at the time prescribed by the charter, you require of the house of representatives, in his majesty's name, to rescind the resolutions which gave birth to the circular letter from the speaker, and to declare their disapprobation of, and dissent to, that rash and hasty proceeding. If the new assembly should refuse to comply with his majesty's reasonable expectations, it is the King's pleasure that you should immediately dissolve them."

In accordance with his instructions, Governor Bernard required the assembly to rescind the resolutions. To this requisition, the house replied: "If the votes of this house are to be controlled by the direction of a minister, we have left us but a vain semblance of liberty. We have now only to inform you that this house have voted not to rescind, and, that on a division on the question, there were ninety-two yeas and seventeen nays." The Governor at once proceeded to dissolve the assembly; but before the act was accomplished, that body had prepared a list of serious accusations against him, and a petition to the King for his removal. Counter circulars were sent to the several colonies, warning them to beware imitating the factious and rebellious conduct of Massachusetts; but they entirely failed to produce the intended effect, and the assemblies in several of the colonies were dissolved by the respective governors.

In 1769, the assemblies of Virginia and North Carolina were dissolved by their governors, for adopting resolutions boldly denying the right of the King and parliament to tax the colonies—to remove offenders out of the country for trial—and other acts which infringed upon the sacred rights of the people.

In 1774, when the various colonial assemblies entertained the proposition for a general congress, they were nearly all dissolved by the respective governors, to prevent the adoption of the scheme and the election of delegates to that national council. But the people assembled in popular conventions, assumed legislative powers, and their delegates to a General Congress, in spite of the efforts of royal millions to restrain them. These dissolutions of "representative houses repeatedly" only tended to inflame the minds of the people and widen the breach between them and their rulers.

*VI.He has refused, for a long time after such dissolutions, to cause others to be elected; whereby the legislative powers, incapable of annihilation, have returned to the people at large for their exercise, the state remaining, in the meantime, exposed to all the dangers of invasion from without and convulsions within.*

Soon after the repeal of the Stamp Act, in 1767, the colonists were again alarmed at the expressed intention of ministers to enforce a new clause in the Mutiny Act. This act granted power to every officer, upon obtaining a warrant from a justice, to break into any house by day or by night, in search of deserters. The new clause alluded to provided that the troops sent out from England should be furnished with quarters, beer, salt and vinegar, at the expense of the colonies. The people justly regarded this as disquised taxation, and opposed it as a violation of the same principles as those upon which the Stamp Act trampled. Besides, the soldiers were insolent and overbearing toward the citizens; they were known to be quartered here for the purpose of abridging and subduing the independent actions of the people, and the supplies demanded were to be drawn from the very men whom they came to injure and oppress.

The Assembly of New York refused to make the required provisions for the troops, and in consequence of this disobedience of royal orders, its legislative functions were entirely suspended. The Assembly was prohibited from making any bill, order, resolution or vote, except for adjourning, or choosing a speaker, until the requirenients were complied with. Consequently "the legislative powers, incapable of annihilation, returned to the people at large for their exercise, the state remaining, in the meantime, exposed to all the dangers of invasion from without and convulsions within" Thus matters stood for several months.

The Assembly of Massachusetts, also, after its dissolution by the governor in July, 1768, was not permitted to meet again until the last Wednesday of May, 1769, and then they found the state house surrounded by a military guard, with cannon pointed directly at the place wherein they met for deliberation. Thus restricted in the free exercise of their functions as legislators, the power they had possessed "returned to the people," because it was annulled in them by restraining their freedom of action.

*VII.   He has endeavored to prevent the population of these states—for that purpose, obstructing the laws for the naturalization of foreigners, refusing to pass others to encourage their migration hither, and raising the conditions of new appropriations of lands.*

John, Earl of Bute, was the pupil and favorite companion of George III, while he was yet Prince of Wales, and when, on the sudden death of his grandfather, George II, he became King, he looked to this nobleman for council and advice. He was one of his first cabinet, and so completely did he influence the mind of the King, at the beginning of his reign, that those who wished for place or preferment, first made their suits to the Earl of Bute.

Among other measures advised by Bute, was the employment of men, in secret service, in different parts of the realm, to keep the King advised of all that in any way effected the power, stability and glory of the crown.

An agent of this kind was sent by Bute to America, and the glowing account which he gave of the rapid growth of the colonists in wealth and number, after the peace of 1763, and the great influx of German immigrants, caused Bute to advise his royal master to look well to those things, lest a spirit of independence should grow side by side with the increase of power, which would finally refuse to acknowledge a distant sovereignty, and defy the authority of the British crown. Some of the colonial governors within whose jurisdiction immigrants had been most freely settled, encouraged this idea, for they found the German people, in general, strongly imbued with principles of political freedom. Added to this innate characteristic, they remembered the German battle-fields where George II, in his efforts to maintain the Electorate of Hanover, had been the cause of the offering of whole hecatombs of their countrymen upon the altar of the Moloch, War.

George III therefore, at the instigation of Bute, took measures to arrest any influence which this Germanic leaven might exert, and he cast obstacles in the way of further immigration to any extent. He also became jealous of the tendency to immigration to the more salubrious states, especially Roman Catholic Maryland, which the French of Canada exhibited, fearing their ancient animosities might, by contact with the English colonies, weaken the loyalty of the latter.

The colonists on the other hand, joyfully hailed the approach of the German immigrants, and extended the right band of fellowship to their now peaceful French brethren. Both interest and policy dictated this course toward the immigrant, and the colonial assemblies adopted various measures to encourage their migration hither. Unwilling to, excite alarm among the colonists the King endeavored to thwart the operation of these measures by instructing his governors to refuse their assent to many of those enactments until the royal consent should be obtained. Such refusals were made under various pretences, and there was so much delay in the administration of the naturalization laws, through which alone foreigners could hold lands in fee, and enjoy other privileges, that immigration in a mea sure ceased. The easy condition too, upon which lands on the frontiers were conveyed to foreigners, were so changed, that little inducement was held out to them to leave their native country; and the bright prospect of the valley of the Ohio peopled and cultivated, which appeared at the peace of '63, faded away, and the gloom of the interminable forest alone met the eye. So much did these obstructions check immigration, that when the war of the Revolution broke out, the current had quite ceased to flow hitherward. Bute, however, was right in his conjecture about the independent spirit which the German immigrants would evince, if occasion should offer, for when the Revolution broke forth, almost the entire German population, numbering about two hundred thousand, took side with the patriots.

## VIII.  He has obstructed the administration of justice, by refusing his assent to laws for establishing judiciary powers.

Under the act already referred to, "For the better regulation of the government of Massachusetts Bay," adopted in March, 1774, the judiciary powers were taken out of the hands of the people. The judges were appointed by the Crown, were subject to its will, and depended upon it for the emoluments of office. These emoluments, too, were paid to them out of moneys extracted from the people of the colonies by the "Commissioners of Customs," in the form of duties; and, therefore, the judges were more obnoxious to the hate and contempt of the colonists. They were also, by this act, deprived, in most cases, of the benefits of trial by jury, and the lives and property of the people were placed in the custody of the myrmidons of royalty. The "administration of justice" was effectually obstructed, and the very rights which the people of England so manfully asserted, and successfully defended in the revolution of 1688, were trampled under foot. In other colonies, too, the administration of justice was so obstructed by the interference of the royal governors, that it had but the semblance of existence left. The people tried every honorable means, by petitions to the King, addresses to the parliament, and votes in legislative assemblies and in popular conventions, to have laws passed, either in the provincial legislature, or in the supreme national council, for "establishing judiciary powers;" but their efforts were ineffectual. Power stood in the place of right, and exercised authority ; and under the goadings of a system of wrong and oppression, the people resorted to arms to "right themselves by abolishing the forms," and in prostrating the power of a monarchy become odious though the maladministration of weak or wicked ministers.

### IX. He has made judges dependent on his will alone for the tenure of their offices, and the amount and payment of their salaries.

In 1773, an act was passed by the British Parliament, on motion of Lord North, to make the governors and judges quite independent of those they governed, by paying their salaries directly from the National Treasury, instead of making them dependent upon the appropriations of the Colonial Assemblies for that purpose. This measure, making the public servants in the colonies wholly dependent upon the Crown for support, and independent of the people, was calculated to make them pliant instruments in the hands of their masters—ready at all times to do the bidding of the King and his council. The various Colonial Assemblies strongly protested against the measure; and out of the excitement and just alarm which followed, that mighty lever of the revolution, the system of Committees of Correspondence, was brought forth and vigorously applied.

Early in 1774, the Massachusetts Assembly required the judges in that colony to state explicitly whether they intended to receive their salaries from the Crown. Chief Justice Oliver declared that to be his intention, and the Assembly proceeded at once to impeach him. By a vote of ninety-six to nine, he was declared to be obnoxious to the people of the colony, and a petition to the Governor for his removal was adopted. The Governor refused compliance with this expressed will of the people, and this was presumptive evidence that the Governor, too, intended to receive his salary from the Crown. This matter produced much irritation, and just cause for bitter complaint on the part of the colonists. The Governor assuming the right to keep a judge in his seat, contrary to the wishes of the people, and the Crown paying his salary, made him dependent upon the will of the King alone for the tenure of his office, and the amount and payment of his emoluments."

X. *He has erected a multitude of new offices, and sent hither swarms of officers to harass our people, and eat out their substance.*

The passage of the Stamp Act, in 1765, called for the establishment of a new officer in every sea-port town, who was entitled Stamp Master. It was his business to dispose of the stamps and collect the revenue accruing from the same.

In 1766, an act was passed for imposing rates and duties, payable in the colonies. This act called for the creation of collectors of the customs, and "swarms of officers" were brought into being.

In 1767 an act was adopted "to enable his majesty to put the customs, and other duties in America, under the management of commissioners," &c., and a board of commissioners was at once erected. The members were paid high salaries, besides having many perquisites—all of which were paid by the colonists.

In 1768 Admiralty and Vice-Admiralty courts were established on a new model, and an increase in the number of officers was made; and thus, by act after act, each receiving the royal signature, were "sent hitlier swarms of officers to harass our people and eat out their substance."

## XI. He has kept among us, in times of peace, standing armies, without the consent of our legislatures.

After the "Peace of Paris," in 1764, when, by treaty, the "Seven Years' War" was ended, and quiet was for a time restored in both Europe and America, Great Britain, instead of withdrawing her regular troops from America, left quite a large number here, and required the colonists to contribute to their support. On the surface of things, there appeared no reason for this "standing army in time of peace;" but there can be little doubt, as we have before said, that growing jealousy of the power and independent feeling of the colonists, and an already conceived design to tax the colonies without their consent, were the true cause of the presence of armed men among a peaceful people. They were doubtless intended to *suppress democracy and republican independence, and to enforce every revenue law, however arbitrary and unjust soever it might be.* The colonists felt this, and hence the presence of the British troops was always a cause for irritation, and unappeased discontent. And, finally, when the people of Massachusetts began openly to resist the encroachments of British power, a large standing army was quartered in its capital, for no other purpose than to awe them into submission to a tyrant's will.

## XII. He has affected to render the military independent of, and superior to, the civil power.

In the spring of 1774, General Gage, who was the commander-in-chief of all the British forces in America, was appointed Governor of Massachusetts; and the first civil duty he was called upon to perform was to carry into effect the provisions of the Boston Port Bill. To sustain and enforce this harsh measure, be introduced two regiments of troops into Boston; and soon afterward they were reinforced by several regiments from Halifax, Quebec, New Fork, and Ireland. By an order of the King, the authority of the commander-in-chief, and under him, the brigadier-generals, was rendered supreme in all civil governments in America. This, be it remembered, was in a time of peace; and thus an uncontrolled military power was vested in officers not known as civil functionaries to the constitution of any colony. The military was rendered "independent of, and superior to, the civil power."

**XIII.  He has combined with others to subject us to a jurisdiction foreign to our constitution, and unacknowledged by our laws, giving his assent to their acts of pretended legislation.**

One of the most prominent acts, obnoxious to this serious charge, was the establishment by act of Parliament, under the sanction of the King, of a Board of Trade in the colonies, independent of colonial legislation: and the creation of resident commissioners of customs, to enforce strictly the revenue laws. This act was passed in July, 1767; and when the news of its adoption reached America, it produced a perfect tornado of indignation throughout the Colonies. The people perceived clearly that they were now not only to be subjected to the annoyance of unqualified assertions that Parliament had "a right to bind the colonies "in all cases whatsoever," but that they were to be subject to the actual control of persons appointed to carry out these principles avowed by the British Ministry.

The establishment of this Board of Trade in the colonies, unto whom was given power to regulate the customs and secure the revenue--the modeling of the admiralty courts upon a basis which quite excluded trial by jury therein--and the supremacy given to the military power in 1774, as alluded to in the next preceding charge--are all evidences that prove the truth and justice of this charge.

The Commissioners of Customs arrived in May, 1768, and at Boston they entered vigorously upon their duties; and the riots which ensued on the seizure by them of a vessel belonging to John Hancock, attest the deep feeling of resistance in the hearts of the people to a "jurisdiction foreign to their constitution, and unacknowledged by *their* laws."

The powers which the Commissioners possessed, in connexion with the Board of Trade, in the appointment of an indefinite number of subordinates, and in controlling legislative action, were dangerous to the liberties of the people; for they claimed the right of adjudicating in all matters connected with the customs. The jurisdiction, too, of the newly-modeled Courts of Admiralty, where, in many cases, a trial by jury was denied, was "foreign to *their* constitution, and unacknowledged by *their* laws."

When, in 1774, the charter of Massachusetts was altered, the character of the colonial council was changed. Before that time, the members of the council, (answering to our senate,) were chosen by the general assembly, but, in the alteration, it was provided that after the first of August of that year they should be chosen by the King, to consist of not more than thirty-six, nor less than twelve ; and to hold their office during his pleasure. To the Governor was given almost unlimited power, and the people were subjected to "a jurisdiction foreign to their constitution," and the assent of the King was given to the acts of "pretended legislation," made by these crown-chosen senators.

## XIV. *For quartering large bodies of armed troops among us.*

In 1767, the patriotic movements of the colonists so alarmed the British ministry, that they determined to repress the republican feeling by force, if necessary. For this purpose, Lord Hillsborough sent a secret letter to General Gage, then in Halifax, telling him that it was the King's pleasure that he should send one regiment, or more, to Boston to assist the civil magistrate and the officers of revenue. About the same time, Governor Bernard, of Massachusetts, requested General Gage to send some troops to Boston. Seven hundred were accordingly sent; and on the first of October, 1774, they landed, under cover of the cannon of armed ships in the harbor. The people refused to provide quarters for them, and they were quartered in the State House.

This unwise movement, which greatly exasperated the people, was repeated the next year, not only at Boston, but in New York, Philadelphia, Charleston, and other seaport towns. At the beginning of 1775, Parliament voted a supply of ten thousand men for the American service, and a large number of them landed at Boston in the spring of that year, accompanied by Generals Howe, Clinton, and Burgoyne. The tragedies of Lexington and Concord soon followed; and in June, the blood of American patriots was profusely spilt upon Bunker Hill by the "large bodies of armed troops quartered among us."

### XV. For protecting them, by a mock trial, from punishment any murders which they should commit on the inhabitants of these states.

In 1768, a dispute occurred between some soldiers and citizens of Annapolis, in Maryland, and two of the Litter were killed by the former. As they were marines, belonging to an armed vessel lying near, they were arraigned before the court of admiralty for murder, on the complaint of some of the citizens. The whole affair assumed the character of a solemn farce, so far as justice was concerned; and, as might have been expected, the miscreants were acquitted.

In 1771, a band of patriots, called the "Regulators," in North Carolina, became so formidable, and were so efficacious in stirring the people to rebellion, that Governor Tryon of that state, determined to destroy or disperse them. Having learned that they had gathered in considerable force upon the Alamance River, he proceeded thither with quite a large body of regulars and militia. They met near the banks of that stream, and a parley ensued. The "Regulators," asking only for redress of grievances, sought to negotiate, but Tryon peremptorily ordered them to disperse. This they refused to do, and some of his men, thirsting for blood, fired upon them and killed several. These soldiers were afterward arraigned for murder, through the clamorous demands of the people; but, after a mock trial had been acted, they were acquitted, and thus they were "protected from punishment for any murders which they should commit on the inhabitants of these states."

**XVI. *For cutting off our trade with all parts of the world.***

The narrow, restrictive policy of Great Britain, begun as early as the middle of the seventeenth century, had a tendency to repress, rather than to encourage, the commerce of the colonies. Instead of allowing them free commercial intercourse with other nations, the home government did all in its power to compel the colonists to trade exclusively with Great Britain.[1] In 1764, the British Minister, under a pretence of preventing *illegal* traffic between the British colonies and foreign American possessions, made the naval commanders revenue officers--directed them to take the usual custom-house oaths--and to conform to the custom-house regulations. By this means a profitable trade with the Spanish and French colonies in America, which the colonists had long uninterruptedly enjoyed, (although in violation of the old Navigation Act,) was destroyed. This trade was advantageous to Great Britain as well as to the colonies; but as the enforcement of these laws was a part of the system of "reforming the American governments,"[2] began by Bute, the advantages to England were over-looked. Under this act, many seizures of vessels were made; and the Americans were so distressed and harassed, that they were obliged to abandon the trade.

Other measures, having a tendency to narrow the commerce of the colonies to a direct trade with Great Britain, were adopted; and finally, in 1775, among the acts projected by Lord North for *punishing* the colonies, was one for effectually stopping the commerce of New England with Great Britain, Ireland, and the West Indies, and also fishing on the Banks of Newfoundland. This restrictive act, first applied to the New England colonies, was afterward extended to all the others, and thus, as far as parliamentary enactments could effect it, "trade with all parts of the world" was cut off.

[1]   The Navigation Act, first adopted in 1651, and extended in 1660, declared that no merchandise of the English plantations should be imported into England in any other than English vessels. There were also restrictive laws respecting the manufactures of the colonies, and their domestic commerce. For the benefit of English manufacturers,

the colonists were forbidden to export, or introduce from one colony into another, hats and woollens of domestic manufacture; and hatters were forbidden to have, at one time, more than two apprentices. They were not allowed to import sugar, rum, and molasses, without paying an exorbitant duty, and forbade the erection of certain iron works.

[2]    See Gordon, vol. i., p. 108.

### XVII. For imposing taxes on us without our consent.

George Grenville, an honest but short-sighted statesman, became the Prime Minister, or "First Lord of the Treasury," of Great Britain, in 1764. He found the treasury drained empty by the vampire appetite of war, and his first care was to devise means to replenish it. Believing that the Crown had an unquestionable right to tax its colonies, and perceiving the capacity of the Americans to pay a tax if levied, he turned his attention to a project for replenishing the treasury, by establishing new duties upon all foreign goods imported by the Americans. They were already submitting to the taxes, in the shape of duties, which the Navigation Act, and the Sugar Act, imposed; and when this new scheme was proposed to Parliament, the people were at once aroused to a sense of their danger--they saw clearly the designed the British Ministry to impose tax upon tax, as long as forbearance would allow it. Action on the subject was taken in the colonial assemblies, and one sentiment. seemed to prevail,--*a denial of the right of Great Britain to tax its colonies without their consent.* The fundamental principle of a free government, that *"Taxation equitable representation are inseparable,"* was boldly proclaimed, and petitions and remonstrances from the colonies were transmitted to the King and Parliament. But the King, instead of heeding these remonstrances, asserted his right to tax the colonies, in his speech to Parliament at the opening in January, 1765, and recommended the adoption of Grenville's measures. Emboldened by this, the Minister proposed his famous Stamp Act in February, and in March it became a law, and received the royal signature.

The ferment which this act produced in America, and the violent opposition it met with from Pitt, and other leading minds in Parliament, caused its repeal in March 1766. The Repeal Act, however, was accompanied by a Declaratory Act, which contained the germ of other oppressions. It affirmed that Parliament had power *to bind the colonies in all cases whatsoever.* Although it was thought expedient to repeal the Stamp Act, yet the Declaratory Act asserted the correctness of the doctrine it contained and exhibited practically.[1]

Again in 1767, another tax was imposed in the shape of duties upon glass, paper, painter's colors, and tea. Here again taxes were imposed upon us "without our consent." The act was strongly condemned throughout the colonies, and the British ministry perceiving a tendency toward open rebellion in America, repealed this act also, excepting the duty upon tea. Finally, in 1773, Lord North attempted to draw a revenue from America by imposing additional duties upon tea; but it was met by firm opposition, and the celebrated Boston Tea Riot ensued. We might cite other proofs of the truth of this charge, but these may suffice.

[1]     As the Stamp Act was the first and chief cause which fully aroused the colonists to a sense of the danger of enslavement by the mother country, and awakened the first notes of universal alarm that led to a general union of the Anglo-Americans in defence of their inalienable rights, and resulted finally in the adoption of a Declaration of Independence, we have inserted it in detail in the Appendix to this work.

### XVIII. *For depriving us, in many cases, of the benefits of trial by jury.*

When the British ministry perceived that their scheme for taxing the colonies without their consent, met with determined opposition, and the Commissioners of Customs, in 1768, were obliged to flee for personal safety from Boston to Castle William, they so modified the Court of Admiralty in America, as to make them powerful aids to these Commissioners, and a strong right arm of oppression An act was passed, in which it was ordained that whenever offences should be committed in the colonies against particular acts, imposing various duties and restrictions upon trade, the prosecutor might bring his action for penalties in the Courts of Admiralty;" by which means the subject lost the advantage of being tried by an honest, uninfluenced jury of the vicinage, and was subjected to the sad necessity of being judged by a single man, a creature of the crown, and according to the course of law, which exempted the prosecutor from the trouble of proving his accusation, and obliged the defender either to evince his innocence, or suffer."[1]

[1]    Address of the first continental congress, to the people of Great Britain.

### XIX. For transporting us beyond seas to be tried for pretended offences.

On the fifteenth of April, 1774, Lord North introduced a bill in Parliament, entitled "A bill for the impartial administration of justice in the cases of persons questioned for any acts done by them in the execution of the laws, or for the suppression of riots and tumults in the province of Massachusetts Bay, in New England." This bill provided that in case any person indicted for murder in that province, or any other capital offence, or any indictment, for riot, resistance of the magistrate, or impeding the revenue laws in the smallest degree, he might, at the option of the Governor, or, in his absence, of the Lieutenant Governor, be taken to another colony, or *transported to Great Britain,* for trial, a thousand leagues from his friends, and amidst his enemies.

The arguments used by Lord North in favor of the measure, had very little foundation in either truth or justice, and the bill met with violent opposition in parliament. The minister seemed to be actuated more by a spirit of retaliation, than by a conviction of the necessity of such a measure. "We must show the Americans," said he, "that we will no longer sit quietly under their insults; and also, that even when roused, our measures are not cruel or vindictive, but necessary and efficacious." Colonel Barre, who, from the fast commencement of troubles with America, was the fast friend of the colonists, denounced the bill in unmeasured terms, as big with misery, and pregnant with danger to the British Empire. "This," said he, "is indeed the most extraordinary resolution that was ever heard in the Parliament of England. It offers new encouragement to military insolence, already so insupportable. By this law, the Americans are deprived of a right which belongs to every human creature, that of demanding justice before a tribunal composed of impartial judges. Even Captain Preston,[1] who, in their own city of Boston, had shed the blood of citizens found among them a fair trial, and equitable judges." Alderman Sawbridge, another warm friend of the Americans, in Parliament, also denounced the bill, not only as unnecessary and ridiculous, but unjust and cruel. He asserted that witnesses against the crown could never be brought over to England; that the Act was meant to enslave the Americans; and he expressed the ardent hope that the Americans would not admit of the execution of any fly of these destructive bills,[2] but nobly refuse them all. If they do not," said he, "they are the most abject slaves upon earth, and nothing the minister can do is base enough for them."

Notwithstanding the manifest inexpediency of such a treasure, the already irritated feeling of the colonists, and the solemn warning of sound statesmen in both[1] houses of Parliament, the bill was passed by one hundred and twenty-seven to forty-four, in the Commons, and forty-nine to twelve in the House of Lords. The king signed the bill, and it was thus decreed that Americans might be "transported beyond the seas, to be tried for pretended offences" or real crime.

[1]   See biography of John Adams.
[2]   The Boston Port Bill; the bill for altering, or rather for abolishing, the constitution of Massachusetts; and the bill under consideration.

## XX. *For abolishing the free system of English laws in a neighboring province, establishing therein an arbitrary government, and enlarging its boundaries, so as to render it at once an example and fit instrument for introducing the same absolute rule into these colonies.*

After the adoption of the Boston Port Bill, the bill for changing the government of Massachusetts, and the bill providing for the transportation of accused persons to England for trial, the British ministry were evidently alarmed at the fury of the whirlwind they themselves had raised; and they doubtless had a presentiment of the coming rebellion which their own cruel measures had engendered and ripened. They therefore thought it prudent to take steps in time to secure such a footing in America as should enable them to breast successfully the gathering storm. Accordingly a bill was introduced in the House of Lords in May, 1774, "for making more effectual provision for the government of the province of Quebec, in North America."

This bill proposed the establishment, in Canada, of a Legislative Council, invested with all powers, except that of levying taxes. It was provided that its members should be appointed by the crown, and continue in authority during its pleasure; that Canadian subjects, professing the Catholic faith, might be called to sit in the Council; that the Catholic clergy, with the exception of the regular orders, should be secured in their possessions and of their tithes, from all those who professed their religion; that the French laws, without jury, should be re-established, preserving, however, the English laws, with trial by jury, in criminal cases. It was also added, in order to furnish the ministers with a larger scope for their designs, that the limits of Canada should be extended, so as to embrace the territory situated between the lakes, and the Ohio and Mississippi rivers.[1]

This was a liberal concession to the people of Canada, nearly all of whom were French, and but a small portion of them Protestants.[2] The nobility and clergy had frequently complained of the curtailment of their privileges, and maintained that they were better off under the old French rule previous to 1763, than now. The measure proposed was well calculated to quiet all discontent in Canada, and make the people loyal. By such a result, a place would be secured in the immediate vicinity of the refractory Colonies, where troops and munitions of war might be landed, and an overwhelming force be concentrated, ready at a moment's warning to march into the territory of, and subdue, the rebellious Americans. This was doubtless the ulterior design of the ministry in offering these concessions, and the eagle vision of Colonel Barre plainly perceived it. In the debate on the bill, he remarked, "A very extraordinary indulgence is given to the inhabitants of this province, and one calculated to gain the hearts and affections of these people. To this I cannot object if it is to be applied to good purposes; but if you are about *to raise a Popish army to serve in the Colonies*, from this time all hope of peace in America will be destroyed."

The bill was so opposed to the religious and national prejudices of the great mass of the people of Great Britain, that it met with violent opposition both in and out of Parliament, yet it passed by a large majority, and on the twenty-first of June it became a law by receiving the royal signature.

[1]    Soon after the introduction of this bill, Thomas and John Penn, son and grandson of William Penn, put in a remonstrance against the boundary proposition, as it contemplated an encroachment upon their territory, they being the proprietaries of Pennsylvania, and the counties of New Castle, Kent, and Sussex, in Delaware. Burke, also, who was then the agent for New York, contended against the boundary proposition, because it encroached upon the boundary line of that Colony.

[2]    General Carleton, then Governor of Canada, asserted, during his Examination before Parliament, that there were then in that province only about three hundred and sixty Protestants, besides women and children; while there were one hundred and fifty thousand Roman Catholics.

## XXI. *For taking away our charters, abolishing our most valuable laws, and altering, fundamentally, the forms of our governments.*

While the Boston Port Bill was before the Lords, Lord North, on the twenty-eighth day of March, 1774, in a Committee of the whole Lower House, brought in a bill "for the better regulating of the government in the province of Massachusetts Bay." It provided for an alteration in the Constitution of that province as it stood upon the charter of William III By this act the people of Massachusetts were, without a hearing, deprived of some of the most important rights and privileges secured to them by their charter; rights which they had enjoyed from the first settlement of the colony. The members of the Council, heretofore chosen under the charter, by the General Assembly, were, after the first of August of that year, to be chosen by the King; to consist of not more than thirty-six, and not less than twelve; and to hold their office during his pleasure. After the first of July the governor was authorized to *appoint* and *remove,* without the consent of the Council, all judges of the inferior Courts of Common Pleas, Commissioners of Oyer and Terminer, the Attorney General, Provosts, Marshals, Justices of the Peace, and other officers belonging to the Council and courts of justice; and was also empowered to *appoint* sheriffs without the consent of the Council, but not to *remove* them without their consent.

The ministers did not confine themselves to these fundamental alterations in the charter of that province, but materially altered or totally repealed the laws relating to town meetings, and the election of jurors; laws which had been in existence from the commencement of the government, and deemed a part of the constitution of the colony. The right of selecting jurors by the inhabitants and freeholders of the several towns, was taken from them, and all jurors were by this act, to be summoned and returned by the sheriffs.[1]

This bill was zealously opposed by the friends of America in the British House of Commons. Barre and Burke, the leaders of this party, opposed it with all their strength of mind and eloquence of speech. "What," said the latter, "can the Americans believe but that England wishes to despoil them of all liberty, of all franchises; and by the destruction of their charters to reduce them to a state of the most abject slavery? As the Americans are no less ardently attached to liberty than the English themselves, can it ever be hoped they will submit to such exorbitant usurpation: to such portentous resolutions?" Governor Pownall, too, lifted up the voice of warning, and plainly told the ministers that their measures would be resisted, not only by the will and sentiment of the whole people, but probably by force of arms. But a false security shut the ears of the British ministry against all of these portentous warnings, and the British legislators seemed to have lost all sense of right and equity. The bill was adopted by an overwhelming majority--two hundred and thirty-nine against sixty-four in the Commons, and ninety-two against twenty in the House of Lords. The King gave the bill his royal signature, and thus he "combined with others for taking away our charters, abolishing our most valuable laws, and altering fundamentally, the forms of our governments."

[1]    Pitkin's Political and Civil History of the United States, vol. 1. p. 266.

## XXII. For suspending our own legislatures, and ring themselves invested with power to legislate for us in all cases whatsoever.

By the act described in the next preceding charge, entitled "For the better regulation of government in the province of Massachusetts Bay," the colonial legislature was virtually and actually" suspended; for, according to the charter under which the people had always lived and been governed, they recognised no legislature but one of their own free choice and election. By that act, the members of the council were chosen by the King, and a free legislature was in fact suspended, and a declaration virtually made that the King and Parliament were "invested with power to legislate for us in all cases whatsoever." In 1767 the powers of the Legislature of New York were suspended indefinitely, because the Assembly refused to furnish the soldiers, quartered among them, with certain articles mentioned in a clause in the Mutiny Act. In the language of the Declaration of Independence, by such an act of suspension of legislative functions, those "powers, incapable of annihilation, returned to the people at large for their exercise;" but the King and his council, by both word and deed, claimed that those powers returned to, and were vested in, the Crown, and thus asserted the principle, that it in connexion with the Council, was invested with power to legislate for the colonies "in all cases whatsoever."

Lord Dunmore, after dissolving the Assembly of Virginia about the beginning of 1775, assumed the same right, and issued proclamations to the people, calling upon them to perform certain duties, which had not been required of them by their own representatives in the House of Burgesses.

## XXIII. *He has abdicated government here, by declaring us out of his protection, and waging war against us.*

As early as the meeting of Parliament in 1774, the King, in his address from the throne, spoke of the colonies as in a state of almost open rebellion, and assured Parliament that he should employ vigorous efforts to suppress the unfolding insurrection. Again, in February, 1775, he sent a message to the Commons, declaring his American subjects to be in a state of open rebellion, and informing them that it would be necessary to augment the naval and military force in the colonies. Toward the close of 1775, he gave his assent to an agreement, with several German princes, to send armies to America to assist in crushing his rebellious subjects; and he sanctioned the barbarous acts of his governors, who sought to engage the Indian tribes in a warfare upon the colonists. In these measures, he personally declared us "out of his protection," and waged war against them.

Through his representatives, his governors of colonies, he, in several instances," abdicated government here." Lord Dunmore, Governor of Virginia, fearing the just resentment of the people, "abdicated government," by fleeing on board the Fowey ship of war. Tryon, of New York, "abdicated government," when, for fear of the resentment of the patriots, he fled on board a Halifax packet ship; and Governor Martin, of North Carolina, also took refuge on board a British ship of war. Lord William Campbell, Governor of South Carolina, also abdicated government, "by withdrawing from the colony, and carrying off with him the royal seals and the instructions to governors; and he "waged war" against the people, by acting in concert with Sir Peter Parker and Sir Henry Clinton, in besieging Charleston. In various ways, both personally and by representatives, did King George "abdicate government here," and waged a "cruel war against us."

### XXIV. He has plundered our seas, ravaged our coasts, burnt our towns, and destroyed the lives of our people.

In 1764, when the provisions of the Navigation Act were strictly enforced, and the commanders of vessels were invested with the power of custom-house officers to enforce the revenue laws under that act, a great many American vessels were seized, by which much distress was produced. Although this was done under the sanction of written law, yet it was nothing more, in the mode of enforcing the law, than "plundering our seas."

In April, 1775, the "lives of our people" were destroyed at Lexington and Concord, by an expedition sent out by Governor Gage, of Massachusetts. In June of that year, he "burnt our towns," and destroyed the lives of our people, "by his troops setting fire to Charlestown, and attacking and slaying our people upon Breed's, and Bunker Hill; and shortly afterward, the unprotected town of Bristol, in Rhode Island, was cannonaded, because the people refused to comply with an order from the commander of the vessels that appeared before it, to supply him with three hundred sheep.

In the autumn of 1775, several royal cruisers ravaging the coasts of New England. Captain Wallace, with the man-of-war, Rose, and two others, pursued a vessel which took shelter in the port of Stonington, Connecticut. He entered the harbor, and opened a fire upon the town, which he kept up nearly a whole day. He killed two men, and carried off some vessels. This was the same Captain (Sir James) Wallace who afterward commanded the flying squadron of small vessels that made a predatory expedition up the Hudson river, and, in connection with Colonel Vaughan of the land force, burnt Esopus, or Kingston, in Ulster county.

On the eighteenth of October, Captain Mowatt, with a few armed vessels, burnt the town of Falmouth, upon the northeastern coast of Massachusetts ; and he asserted that he had orders to destroy, by fire, all the sea-port towns from Boston to Halifax.

In December, 1775, Governor Dunmore, of Virginia, having been obliged to take refuge on board the Fowey, a British armed vessel at Norfolk, tried every means in his power to bring the people to subjection under him. Finally, the frigate Liverpool arrived, and the Governor felt quite strong in his resources, believing, that with the two vessels and the armed force of tories and blacks which he had collected on board, he should be able to regain his lost power. He sent a peremptory order to the inhabitants of Norfolk to supply the vessels with provisions. The order was of course disobeyed; and on the first of January, 1776, the two vessels opened a destructive cannonading upon the town. At the same time, some marines were landed, who set fire to the town, and reduced it to ashes.

In June, 1776, while the proposition of independence was before Congress, a naval armament under Admiral Sir Peter Parker, and a land force under Sir Henry Clinton, made a combined attack upon Charleston, South Carolina, and many Americans were killed. And after the Declaration of Independence went forth, the King's minions continued to "plunder our seas, ravage our coasts, and destroy the lives of our people."

*XXV. He is at this time transporting large armies of foreign mercenaries to complete the works of death, desolation, and tyranny, already begun, with circumstances of cruelty and perfidy scarcely paralleled in the most barbarous ages, and totally unworthy the head of a civilized nation.*

Toward the close of 1775, Lord North introduced a bill in Parliament, which provided for prohibiting all intercourse with the colonies, until they should submit, and for placing the whole country under martial law. This bill included a clause for appointing resident commissioners in America, who should have discretionary powers to grant pardons and effect indemnities, in case the Americans should come to terms. Having thus determined to place the country under martial law, and to procure the submission of the colonies by force of arms, the next important consideration. was to procure the requisite force. The estimated number of men sufficient to carry out successfully the designs of the ministry, was twenty-eight thousand seamen, and a land force of fifty-five thousand men.

This was a large force to raise within the brief space which the exigency of the case required, for the peace establishment at home was small enough already, and the delay in procuring volunteers, or waiting for the return of troops from foreign stations, might prove fatal to their plans. Ministers therefore resolved to *hire soldiers of some of the German princes,* and they at once appointed a commissioner for the purpose. Early in 1776, a treaty was concluded, and the Landgrave of Hesse-Cassel agreed to furnish twelve thousand one hundred and four men; the Duke of Brunswick, four thousand and eighty-four; the Prince of Hesse, six hundred and sixty-eight; the Prince of Waldeck, six hundred and seventy; making in all, seventeen thousand five hundred and twenty-six. The masters of these mercenaries, perceiving the stern necessity which had driven the British government to this atrocious resort, in its endeavor to crush the spirit of freedom in its American colonies, extorted hard terms--terms which none but a desperate suitor for favor would have agreed to. It was stipulated that they were to receive *seven pounds, four skillings and four-pence sterling for each man, besides being relieved from the burden of maintaining them.* In addition, the princes were to receive a certain stipend, amounting in all to one hundred and thirty-five thousand pounds sterling, or about *six hundred and seventy-five thousand dollars.* And Great Britain further agreed to guaranty the dominions of those princes against foreign attacks during the absence of their soldiers.

This hiring of the bone and sinew, and even the *lives,* of foreign troops--purchased assassins--to aid in enslaving its own children, whose only crime was an irrepressible aspiration for freedom, is the foulest blot upon the escutcheon of Great Britain, which its unholy warfare against us during the revolution produced.

The best friends of Great Britain, in and out of Parliament, deeply deplored the measure; and the opposition in the National Legislature, with a sincere concern for the fair fame of their country, did all in their power to prevent the transaction. But Parliament, as if madly bent on the entire destruction of British honor, and on pulling down the very pillars of the Constitution, seconded the views of Ministers, and adopted the measure by an overwhelming majority.

For this act, the King and his Ministers were obliged to hear many home truths from statesmen in both Houses of Parliament. Among others, the Earl of Coventry inveighed most heartily against the employment of foreign mercenaries to fight the battles of England, even in a *just* war. He maintained that the war in question was an unnatural and unrighteous one, and, as such, would not terminate favorably to the oppressor. "Look on the map of the globe," said he; "view Great Britain and North America; compare their extent; consider their soil, rivers, climate, and increasing population of the latter; nothing but the most obstinate blindness and partiality can engender a serious opinion that such a country will long continue under subjection to this. The question is not, therefore, how we shall be able to realize a vain, delusive scheme of dominion, but how we shall make it the interest of the Americans to continue faithful allies and warm friends. Surely that can never be effected by fleets and armies. Instead of meditating conquest, and exhausting our strength in an ineffectual struggle, we should wisely, abandoning wild schemes of coercion, avail ourselves of the only substantial benefit we can ever expect, the profits of an extensive commerce, and the strong support of a firm and friendly alliance and compact for mutual defence and assistance."

What blood and treasure would have been spared had such statesmanlike views prevailed in the British Parliament. But national pride was wounded, and its festerings produced relentless hate, whose counsels had no whispers of justice or of honorable peace. "Large armies of foreign mercenaries, to complete the work of death, desolation and tyranny, already begun," were sent hither, and the odious Hessians (the general title given to those German troops) performed their first act in the bloody drama, in the Battle of Long Island, on the twenty-ninth of August, 1776.

**XXVI.** *He has constrained our fellow-citizens, taken captive on the high seas, to bear arms against their country, to become the executioners of their friends and brethren, or to fall themselves by their hands.*

About the last of December, 1775, the British Parliament passed an act for prohibiting all trade and commerce with the colonies, and authorizing the capture and condemnation, not only of all American vessels with their cargoes, but all other vessels found trading with the colonies, and the crews were to be treated, not as prisoners, but as slaves. By a clause in the act, it was made lawful for the commander of a British vessel to take the masters, crews, and *other persons,* found in the captured vessels, and to put them on board any other British armed vessel, enter their names on the books of the same, and, from the time of such entry, such persons were to be considered in the service of his majesty, to all intents and purposes, as though they had entered themselves voluntarily on board such vessel.[1] By this means, the Americans were compelled to fight *even against their own friends and countrymen*--to become the executioners of their friends and brethren, or to fall by their hands." This barbarous act was loudly condemned on the floor of Parliament, as unworthy of a Christian people, a "refinement of cruelty unknown among savage nations," and paralleled only "among pirates, the outlaws and enemies of human society." But the act became law, and to the disgrace of Great Britain it was put in force.

It was the provisions of this odious act which laid the British government under the necessity of providing a force to carry out its designs in America, which its resources in men were inadequate to do; and ministers resorted to the foul measure of hiring German soldiers to fight their battles against their brethren here.

¹   Pitkin, vol. i., p 357.

## XXVII. He has excited domestic insurrections among us, and has endeavored to bring on the inhabitants of our frontiers, the merciless Indian savages, whose known rule of warfare is an undistinguished destruction of all ages, sexes and conditions.

Lord Dunmore, one of the most unpopular governors Virginia ever had, became involved in difficulties with the people, soon after his accession. Like too many of the native-born Englishmen at that time, he regarded the colonists as inferior people, and instead of using conciliatory measures, which might have made his situation agreeable to himself, he maintained a haughty carriage and aristocratic reserve. These private matters would have been tolerated, had not his public acts partaken of the same spirit. He seemed to be exceedingly deficient in judgment, and by various acts of annoyance he greatly exasperated the people. At length they arose in arms in consequence of his removing the powder of the colonial magazine on board of a ship of war, and he was obliged to fly thither himself, with his family, for fear of personal injury. This was early in May, 1775, and during the summer and autumn he attempted to regain his lost power. All moderate attempts having failed, he resolved on a bolder and more cruel measure. He issued his proclamation, and authoritatively summoned to his standard all capable of bearing arms; and in that proclamation as well as through private emissaries, he offered freedom to the slaves if they would take up arms against their masters. Thus, he "excited domestic insurrection."

In the spring of 1775, this same Governor Dunmore was an accomplice in, and an active promoter of, a scheme to "bring on the inhabitants of our frontiers, the merciless Indian savages." The plan adopted was to organize an active co-operation of all the various Indian tribes on the frontier, with the Tories. John Connelly, a Pennsylvanian, has the honor of originating the plot; and he found in Governor Dunmore a zealous coadjutor and liberal patron in the enterprise. Fort Pitt (now Pittsburgh) was to be the place of rendezvous, and ample rewards were offered to the chiefs of the Indians, as well as to the militia captains, who should join their standard.

In order to connect the plan, give it wider scope, secure more efficiency, and have higher sanction, a messenger was sent to Governor Gage, at Boston, then commander-in-chief of all the British forces in America. Gage entered heartily into the atrocious scheme, and gave Connelly a commission as Lieutenant-Colonel. He also sent an emissary named John Stuart, to the nation of the Cherokees on the borders of the Carolinas. General Carleton, governor of Canada, sent Colonel Johnson to the Indians of St. Francis, and others, belonging to the Six Nations, and in every case heavy bribes were offered. Too well did these emissaries succeed, for during the summer hundreds of innocent old men, women, and young children, were butchered in cold blood upon the frontiers of Virginia and the Carolinas.

This charge was true, not only at the time it was made in the Declaration of Independence, but on several subsequent occasions it might with verity have been made. When Burgoyne prepared to invade the States from Canada, he, by express orders of ministers, put under arms, and secured for the British service several tribes of Indians inhabiting the country between the Mohawk river and Lake Ontario. And just before going to attack Ticonderoga, he gave a great war feast to the Indians, and issued a proclamation calling upon the Americans to surrender or suffer the consequences of savage ferocity.

The American Congress, in its Declaration of Independence, after asserting that "The History of the present King of Great Britain is a history of repeated injuries arid usurpations, all having, in direct object, the establishment of absolute tyranny over these states," and submitting the foregoing charges as proofs of the truth of their declaration, they asserted:--

First: *That in every stage of these oppressions, we have petitioned for redress in the most humble terms. Our repeated petitions have been answered only by repeated injury.*

For ten long years, "in every stage of these oppressions," did the colonists "petition for redress in the most humble terms." It was done by the Colonial Congress which assembled in 1765, in consequence of the passage of the Stamp Act. They put forth a *Declaration of Rights,* the thirteenth section of which asserted, "That it is the right of the British subject in these colonies to petition the King, or either House of Parliament." This right was denied by the colonial governors, claiming it exclusively for the assemblies in their legislative capacity. But acting upon their declared right, that Congress sent a most humble petition to the King, setting forth the grievances which the acts for taxing the colonies imposed upon the people, and beseeching him to lay the subject before the Parliament and obtain redress for them. But this petition was unheeded, as well as those of the popular provincial conventions, and "repeated injuries" were inflicted, in the form of new and oppressive acts for taxing the colonists without their consent.

The first Continental Congress, that convened in September, 1774, humbly petitioned the King, and set forth the various measures of his government which bore heavily upon their prosperity and curtailed their rights as British subjects. The General Congress that met in May, the next year, also sent another humble petition to the King, but both were "answered only by repeated injuries." Instead of listening to their loyal importunities for redress, he deprived them in many cases of "trial by jury;" he prepared to "transport them beyond seas, to be tried for pretended offences ;" he "abolished the free system of English laws in a neighboring province;" he took away their charters, abolished their "most valuable laws," and "altered, fundamentally, the *forms*" of their government ; he "plundered their seas, ravaged their coasts, burnt their towns, and destroyed the lives of their people;" and he transported "large armies of foreign mercenaries to complete the works of death, desolation, and tyranny, already begun, with circumstances of cruelty and perfidy scarcely paralleled in the most barbarous ages, and totally unworthy the head of a civilized nation."

Secondly: *We have not been wanting in attention to our British brethren.*

This assertion the journals of the Continental Congress, and the proceedings of the British Parliament, fully corroborate. The first address put forth by the Continental Congress, in 1774, was *to the people of Great Britain,* in which the most affectionate terms of brotherhood, expressive of the strongest feelings which the ties of con sanguinity could produce, were used. They concluded their address by expressing a hope "that the magnanimity and justice of the British nation will furnish a parliament of such wisdom, independence, and public spirit, as may save the violated rights of the whole empire from the devices of wicked ministers and evil counsellors, whether in or out of office ; and thereby restore that harmony, friendship, and fraternal affection, between all the inhabitants of his majesty's kingdoms and territories, so ardently wished for by every true and honest American."

The second Continental Congress, in 1775, sent an affectionate address to the people of Ireland, in which they thanked them for the friendly disposition which they had always shown toward Americans; expressed a strong sympathy for them, on account of the grievances which the inhabitants of that fertile island suffered at the hands of the same arbitrary rulers, and closed with a "hope that the patient abiding of the meek may not always be forgotten;" and that God would "grant that the iniquitous schemes for extirpating liberty from the British empire might be soon defeated."

But, not only were British rulers unmindful of their petitions and of their remonstrances; their "British brethren" also were deaf to the "voice of justice and consanguinity;" and the colonists were obliged to acquiesce in the necessity which denounced their separation ; and they held them, as they held the rest of mankind, "ENEMIES IN WAR--IN PEACE, FRIENDS."

# APPENDIX C

## *Hillsdale College's Courses*

All course Lectures are archived and available to view at your convenience. Questions about the courses? Check out their Frequently Asked Questions page.

### Introduction to the Constitution
Lecture series by Hillsdale President Larry P. Arnn

### Constitution 101
"The Meaning and History of the Constitution" (typical separate lectures listed below)

### Constitution 201
"The Progressive Rejection of the Founding and trhe Rise of Bureaucratic Despotism"

### History 101 – Western Heritage
"From the Book of Genesis to John Locke"

### History 102 – American Heritage
"From Colonial Settlement to the Reagan Revolution"

### Economics 101: The Principles of Free Market Economics
Workbook available

Here is an example of what you can expect from Hillsdale's courses. Each course is made up of separate lectures. Here are the lectures for the "Welcome" portion of the course:

## Welcome to Constitution 101!
## "The Meaning and History of the Constitution"

Introductory Materials
The American Mind, Larry P. Arnn
The Declaration f Independence, Thomas G. West
The Problem of Majority Tyranny, David Bobb
Separation of Powers: Preventing Tyranny, Kevin Portteus
Separation of Powers: Ensuring Good Government, Will Morrisey
Religion, Morality and Property, David Bobb
Crisis of Constitutional Government, Weill Morrisey
Abraham Lincoln and the Constitution, Kevin Portteus
The Progressive Rejection of the Found, Ronald J. Pestritto
The Recovery of the Constitution, Larry P. Arnn
Course Conclusion

### Other Hillsdale's Lectures and Programs

### Hillsdale's Dialogues: A Survey of Great Books, Great Men and Great Ideas
Weekly series featuring Hillsdale President Larry Arnn, national radio host Hugh Hewitt, and members of the Hillsdale College faculty.

### Kirk Center Lecture Series Archive
Hillsdale College's Allan P. Kirby, Jr. Center for Constitutional Studies NS Citizenship in Washington, D.C.

### Hillsdale College is also on YouTube

# NOTES

## Introduction
1. Data from *www.infoplease.com/ipa/A0004986.html*);

## Chapter 1 – What Do You Know?
1. Justice John Jay, Original Chief Justice of the Supreme Court, *The Papers of John Adams*, Robert J. Taylor, editor (Cambridge: Belnap Press, 1977) Vol. I, p.81, from "'U' to the Boston Gazette" written on August 29, 1763. David Barton, *Restraining Judicial Activism*, (WallBuilders Press, Aledo, TX), p. 51.
2. President Woodrow Wilson, Denver Rally, 1911. America's God and Country Encyclopedia, William J. Federer (FAME Publishing Inc, Coppell, TX.) p. 697

## Chapter 2 – The Declaration of Independence
1. Declaration of Independence: A History:
   http://www.archives.gov/exhibits/charters/declaration_history.html

Re: Declaration of Independence - The signers of the Declaration of Independence were a profoundly intelligent, religious and ethically-minded group. Four of the signers of the Declaration of Independence were current or former full-time preachers, and many more were the sons of clergymen. Other professions held by signers include lawyers, merchants, doctors and educators. These individuals, too, were for the most part active churchgoers and many contributed significantly to their churches both with contributions as well as their service as lay leaders. The signers were members of religious denominations at a rate that was significantly higher than average for the American Colonies during the late 1700s.

These signers have long inspired deep admiration among both secularists (who appreciate the non-denominational nature of the Declaration) and by traditional religionists (who appreciate the Declaration's recognition of God as the source of the rights enumerated by the document). Lossing's seminal 1848 collection of biographies of the signers of the Declaration of Independence echoed widely held sentiments held then and now that there was divine intent or inspiration behind the Declaration of Independence. Lossing matter-of-factly identified the signers as "instruments of Providence" who have "gone to receive their reward in the Spirit Land."

From: B. J. Lossing, *Signers of the Declaration of Independence*, George F. Cooledge & Brother: New York (1848) [reprinted in *Lives of the Signers of the Declaration of Independence*, WallBuilder Press: Aledo, Texas (1995)], pages 7-12:

## Chapter 3 – The Signers of the Declaration of Independence

1. The material on the biographies of the signers of the Declaration of Independence was derived from USHistory.org. The author of the material, Mr. Thomas Kindig, graciously allowed his material to be included in this compilation (USHistory.org/declaration/kindig.htm); "I am very happy to acknowledge my authorship of these modest little biographical sketches. I derived facts for these sketches from *A Biography of the Signers of the Declaration of Independence: And of William and Patrick Henry*, L. Carroll Judson. The publication date was 1839. I accepted a very carefully packed edition of this book via the inter-library loan program, shared by the Coe College library in Cedar Rapids, Iowa (where I was in fact born and raised). The librarian here in Las Cruces, New Mexico, was very concerned that I should treat the volume with great care and even urged me to wear gloves while handling it. The book is available today on line at Google Books.

"I was at the time working on an online and ebook publishing business LeftJustified.com when I was contacted by someone at USHistory.org for permission to re-publish my work Account of a Declaration, based on letters of Thomas Jefferson. I further supplied these biographical sketches by email. I wrote them as part of a collection of historical content on the subject of the Declaration of Independence which I never completed."

All of the biographies of the signers are from Mr. Kindig's work.

Another excellent source for material on each of the signers can be found at, *Signers of the Declaration of Independence*, Benson J. Lossing, 1848 (George F. Cooledge & Brother: New York) [reprinted in *Lives of the Signers of the Declaration of Independence*, WallBuilder Press: Aledo, Texas (1995)]", and *"The Pictorial Field-Book of The Revolution* Benson J. Lossing, 1850 (illustrations by Lossing and Barritt) (Harper & Brothers, New York)

Additional verification of the Christian background of each of the signers was obtained from: http://www.adherents.com/gov/Founding Fathers Religion.html#Declaration.

## Chapter 4 – Religion and the Congress of the Confederation
1. The Library of Congress at http://loc.gov/exhibits/religion/rel04.html

## Chapter 5 – A More Perfect Union
1. Roger A. Bruns to *A More Perfect Union: The Creation of the United States Constitution. Washington, DC: Published for the National Archives and Records Administration by the National Archives Trust Fund Board, 1986. p. 33.* http://www.archives.gov/exhibits/charters/constitution_history.html

## Chapter 6 – Continental-Confederation Congress Delegates
All biographies are from the *American History* with the approval of, University of Groningen -http://www.let.rug.nl/usa/biographies. Religious affiliations from www.adherents.org citing

1. Political Graveyard website: http://politicalgraveyard.com/bio/ellsworth.html#R9MoIW34R viewed 7 December 2005)
2. Identified as a Presbyterian by the *1995 Information Please Almanac*. The Library of Congress; M. E. Bradford, *A Worthy Company: Brief Lives of the Framers of the United States Constitution*, (Source: Ian Dorion, "Table of the Religious Affiliations of American Founders", 1997). Robert G. Ferris (editor), *Signers of the Constitution: Historic Places Commemorating the Signing of the Constitution*, The United States Department of the Interior, National Park Service: Washington, D.C. (revised edition 1976), p. 178-180.
3. The Congregationalist Library; the Library of Congress and M. E. Bradford, *A Worthy Company: Brief Lives of the Framers of the United States Constitution* (Source: Ian Dorion, "Table of the Religious Affiliations of American Founders", 1997).

4. Abraham Baldwin was a Congregationalist, an Episcopalian and/ or a Presbyterian according to various sources. M. E. Bradford, *A Worthy Company: Brief Lives of the Framers of the United States Constitution;* Georgia Public Library Service. The Library of Congress was cited as the source stating he was later a Presbyterian. (Source: Ian Dorion, "Table of the Religious Affiliations of American Founders", 1997). Robert G. Ferris (editor), *Signers of the Constitution: Historic Places Commemorating the Signing of the Constitution,* published by the United States Department of the Interior, National Park Service: Washington, D.C. (revised edition 1976), p. 140-141.

5. M. E. Bradford, *A Worthy Company: Brief Lives of the Framers of the United States Constitution;* Georgia Public Library Service; The Library of Congress. (Source: Ian Dorion, "Table of the Religious Affiliations of American Founders", 1997). Robert G. Ferris (editor), *Signers of the Constitution: Historic Places Commemorating the Signing of the Constitution,* United States Department of the Interior, National Park Service: Washington, D.C. (revised edition 1976), pp. 161-162.

6. Political Graveyard website: (http://politicalgraveyard.com/bio/ houstoun-howan.html#RIU0U3XQ5; viewed 7 December 2005).

7. Political Graveyard website (http://politicalgraveyard.com/bio/pierce. html#RB60V6FQY; viewed 7 December 2005).

8. M. E. Bradford, *A Worthy Company: Brief Lives of the Framers of the United States Constitution* (Source: Ian Dorion, "Table of the Religious Affiliations of American Founders", 1997); Political Graveyard website (http://politicalgraveyard.com/bio/gerry.html#R9MoIXWKX; viewed 23 November 2005):

9. The Library of Congress and *A Worthy Company: Brief Lives of the Framers of the United States Constitution,* written by M. E. Bradford. (Source: Ian Dorion, "Table of the Religious Affiliations of American Founders", 1997).

10. Episcopalian, M. E. Bradford, *A Worthy Company: Brief Lives of the Framers of the United States Consti-tution.* Congregationalist, The Library of Congress. (Source: Ian Dorion, "Table of the Religious Affiliations of American Founders", 1997).

11. Political Graveyard website (http://politicalgraveyard.com/bio/strong. html#R9MoJEB1Z; viewed 7 December 2005).

12. Robert G. Ferris (editor), *Signers of the Constitution: Historic Places Commemorating the Signing of the Constitution,* published by the United States Department of the Interior, National Park Service: Washington, D.C. (revised edition 1976), p. 148-149.

13. Presbyterian, The Library of Congress; M. E. Bradford *A Worthy Company: Brief Lives of the Framers of the United States Constitution* later an Episcopalian. (Source: Ian Dorion, "Table of the Religious Affiliations of American Founders", 1997).

14. Political Graveyard website: (http://politicalgraveyard.com/bio/houston.html#RIUoOWLCo)

15. The Library of Congress; M. E. Bradford *A Worthy Company: Brief Lives of the Framers of the United States Constitution* (Source: Ian Dorion, "Table of the Religious Affiliations of American Founders", 1997). Robert G. Ferris (editor), *Signers of the Constitution: Historic Places Commemorating the Signing of the Constitution*, The United States Department of the Interior, National Park Service: Washington, D.C. (revised edition 1976), pp. 185-186.

16. *1995 Information Please Almanac*; The Library of Congress; M. E. Bradford, *A Worthy Company: Brief Lives of the Framers of the United States Constitution* (Source: Ian Dorion, "Table of the Religious Affiliations of American Founders", 1997).

17. The Library of Congress, The North Carolina State Library and M. E. Bradford, *A Worthy Company: Brief Lives of the Framers of the United States Constitution* were cited as the sources stating he was later a Presbyterian. (Source: Ian Dorion, "Table of the Religious Affiliations of American Founders", 1997).

18. Political Graveyard website: (http://politicalgraveyard.com/bio/davie-davila.html#RDHoQoLE7).

19. Alexander Martin was a Presbyterian. http://www.adherents.com/people/pm/Alexander_Martin.html

20. North Carolina State Library; the Library of Congress; M. E. Bradford, *A Worthy Company: Brief Lives of the Framers of the United States Constitution* by. (Source: Ian Dorion, "Table of the Religious Affiliations of American Founders", 1997): Robert G. Ferris (editor), *Signers of the Constitution: Historic Places Commemorating the Signing of the Constitution*, The United States Department of the Interior, National Park Service: Washington, D.C. (revised edition 1976), pp. 212-213.

21. North Carolina State Library; the Library of Congress. M. E. Bradford, *A Worthy Company: Brief Lives of the Framers of the United States Constitution* cited as the source stating he was a Deist. (Source: Ian Dorion, "Table of the Religious Affiliations of American Founders", 1997); Robert G. Ferris (editor), *Signers of the Constitution: Historic Places Commemorating the Signing of the Constitution*, The United States Department of the Interior, National Park Service: Washington, D.C. (revised edition 1976), pp 218-220.

22. M. E. Bradford, *A Worthy Company: Brief Lives of the Framers of the United States Constitution*. Roger A. Martin *A History of Delaware Through its Governors 1776-1984*by. (Source: Ian Dorion, "Table of the Religious Affiliations of American Founders", 1997). Pierce Butler should *not* be confused with the similarly named U.S. Supreme Court justice who served in the Supreme Court from 1923 until 1939.

23. The Library of Congress and M. E. Bradford, *A Worthy Company: Brief Lives of the Framers of the United States Constitution* (Source: Ian Dorion, "Table of the Religious Affiliations of American Founders", 1997).

24. The Library of Congress and M. E. Bradford, *A Worthy Company: Brief Lives of the Framers of the United States Constitution*. (Source: Ian Dorion, "Table of the Religious Affiliations of American Founders", 1997).

25. The Library of Congress and M. E. Bradford. *A Worthy Company: Brief Lives of the Framers of the United States Constitution* (Source: Ian Dorion, "Table of the Religious Affiliations of American Founders", 1997).

26. Robert G. Ferris (editor), *Signers of the Constitution: Historic Places Commemorating the Signing of the Constitution*, The United States Department of the Interior, National Park Service: Washington, D.C. (revised edition 1976), pp. 145-146.

27. M. E. Bradford, *The 1995 Information Please Almanac*; *A Worthy Company: Brief Lives of the Framers of the United States Constitution* by; and the Library of Congress. *Memoirs & Correspondence of Thomas Jefferson, IV*, p. 512 citing as the source stating explicitly that Madison was a "theist." (Source: Ian Dorion, "Table of the Religious Affiliations of American Founders", 1997). Robert G. Ferris (editor), *Signers of the Constitution: Historic Places Commemorating the Signing of the Constitution*, The United States Department of the Interior, National Park Service: Washington, D.C. (revised edition 1976), pp. 189-193.

28. Political Graveyard website (http://politicalgraveyard.com/bio/mason. html#RIT0GNK79; viewed 7 December 2005).

29. http://www.potiori.com/James_McClurg.html

30. Political Graveyard website (http://politicalgraveyard.com/bio/randolph.html#RAV0UVJ9Q; viewed 7 December 2005).

31. The *1995 Information Please Almanac*; the Library of Congress. M. E. Bradford. *A Worthy Company: Brief Lives of the Framers of the United States Constitution*. *Memoirs & Correspondence of Thomas Jefferson, IV*, p. 512 was cited as the source stating that Washington

was a "theist." (Source: Ian Dorion, "Table of the Religious Affiliations of American Founders", 1997).

32. M. E. Bradford, *A Worthy Company: Brief Lives of the Framers of the United States Constitution* by. (Source: Ian Dorion, "Table of the Religious Affiliations of American Founders", 1997).

33. United Methodist Church, M. E. Bradford, *A Worthy Company: Brief Lives of the Framers of the United States Constitution; A History of Delaware Through its Governors 1776-1984*by Roger A. Martin; and the Library of Congress. (Source: Ian Dorion, "Table of the Religious Affiliations of American Founders", 1997). Robert G. Ferris (editor), *Signers of the Constitution: Historic Places Commemorating the Signing of the Constitution,* The United States Department of the Interior, National Park Service: Washington, D.C. (revised edition 1976), pp. 142-143.

34. M. E. Bradford, *A Worthy Company: Brief Lives of the Framers of the United States Constitution;* Roger A. Martin, *A History of Delaware Through its Governors 1776-1984* (Source: Ian Dorion, "Table of the Religious Affiliations of American Founders", 1997).

35. Robert G. Ferris (editor), *Signers of the Constitution: Historic Places Commemorating the Signing of the Constitution,* published by the United States Department of the Interior, National Park Service: Washington, D.C. (revised edition 1976), pages 150-151. (Jacob Broom was a Lutheran, according to most sources. Broom devoted time to serving his church. Some sources indicate he was a Quaker and/or an Episcopalian.)

36. Quaker- M. E. Bradford, *A Worthy Company: Brief Lives of the Framers of the United States Constitution; A History of Delaware Through its Governors 1776-1984* by Roger A. Martin; The Library of Congress. Episcopalian- M. E. Bradford, *A Worthy Company: Brief Lives of the Framers of the United States Constitution* (Source: Ian Dorion, "Table of the Religious Affiliations of American Founders", 1997).

37. M. E. Bradford the Library of Congress; *A Worthy Company: Brief Lives of the Framers of the United States Constitution.* Roger A. Martin *A History of Delaware Through its Governors 1776-1984* (Source: Ian Dorion, "Table of the Religious Affiliations of American Founders", 1997).

38. U.S. Catholic Historical Society; M. E. Bradford, *A Worthy Company: Brief Lives of the Framers of the United States Constitution* by; and the Library of Congress. (Source: Ian Dorion, "Table of the Religious Affiliations of American Founders", 1997). Robert G. Ferris

(editor), *Signers of the Constitution: Historic Places Commemorating the Signing of the Constitution*, The United States Department of the Interior, National Park Service: Washington, D.C. (revised edition 1976), p. 153-154. Adherents.com.

39. M. E. Bradford, The Library of Congress and *A Worthy Company: Brief Lives of the Framers of the United States Constitution*, (Source: Ian Dorion, "Table of the Religious Affiliations of American Founders", 1997).

40. Political Graveyard website (http://politicalgraveyard.com/bio/martin6.html#RIU0QFQ0W; viewed 7 December 2005).

41. The Library of Congress; M. E. Bradford, *A Worthy Company: Brief Lives of the Framers of the United States Constitution*, (Source: Ian Dorion, "Table of the Religious Affiliations of American Founders", 1997).Robert G. Ferris (editor), *Signers of the Constitution: Historic Places Commemorating the Signing of the Constitution*, The United States Department of the Interior, National Park Service: Washington, D.C. (revised edition 1976), p. 189.

42. Political Graveyard website (http://politicalgraveyard.com/bio/mercer.html#R9M0J6I6Q; viewed 7 December 2005).

43. The Library of Congress; M. E. Bradford *A Worthy Company: Brief Lives of the Framers of the United States Constitution*, (Source: Ian Dorion, "Table of the Religious Affiliations of American Founders", 1997).

44. The Library of Congress; M. E. Bradford *A Worthy Company: Brief Lives of the Framers of the United States Constitution*, (Source: Ian Dorion, "Table of the Religious Affiliations of American Founders", 1997).

45. The Library of Congress; M. E. Bradford *A Worthy Company: Brief Lives of the Framers of the United States Constitution*, written by. (Source: Ian Dorion, "Table of the Religious Affiliations.

46. Political Graveyard website (http://www.newnetherlandinstitute.org/history-and-heritage/dutch_americans/john-lansing-jr/.

47. Political Graveyard website (http://politicalgraveyard.com/bio/yates.html#RIU0O4CG)

48. Quaker - The Library of Congress; M. E. Bradford *A Worthy Company: Brief Lives of the Framers of the United States Constitution*, also cited as the source stating he was later an Episcopalian. (Source: Ian Dorion, "Table of the Religious Affiliations of American Founders", 1997).

49. Robert G. Ferris (editor), *Signers of the Constitution: Historic Places Commemorating the Signing of the Constitution*, The United States

Department of the Interior, National Park Service: Washington, D.C. (revised edition 1976), pp. 163-164.

50. The Library of Congress. M. E. Bradford, *A Worthy Company: Brief Lives of the Framers of the United States Constitution,* also cited as the source stating he was later a Deist. (Source: Ian Dorion, "Table of the Religious Affiliations of American Founders", 1997). (Catherine Drinker Bowen. *Miracle at Philadelphia: The Story of the Constitutional Convention,* May to September 1787. New York: Book-of-the-Month Club, 1966, pp. 125-126).

51. The Library of Congress; M. E. Bradford *A Worthy Company: Brief Lives of the Framers of the United States Constitution.* (Source: Ian Dorion, "Table of the Religious Affiliations of American Founders", 1997).

52. Robert G. Ferris (editor), *Signers of the Constitution: Historic Places Commemorating the Signing of the Constitution,* The United States Department of the Interior,

53. National Park Service: Washington, D.C. (revised edition 1976), pp. 193-194.

54. M. E. Bradford, *A Worthy Company: Brief Lives of the Framers of the United States Constitution.* The Library of Congress and *Memoirs & Correspondence of Thomas Jefferson, IV,* p. 512, cited as the sources stating that Morris was a Deist. (Source: Ian Dorion, "Table of the Religious Affiliations of American Founders", 1997).

55. The Library of Congress and M. E. Bradford *A Worthy Company: Brief Lives of the Framers of the United States Constitution,* (Source: Ian Dorion, "Table of the Religious Affiliations of American Founders", 1997).

56. *Episcopalian, 1995 Information Please Almanac.* Presbyterian, The Library of Congress and Presbyterian Church, USA. "Deist," M. E. Bradford, *A Worthy Company: Brief Lives of the Framers of the United States Constitution* (Source: Ian Dorion, "Table of the Religious Affiliations of American Founders", 1997). B. J. Lossing, *Signers of the Declaration of Independence,* George F. Cooledge & Brother: New York (1848) [reprinted in *Lives of the Signers of the Declaration of Independence,* WallBuilder Press: Aledo, Texas (1995)], p. 129.

## Chapter 7 – The Bill of Rights

1. http://www.archives.gov/exhibits/charters/constitution_history.html

## Chapter 8 - Constitutions of the Individual States

1. The State's Constitutions: "What was the Government BEFORE the U.S. Constitution?" *American Minute*, William Federer, March 1, 2013 http://archive.constantcontact.com/fs155/1108762609255/archive/1112628521154.html (Emphasis in these quotes from William Federer's *American Minute* are by Mr. Federer)
2. Martin Kelly, http://americanhistory.about.com/od/colonialamerica/p/great_awakening.htm

## Chapter 9 – So, what now?

1. David Barton, Keys to Good Government (WallBuilders, Aledo TX) 1994, p.35
2. Ibid, p 24.
3. *Supreme Court Decision, 1892 Church of the Holy Trinity Decision* v *United States.*

For an excellent recap of the History of the Constitution, including The Bill of Rights, see: *http://www.archives.gov/exhibits/charters/print_friendly.html?page=constitution_history_content.html&title=NARA%20%7C%20The%20Constitution%20of%20the%20United%20States%3A%20A%20History*

For a Biographical recap of Congress from 1774 to present: *bioguide.congress.gov/*

For research in the US National Archives: *http://www.archives.gov/research/*

As can be seen from the recommended reading and DVD lists, I highly recommend David Barton's *WallBuilders* and William J. Federer's *Amerisearch* as the basis for *any* search on the Christian history of the United States. Federer has a daily column on Christianity and the United States. It can be found at www.AmericanMinute.com. He also has lectures on-line called *Faith in History*.

# RECOMMENDED READING
# & VIEWING

## Books

Allen, Leslie, *Liberty, The Statue and The American Dream* (NY, NY. Goodwill Publ.) 1993

American History Series, *The Coming Insurrection* (Cambridge, MA. MIT Press) 2009

Amar, Akhil, Reed *The Bill of Rights* (New Haven, CT. Yale Publ.) 1998

Bailyn, Bernard, *The Debate on the Constitution, volume I & II* (NY, NY. Penguin Books)

Barton, David, *American History in Black & White* (Aledo, TX, WallBuilders) 2004

Barton, David, *Benjamin Rush* (Aledo, TX, WallBuilders) 1999

Barton, David, *The Bulletproof Washington* (Aledo, TX, WallBuilders) 1990

Barton, David, *Celebrate Liberty* (Aledo, TX, WallBuilders) 2003

Barton, David, *Four Centuries of American Education* (Aledo, TX, WallBuilders) 2004

Barton, David, *The Jefferson Lies* (Aledo, TX, WallBuilders) 2012

Barton, David, *Keys to Good Government* (Aledo, TX, WallBuilders) 1994

Barton, David, *The Myth of Separation* (Aledo, TX, WallBuilders) 1992

Barton, David, *Restraining Judicial Activism* (Aledo, TX, WallBuilders) 2003

Barton, David, *The Role of Pastor & Christians* (Aledo, TX, WallBuilders) 2003

Barton, David, *Separation of Church & State* (Aledo, TX, WallBuilders) 2007

Barton, David, *Original Intent* (Aledo, TX, WallBuilders) 1996

Barton, David, *Second Amendment* (Aledo, TX, WallBuilders) 2006

Bastuat, Frederick, *The Law* (NY, NY. Irvington on the Hudson) 1987

Beck, David, *Common Sense,*

Beck, Glenn, *Miracles & Massacres* (NY. Threshold Publ.) 2013

Bennett, Wm. J., *Our Sacred Honor* (NYC. Simon & Schuster) 1997

Bilhartz, Terry D., *Francis Asbury's America* (Grand Rapids, MI. Francis Ashbury Press) 1984

Bishop, Jim, *The Day Lincoln Was Shot* (NYC. Harper & Brothers) 1955

Bloom, Sol, *The Story of the Constitution* (Washington, DC, House Office) 1935

Boudreau, Michael, *The Gospel's Triumph over Communism* (Minn., MN. Bethany House) 1991

Brown, Stuart Gerry, *Thomas Jefferson* (NY, NY, Wilmington Square Press) 1963

Carson, Benjamin F., *America the Beautiful* (Grand Rapids, MI, Zondervan Press) 2012

Catton, Bruce, *Civil War (3-in-1 volume),* (NYC. Fairfax Press) 1984

Chan, Rabbi Jonathan, *The Harbinger* (Cherry Hill, NJ. Frontline Publ.) 2012

Christian Defense, *One Nation Under God* (Springfield, VA. Christian Defense Fund) 1987

Cole, Franklin P., They Preached Liberty (Ft. Lauderdale, FL. Coral Ridge Ministries)

Collins, Alan C., The Story of America in Pictures (NY, NY. Doubleday, Doran & Co.) 1944

de Tocqueville, *Democracy in America* (NYC. Oxford University Press) 1947

Donald, David Herbert, *Lincoln; A Biography,* (London. Jonathan Cape) 1995

Draper Edward, *Primer*

Dugan, Robert, *Stand and Be Counted* (Sisters, OR. Multnomah Books) 1995

Ellisen, Stanley A., *Who Owns The Land?* (Portland, OR. Multinomah) 1991

Federer, Susie, *Miracles in American History* (St. Louis, Amerisearch) 2012

Federer, William J., *America's God & Country* (Coppell, TX, Fame Publish.) 1996

Federer, William J., *Back Fired* (St. Louis, Amerisearch) 2010

Federer, William J., *The Original 13* (St. Louis, Amerisearch) 2010

Foster, Marshall, *American Covenant: The Untold Story* (Mayflower Institute) 1981

Fuson, Robert H., *Log of Christopher Columbus* (Camden, ME. International Marine Publ.) 1992

Garrity, Patrick J., *A Sacred Union of Citizens* (Lanham, MD, Rowman & Littlefield) 1996

Gerson, Noel B., *Give Me Liberty: A Novel of Patrick Henry* (NY, NY. Doubleday) 1966

Grafton, John, *Abraham Lincoln, Great Speeches* (NY. Dover Publications) 1991

Hayek, Frederick, *The Road to Serfdom* (DC. Heritage Foundation) 1994

Haley, J. Evetts, *Illegitimate Power, Lyndon Johnson* (Canyon, TX. Palo Duro Press) 1964

Halverson, Richard C., *We, the People* (Ventura, CA. Regal Books) 1987

Hillsdale College, *The U. S. Constitution* (Hillsdale, MI. Hillsdale Press) 2012

Hoover, Herbert, The Challenge to Liberty (NYC. Charles Scribner's Sons) 1934

Hutchinson, Frederick J., *Restoring History, Western Cultural & Political...* (JFK Administrative Services), 2012

Kennedy D. James, *A Nation in Shame* (Ft. Lauderdale, FL. CRM Publishing) *1987*

Kennedy, D. James, *Messiah Prophecies Fulfilled* (Ft. Lauderdale, FL. CRM Publishing)

Kennedy, D. James, *Reclaiming the Lost Legacy* (Ft. Lauderdale, FL. CRM Publishing) *2001*

Kennedy, D. James, *They Preached Liberty* (Ft. Lauderdale, FL. CRM Publishing)

Kennedy, D. James, *What If America were a Christian Nation Again?* (Nashville, TN. Thomas Nelson Publishing) 2003

Kennedy, D. James, *What They Believed* (Ft. Lauderdale, FL. CRM Publishing) *2003*

Kessler, Ronald, *In the President's Service* (NY, NY. Three Rivers Press) 2010

Lacy, Dr. Sterling, *Valley of Decision* (Texarkana, TX. Dayspring Prod.) 1988

Levin, Mark R., *Liberty & Tyranny* ((NYC. Threshold) 2009

Levin, Mark R., The *Liberty Amendments* (NYC. Threshold) 2013

Levin, Mark R., *Men in Black* (DC. Regney Publ.) 2005

Locke, John, *Two Treatises of Government* (Merchant Books) 2011

Lossing, B. J., *Lives of the Signers of the Declaration* (Aledo, TX, WallBuilders) 1990

Madison, James, *The Federalist Papers* (Tribecka Books)

Mapp, Jr., Alf J., *The Faith of Our Fathers* (Lanham, MD. Rowman & Littlefield Publ.) 2003

Marshall, Rev. Peter, *From Sea to Shining Sea* (Grand Rapids, MI, Revell Books) 2009

Marshall, Rev. Peter, *The Light and The Glory* (Old Tappan, NJ. Fleming H Revell) 1977

Martin, Bess, *The Tomb of Abraham Lincoln* (Springfield, IL) 1941

McCullough, David, *1776* (NY, NY. Simon & Schuster) 2005

McCullough, David, *John Adams* (NY, NY. Simon & Schuster) 2001

Mills, Sgt. Dan, *Sniper One* (St. Martin's Griffin) 2007

Mr. Cotton, *The New England Primer - 1777* (Aledo, TX, WallBuilders) 1991

Morris, Benjamin F., *Christian Life & Character* (NY, NY. Benediction Classics, 1868) 2010

Motley, Raymond, *The American Legion Story* (NY, NY. Van Rees Press) 1966

Pangle, Thomas L., *The Spirit of Modern Republicanism* (Chicago, IL. University of Chicago Publishing) 1988

Peterson, Merrill D., *Thomas Jefferson's Writing* (London. Routledge) 1997

Prange, Gordon, *At Dawn We Slept" (Pearl Harbor)* (NYC. McGraw-Hill) 1987

Quigley, Charles N., *We the People* (Washington, DC, Center for Civic Education) 2007

Readers Digest, *The Story of America* (Pleasantville, NY. Readers Digest Publ.) 1975

Robertson, Wilmot, *The Dispossessed Majority* (Cape Canaveral, FL. Howard Allen Enter.) 1981

Sandburg, Carl, *Abraham Lincoln,* vol. 1 (NYC. Harcourt Brace & Co.) 1967

Schweikart, Larry, *A Patriot's History of the US,* (NYC. Penguin Books) 2004

Scudder, Horace, *A History of the United States of America* (Boston. Wm. Ware & Co.) 1884

Shlaes, Amity, *Coolidge* (NY, NY. HarperCollins Publishers) 2013

Shlaes, Amity, *The Forgotten Man (Coolidge),* (NY, NY. HarperCollins Publishers) 2007

Sittser, Gerald L., *A Cautious Patriotism* (Chapel Hill, NC. U of North Carolina Press) 2010

Smith, Adam, *The Theory of Moral Sentiments* (Lexington, KY.) 2013

Smith, Adam, *The Wealth of Nations, Book I-III* (London. Penguin) 1999

Spalding, Matthew, A *Sacred Union of Citizens* (Lanham, MD. Rowann & Littlefield) 1998

Suriano, Gregory R., *Great American Speeches* (NYC. Gramercy Books) 1993

Waldman, Steven, *Founding Faith* (NY. Random Heights) 2008

Whitney, David C., *American Presidents* (Readers Digest Association) 1996

Wirt, Sherwood Eliot, *Living Quotations for Christians* (NY, NY. Harper & Row) 1974

# DVDs

*Declaration of Independence,*

*A More Perfect Union,*

*Obsession*, New Liberty Videos, 2004

*Runaway Slaves*, Ground Floor, LLC 2012

*United States Constitution and Bill of Rights* (San Francisco, CA. Full Circle) 2008

*We Still Hold These Truths. Do you?* (Washington, DC. The Heritage Foundation) 2010

Ancestry, *Our History in Pictures,*

Barton, David, *The American Heritage Series.* (Aledo, TX. WallBuilders) 2000

Barton, David, *American History in Black & White* (Aledo, TX. WallBuilders) 2006

Barton, David, *America's Godly Heritage* (Aledo, TX, WallBuilders)

Barton, David, *Building on The American Heritage Series* (Aledo, TX. WallBuilders)

Barton, David, *Drive thru History, vol. 1* (Coldwater Media)

Barton, David, *Foundations of American Government* (Aledo, TX.)

Barton, David, *Keys to Good Government* (Aledo, TX. WallBuilders) 1994

Barton, David, *The Influence of the Bible on America* (Aledo, TX. WallBuilders)

Durham, Crane, *Miracles in American History,* Amer. Family
Prod., 2012

Farah, Joseph, *Isaiah 9:10,* (WND Prod.) 2012

Giamatti, Paul, *John Adams Series,* (HBO Films) 2012

Gingrich, Newt, *Rediscovering God in America,* Cities United
Foundation, 2007

Kennedy, D. James, *Who is This Jesus?,* Ft Lauderdale, FL; CRM
Productions, 2006

Marshall, Rev. Peter, *Restoring America Series* (Orleans, MA;
Peter Marshall Ministries) 2006

New Liberty, A *Nation Adrift*

Sherwood, Carlton, *Stolen Honor (*PA; Red, White & Blue
Productions) 2004

Williams, John, *Another Conversation with Thomas Jefferson*
(Chicago, IL; WGN Radio) 2001

Printed in the United States
By Bookmasters